T0356141

Enlightened Self-Interest

Enlightened Self-Interest

Individualism, Community, and the Common Good

Thomas J. Bussen with Henry Biggs and Timothy Bono

Georgetown University Press / Washington, DC

Portions of chapter 5 were adapted from the article by Thomas J. Bussen, "The Power of Play," which first appeared in *Our Canada* (March 2022) magazine and is adapted by permission of the publisher, Reader's Digest. Portions of chapter 12 were adapted from the article by Thomas J. Bussen, "The Tip of the Spear: Heritage Reclaimed at 13,000 Feet," which first appeared in *Light of Consciousness Journal* (Spring–Summer 2022) and is adapted by permission of the publisher, Truth Consciousness.

The publisher is not responsible for third-party websites or their content. URL links were active at time of publication.

Library of Congress Cataloging-in-Publication Data

Names: Bussen, Thomas J., author. | Biggs, Henry, author. | Bono, Tim, author.
Title: Enlightened self-interest : individualism, community, and the common good / Thomas J Bussen with Henry Biggs and Timothy Bono.
Description: Washington, DC : Georgetown University Press, 2024. | Includes bibliographical references and index.
Identifiers: LCCN 2023000444 (print) | LCCN 2023000445 (ebook) | ISBN 9781647123901 (hardcover) | ISBN 9781647123918 (ebook)
Subjects: LCSH: Self-interest. | Conduct of life. | Common good. | Individualism—United States. | United States—Civilization—1970–
Classification: LCC BJ1474 . B88 2024 (print) | LCC BJ1474 (ebook) | DDC 171/.8—dc23/eng/20231108
LC record available at https://lccn.loc.gov/2023000444
LC ebook record available at https://lccn.loc.gov/2023000445

∞ This paper meets the requirements of ANSI/NISO Z39.48-1992 (Permanence of Paper).

25 24   9 8 7 6 5 4 3 2   First printing

Printed in the United States of America

Cover design by Jim Keller
Interior design by BookComp, Inc.

To all those drowning beneath the waves.
To all those aspiring to help others swim.

With love, with hope,
we rise as one.

Contents

Introduction

An Anti-American Love Letter

I am an American abroad. Worn-out tennis shoes, blue jeans, a rotating cast of collared t-shirts, close-cropped hair, I look the part. I write from the lush surrounds of Rwanda, a highland country in the remote parts of Central Africa. I sit on a veranda, the weather edging just toward warm, rarely if ever hot, thanks to an elevation similar to that of Denver, Colorado's mile-high city.

Plants flourish, and my small yard includes two palm trees, an avocado tree, and a banana tree with thick leaves soaking up the sun. Home is in a rather upscale part of Kigali, the capital—with the Malian, Algerian, and French embassies nearby, the roads paved with a cobblestone evoking Old World Europe—yet my roommates include not just an Egyptian banker with the build of a butcher but also two dogs, the occasional puppies, rabbits, and a chicken, which most days gifts a fresh egg.

I teach on the city's outskirts, riding to school twenty minutes on the back of a motorcycle for the cost of one dollar. We twist through traffic, pass cars and other motorcycles so closely I hold my knees tight against the vehicle's metal frame. We pass pedestrians, bikers, men in Western attire and Muslim garb, women in head coverings and bright African dresses with babies tied to their backs and fruit baskets balanced on their heads.

We reach African Leadership University, my current work home, situated atop a 1,500-foot-tall hill and looking down across Kigali—a city nicknamed The Land of a Thousand Hills. The campus is modern yet artsy, opened in 2020 and home to an assortment of overachieving but mostly underprivileged students from across the vast expanse known here as The Continent. For most this education is, despite the cliché, an opportunity of a lifetime. It is a chance, perhaps the only chance, to get out of the village, to avoid a life of farm work, which remains the vocation of necessity for around two-thirds of Rwandans and Africans (FAO in Rwanda, 2022; Goedde, Ook-Ombaka, & Pais, 2019).

I hear my students' stories and wonder at their lives—the death of a brother, an uncle, a mother, all leaving students in mourning at a regularity far exceeding that of any American classroom I have known. The floods and other natural disasters visited upon my West African students, the political conflicts, terrorism, and war in Nigeria, Central African Republic, South Sudan, Mozambique, are further reminders of this world's harsh edges.

Hope and optimism are also apparent, as is the belief in a bright future. I share their hope, but fear for the world they envision, for in many ways the world of which they dream is the world from which I come, and it is a world that has grown sick—though, I must believe, not yet terminal. It is a world of hypercompetitive business professionals. Of moneymaking, status-claiming, Mercedes-driving McMansion living. Of vast inequalities. Of aristocracy masquerading as meritocracy.

I hope that as countries across Africa and elsewhere continue to rise, they take the best of the West and leave the rest. As rural Africans own cell phones but bypass landlines, so too may they achieve prosperity without materialism, personal success with social equity, professional success and work-life balance.

Teaching at the confluence of culture, psychology, and business to a class of African students, I speak of the numerous and growing assortment of studies that affirm the old saw that money does not bring happiness—at least not in the way that conventional materialists might expect. Do they believe me? Some do, I think. Will they act on what I say and balance their personal passions, relationships, and charity alongside their pursuit of material wealth? With wealth at their fingertips for the first time in perhaps generations, most probably won't, at least not at this stage of their lives.

Yet the time will come when these young people—mostly among the disfavored portion of the world who find themselves fortunate enough to escape misfortune—take jobs at McKinsey, KPMG, Microsoft, and Goldman Sachs. They will find relative wealth, but if research from the organizational sciences is any indication, the most extrinsically oriented among them will also confront a growing sense of dissatisfaction. The long hours, the solitary social lives, and the diminishing satisfaction that comes from each additional material accumulation will build into simmering discontent.

Then perhaps they will have something that many of the capitalistic pioneers of the United States and elsewhere did not—the vision of another way, of an altogether different value set through which prosperity and personal fulfillment mingle with cooperation and concern for people and planet. In that moment, five, ten, or even twenty years from now, they just may remember a gangly, (over)zealous American professor sermonizing about all the things they could learn from the successes and mistakes of the West.

They may at last join the ranks of people such as Jerry White, whose work in land mine eradication led to a Nobel Peace Prize, or the Harvard lawyer–cum–Peace Corps volunteer, or the Rwandan community leader growing up in the shadow of genocide, or the Persian Canadian building playgrounds in war zones, or the pro-business social justice warrior, or all the others profiled in the coming pages—trading dogged self-interest for shared benefits.

How did I get to this place, lecturing young Africans about a value set that is in sharp contradiction to the one by which I was raised and in which I long believed? Flashback to 2012, when I was a newly minted JD and MBA. I am no Einstein, though these degrees were enough to inspire reasonably positive impressions among certain employers in my hometown, St. Louis. I soon gained employment litigating at a boutique law firm, unduly proud to wear tailored suits to work each day.

The big payday had not yet come, and this position seemed only a stepping stone, one more badge of honor as I climbed to fame, or at least to fortune, which is what I really sought. Before long, offers promising modest riches trickled in—with global travel perks from a multinational firm in Chicago, another with good pay (and boring work) from a financial investor in New York.

I was, to this point, a characteristically ambitious, competitive young man. I considered myself a good person, and to friends and family I probably was, most of the time. But I also spent more time thinking about my own advancement than advancing some greater cause, and to the extent I thought about others or about the social issues of my country and world, I usually thought about them as something that someone else *really* should fix but for which certainly I had no responsibility.

Less than two years into the career I had spent the better part of my life building, I walked away. And while my departure may have appeared sudden, in fact a gnawing level of dissatisfaction had long ago set in. A sense that surely this could not represent the full measure of life.

The A-ha moment came while jogging laps one night at a pleasant little park near my pleasant little home. I ran the math while jogging—how many years until I had enough money to retire? How long to get the things I wanted—a bigger house, a nicer car, a travel budget, and a family. Okay: thirty-five years until retirement, twenty-five if things went well.

And my heart sank. I remember exactly where I was in that park, the exact moment the realization hit. I envisioned doing a job for decades into the future but for which I had little passion. I could see little else but that unrewarding work, and I wasn't wrong: the long hours required of successful lawyers are hardly a secret. All of that, for what? For reaching not a point of something great or transformative but simply where I would no longer have to *do*, and would instead live out my days in hedonic pleasure on a golf course, whiskey tumbler in hand—neither of which I particularly liked.

My future life looked too much like my run that night: a series of laps giving only an illusion of progress. Perhaps, you may say, I lacked the imagination to see all that could have been. Perhaps. But my mind's eye could only see a materially prosperous but emotionally bankrupt future.

I had been following what author Steve Collins (2009) terms negative motivations—rejecting a certain set of values and the lifestyle that came with it but unsure of what I was walking toward. I had few role models and felt surrounded by young professionals living out little microcosms of my retirement dream—grinding away Monday to Friday (and usually Saturday) then drowning the weeks' stress in booze, drugs, sex, and food. The jaded older lawyers who surrounded me in courtrooms and in the office—including a prosperous and well-meaning but painfully unfulfilled supervisor—offered little hope of redemption.

One person I had long admired had taken a different path. Henry Biggs, my longtime friend and coauthor, quickly became worthy of emulation. A Harvard graduate, Biggs chose a less remunerative academic path, and in his alternate universe money did not seem to rule his life—the relentless elevation of knowledge, family, independence, and compassion reigned supreme.

Having earned his PhD at UCLA, he continued his advanced studies in a variety of fields while serving as a professor and dean—a master's in computer science, an MBA, a JD, and an LLM all followed. He did not shy either from extreme athletic challenges—running a collection of fast-paced marathons, completing the brutal Marathon des Sables (the "toughest foot race on Earth"), swimming across the English Channel, and then circling Manhattan Island and raising $120,000 for charity. With boundless energy he published a musical collection in 2019, a documentary starring sports commentator Joe Buck in 2020, and scored a musical production that premiered in New York City in 2021.

All of this would have meant little if Biggs had become a stressed-out curmudgeon. He is not such a person. To the contrary, he appears to be the happiest person I know, seeming to relish a moment rather than live in a state of eternal deferment. I witnessed this in part during animated dinners at the Biggs household, watching as he doted on his brood of children and welcomed a wide circle of diversely accomplished friends.

Over dinner one night I asked, almost embarrassed, whether he thought it a good idea to quit it all and join the Peace Corps. "Sometimes," he said, "you don't know whether you can swim until you jump." He paused. "I think you can swim, though."

A few months later I descended into the waters of an unlikely new home: Kyrgyzstan, Central Asia—seeking a new perspective and a new path. It is now nearly ten years later, and I still do not have all the answers. I never will. In fact, the countless hours of research for this book represent only a continuation of my education; much as I try to implement the lessons shared here, I implore the reader to do as I say and not as I sometimes still do.

Still, I reflect on the moment I walked away from all that I thought mattered as a decision par excellence, as my life transitioned from the Collins-like rejection of that which did *not* work, to the positive motivation for that which *does*. It is this journey that motivates this book and my teaching: to offer a recipe not just for excluding the ingredients of all things toxic, but for infusing life with its forgotten but true fruits.

My coauthors and I speak throughout this book, however, not of anecdotes nor, beyond the occasional indulgence, of personal experience. Rather, our ancestors and genetic inheritances, our histories, our cultures, and perhaps especially our psychologies are all mined to better understand American culture and the wider Western cultural milieu. From this scholarly perch, evolutionary psychology dances with positive organizational psychology, organizational behavior, and cross-cultural studies to create what amounts to an ardent dismissal of the individualistic underpinnings that drive Americans to selfishness, alienation, and in many cases personal tragedy. Along the way we find answers to explain our own happiness and have learned of our own biases and limitations—I hope all of you reading may grow similarly.

For those unfamiliar with the explanatory power of the social sciences, consider two of the field's pioneers, Martin Seligman and Mihaly Csikszentmihalyi (2014). They write: "The social and behavioral sciences . . . can articulate a vision of the good life that is empirically sound while being understandable and attractive. They can show what actions lead to well-being, to positive individuals, and to thriving communities. Psychology should be able to help document what kinds of families result in the children who flourish, what work settings support the greatest satisfaction among workers, what policies result in the strongest civic engagement, and how people's lives can be most worth living" (279).

Articulated in these chapters is the understanding that an American culture espousing individual achievement, ostentatious materialism, and cutthroat competition undermines well-being and divides society into haves and have-nots. The lose-lose consequences from the insatiable desire for more, bigger, better are delineated to reveal the essential ways in which American culture is misguided.

Moving beyond clichés, money, power, and fame are the lens we use to see why it is that Americans—but not all peoples of this world—feel such a need to keep up with the Joneses. Power is not all-corrupting, we will show, unless you are an American. Materialism, for its part, is revealed as farce and little more than a race on a hedonic treadmill.

This is the negative motivation, akin to the one that animated my departure from the practice of law. Shining a light on America's societal ills is essential. Without doing it we may lack the urgency and needed intensity to reform our ways. By doing it we highlight societal norms that together represent a dominant American culture.

Yet we do not claim that all Americans fall prey to these malevolent forces. In truth, not even a *single* American likely encapsulates American culture perfectly. This is in part because national culture—and especially the culture of the highly diverse American people—can be subdivided into countless subcultures, some of which align more closely with dominant norms than others. In addition, people are complex; if national cultures constitute some sort of collective average, then individuals within that nation are humans possessing multitudes of layered and sometimes contradictory inner values.

Still, culture might be thought of as the point at which a group departs from a universal human tendency. In highlighting dominant American cultural values, therefore, we emphasize norms that distinguish what is found in the United States from the remaining mass of humanity. We do this through reference to empirical data and scholarly studies rather than through assumptions, stereotypes, and personal biases. Even if a given American does not perfectly exemplify American culture—and, naturally, many do not—it is the dominant cultural trends that give birth to the customs of a nation: workplace norms, communal ethos, and the laws of society. These norms stalk all from cradle to grave and impact everyone from the paradigmatic American to the eccentric nonconformist.

Furthermore, we emphasize the cultural norms, that are particularly relevant to the college-educated and/or professional sector American subculture. This subculture has before it opportunities not available to most Americans, and therefore has less excuse to engage in cutthroat competition and the unrelenting pursuit of money, power, and position because almost by definition this group already has enough to meet its basic needs. With enough in hand, those unremitting questions of equity must finally be heard—particularly when considering that those very inequities have left the college-educated and professional sector disproportionately white and male (Gee, 2018).

Important thought it is to look into the depths of American culture gone awry, we go beyond this recitation of societal ills. Positive motivations, too, are articulated, and in so doing a new path is illuminated through which clear, actionable steps can be taken to wean oneself from the intoxicating power of an American culture that rewards unbridled self-seeking. While walking this path it becomes clear that money, power, and fame are not the invasive species they once appeared in the hands of an unwell society, but—consciously framed—are part of a healthy ecosystem that promotes both self and other interests.

By definition, a self-help book is intended to *help* the reader, perhaps with a handy to-do list close by. We, too, hope to help, but impose upon the reader a degree of responsibility as well. The burden of change falls most heavily upon the privileged among us. "Privilege" is broadly defined in an unequal world, and many of us are unconsciously and unintentionally complicit in the current state of affairs.

To remain on the current path is therefore not just a personal choice that can be delayed until a more providential time. It is, rather, a choice with very real consequences—yes, for you, but perhaps more importantly for others. It is the source of inequality that, should we ever stop and look at it, should make us all blush in shame. It is the *cause of*—more than a reaction to—the dog-eat-dog world that leaves us and everyone else fighting or flighting. Far from working less in these times of historic prosperity, Americans work more, stress more, and burn out more, lest others get more.

Sadly, many Americans glorify this ideology. Parents tell their children to care for others and yet through competitive sports and school systems, through their words and actions, signal that they practice not as they preach. America is meanwhile exporting this ideology abroad, indiscriminately damning future generations from Pakistan to Peru (Belk, 1988).

It is therefore not just that you should reframe your perspective for your own benefit, but rather that failing to do so is in fact, yes, unethical. A cultural reckoning is overdue. A recalibration is needed in favor of the cooperative, the modest, and the self-interested but also the other-oriented and the globally conscious.

Scholars refer to the concept of enlightened self-interest (ESI), in which self-interests and other-interests align such that both flourish (Frimer, Walker, Dunlop, Lee, & Riches, 2011). Offering a more holistic and detailed understanding of this term, we chart a pathway to enlightened self-interest and help identify win-win outcomes across a variety of life circumstances. Those individuals acting with enlightened self-interest, or the ESIs, as we refer to them here, are the people who follow their hearts and passions and not just the passions of the crowd. ESIs don't seek favor and esteem from strangers. Instead, they experience what social psychologists call optimal self-esteem derived from intrinsic self-worth. They operate not from a place of scarcity, but of abundance, of cooperation and not competition. Instead of aspiring to greatness, ESIs overflow with ethical ambition to use skills and talents to benefit self and others. Those acting from enlightened self-interest find that when they no longer waste energy on a pursuit of greatness before others, they gain the energy to do truly great things.

Admittedly, all of this is bigger than any one of us. Entrenched politics in a polarized society; economic policy in an unequal society; environmental inaction in a world that is burning—as well intentioned as calls for systemic change may be, the end result is to leave many feeling helpless, dispirited, and, most important, apathetic when facing this immovable force. Yet apathy may also be the *cause* for some of these intractable outcomes. We, all of us, comprise society, and when we cease to hold ourselves accountable, we lose the moral integrity to demand more of others. As Mahatma Gandhi said, "If we could change ourselves, the tendencies in the world would also change. . . . We must not wait to see what others do" (1968). By acting within our own spheres of interest—say, spending a bit extra on an electric vehicle or joining the local school board—the needle may quiver. This is not a panacea to the world's ills, and we must know, with a certainty that is rare in this complex and confusing world, that to change any life is to change an entire universe.

This book is, yes, a call to action. You and all of us are the products of our genes, of individualistic societies, of national myths. This is a call to recognize the bounty you may already possess, to challenge the self-serving narratives of modern America, and then? To do something about it. With humility, with patience and empathy for self and others, and with a new lens through which to view each of our worlds, let us shake the foundations on which we stand.

About the Book

Chapter 1 describes American culture within the context of a 2X2 cultural typology. Chapter 2 offers insights into the societal and individual consequences of this cultural practice. Chapter 3 concludes by calculating individual responsibilities under this system, while offering the first glimpses of an alternative path.

Chapter 4 reveals how American culture leads to a disproportionate emphasis on money, power, and fame in the pursuit of status and standing. The remaining chapters of part 2 explore sharply contrasting attitudes and behaviors about money, power, and fame, for those beholden to traditional American values and those enacting the ESI identity. Part 2 concludes by articulating a series of steps to transition from the vertical individualism of old to the new system of enlightened self-interest.

Having revealed in part 1 the dangers of current American ideologies and in part 2 having delved into the benefits of acting with enlightened self-interest, part 3 assesses ESIs in theory and practice. The prospects for a mainstream ESI identity are assessed, before the book concludes with a series of recommendations to jump-start the ESI transition within each of us.

A theoretical note: Frimer et al. (2011) define ESI as an environment in which self-interests align with other-interests to mutual benefit. However, Frimer and colleagues operationalize their theory in part by using Shalom Schwartz's (2012) construct of self-transcendence versus self-enhancement, which Schwartz argues operates in opposition. Horizontal individualism and collectivism, in contrast to self-enhancement and self-transcendence, are clearly distinguishable yet *complementary* representations of self-interest (horizontal individualism) and other interests (horizontal collectivism), respectively. An operationalization that combines horizontal individualism and horizontal collectivism better exemplifies the ESI conceptualization. It must be acknowledged that the literature on horizontal and vertical individualism/collectivism is limited. Nonetheless, we rely on a variety of scholarly sources to draw our conclusions. This includes the measure of assertiveness (House et al., 2004), or competition, as a proxy for the competitive element that helps to distinguish horizontalism from verticalism. To encompass the view of self as connected to others, as is seen particularly among horizontal collectivists, we proxy Schwartz's self-transcendence values. In turn, they share attitudes, values, and behaviors linking vertical individualists with Schwartz's self-enhancement and allow self-enhancement studies to inform our understanding of vertical individualism. We also explore the concept of universal identities and postmaterialism, both of which share important characteristics with the integrated values of horizontal individualism and collectivism.

Authors' Note: This work is the joint product of Thomas Bussen, Henry Biggs, and Timothy Bono, but all first-person reflections are provided by Bussen alone. The introduction was written in the summer of 2021, when Bussen was teaching at the African Leadership University in Kigali. In the fall of 2022 Bussen began teaching at Miami University in Oxford, Ohio.

Part 1

Culturally Extreme

Vertical Individualism in the American Context

1

A Cultural Toolbox

Social Conformity in a Culture of Individualism

It's 1:26 p.m. on a rainy Friday afternoon. A long, busy, productive, and tiring week is nearly complete. I consider stopping for the day, to either binge on a historical fiction book, take a run with one of the dogs through the misty streets, or, perhaps the wisest of all options, stop cold and allow my busy mind to slow.

After five minutes of mindless stupor, a pang of guilt springs up in my stomach and I jump back to writing the words you are now reading. You know the feeling? The pang that says hard work is morally superior to relaxation. That work is worthwhile, above and beyond the gains that it produces.

Have you ever wondered why it is that so many of us feel the need to work so hard, so often? Why, if you are anything like me, do you feel a twinge of guilt if you take an hour or a day away from the office? These emotions are often attributed to a "Protestant work ethic," but these emotions exceed any one religion, ethnicity, or society. In fact, this need for achievement is but one manifestation of the highly competitive cultures of the United States, in much of the West, and in large parts of the East, too (Scott, Ciarrochi, & Deane, 2004). My gnawing unease on this Friday afternoon is a feeling familiar to the many Americans who internalize their society's values, and it reflects a deep-seated desire to conform to cultural norms—in my case, it's a gravitational pull even when I'm away from home, halfway around the world.

Conformity, or acting differently from how one might act if alone, is a powerful phenomenon (Cialdini & Trost, 1998). Consider Stanley Milgram's famous experiments from the early 1960's, better known to some as the "shock experiments." In Milgram's study, participants complied with the directions of an apparent authority figure dressed in a lab coat and willingly unleashed one electric shock after another on fellow research subjects.

Unbeknownst to the test subjects, the shocks were fake and the target subjects were actors who feigned the pain. Yet the vast majority of subjects proved ready to obey the exhortations of this man in a lab coat because society had taught them that such official men are important, not to be questioned. Milgram used this study to help explain the conformity that fueled the barbarism of the many seemingly ordinary Nazi concentration camp guards during the Holocaust (Milgram, 1963).

Nearly a decade before Milgram, social scientist Solomon Asch (1956) revealed how social pressure leads to conformity. In Asch's classic study, participants were asked to compare the lengths of different lines on a screen. Several actors secretly participated in the study—leaving just one outnumbered actual participant. Participants answered correctly more than 99 percent of the time in ordinary conditions. Yet when the actors unanimously offered an obviously incorrect answer, around three-quarters of the non-actor participants bowed to social pressure 36.8 percent of the time and agreed with their supposed peers rather than express disagreement.

A considerably less well-known study took place in the Central African highlands of Rwanda. Rwanda is associated in the minds of many Americans with genocide. Memorialized in the Hollywood film *Hotel Rwanda*, the year 1994 marked the bloody culmination of decades—if not centuries—of disharmony, distrust, and sporadic but significant violence between the country's ethnic Hutu majority and its powerful Tutsi minority.

That year, the Hutu majority, fearing a pending incursion by Tutsi forces stationed in nearby Uganda, engaged in a systematic, genocidal campaign against the Tutsis. Within months nearly a million Tutsis and moderate Hutus were dead—the majority of Tutsis then living in Rwanda. After Tutsi military forces regained control over the country, retributive campaigns on Hutu refugee camps in Congo and elsewhere resulted in several hundred thousand additional murders (Van Reybrouck, 2014).

Today, a mere thirty years on, Rwanda is in many ways a country reborn. It is not perfect and its government is subject to criticism for behavior that falls short of liberal democratic standards. As to absolute levels of violence, however, Rwanda is now one of Africa's safest countries (World Economic Forum, 2017). Physically decimated in 1994, the country is now renowned for its strong and growing infrastructure and its universal if incipient education and health care programs. Its economy has grown year after year, and the country serves as something of a regional oasis—a place where aid workers position their headquarters so that they may access troubled surrounding countries, while also enjoying the pleasant cafes, restaurants, and perennial spring weather that leaves trees and plants in colorful bloom.

The animosity between the Hutus and the Tutsis has meanwhile declined from view. It is illegal in Rwanda today to claim membership in either ethnic group. It is also taboo to do so, indicative of a cultural as well as legal shift. Today, all are Rwandans.

A 2018 episode on National Public Radio's *Hidden Brain* can shed some light on the psychological mechanisms underpinning this cultural transformation. NPR's Shankar Vedantam tells the story of a nationally popular radio soap opera, *Musekeweya*. The writers and producers developed *Musekeweya* with the assistance of psychologist Ervin Staub, a Holocaust survivor. They sought to convince viewers of three points in the hope of preventing future genocides:

Genocidal tendencies accumulate slowly as individuals are devalued
   over time;
Innocent bystanders have an obligation to stand up to wrongdoing; and
Intermarriage between ethnic groups helps reduce intergroup tensions.

In the NPR episode, Vedantam tracks down Princeton psychologist Betsy Paluck. While a graduate student at Yale University, Paluck wanted to determine whether *Musekeweya* effectively shaped minds. She found that most Rwandans did not accept the three theories presented in the show. Though historians document the slow burn that heralded the genocidal eruption, for instance, the lived experience of many survivors was that the genocide came "like a sudden rain" upon their remote hamlets.

Locals also reported that, contrary to *Musekeweya's* message about the importance of bystanders standing up to wrongdoers, many bystanders felt helpless in the face of the genocidal flood. Many recalled Hutu husbands who had turned against their Tutsi wives or other family members, leading them to dismiss the claim that intermarriage reduced ethnic tensions (Vedantam, 2018). In a twist on the expected causal direction, however, Paluck found that the show changed people's *behaviors*, if not their attitudes. She reported on village peacemakers confronting violent agitators and of increased acceptance of intermarriage. She noted that many still privately believe intermarriage to be wrong, but, as it has become the norm, they *conformed* and publicly claimed to agree to that norm—just as Asch's participants had done decades earlier.

The show's *consequences* were probably somewhat more complex than reported by NPR. Likely the radio program changed the attitudes of at least some listeners. For others it offered the imprimatur of legitimacy for attitudes long held. Both groups were probably in the minority, but these first movers altered what the more stubborn majority viewed as acceptable norms of behavior. Once those norms changed, however, the majority conformed—which is to say they acted differently than they might have acted without societal pressure.

At this point the conforming majority might experience a disconnect between their attitudes and their behaviors, producing what is known as cognitive dissonance. Why, their subconscious minds might inquire, would I do something in which I don't believe? Because I actually *do* believe it, the mind eventually says, in an effort to restore psychological consistency.

Asch had illustrated this process to restore cognitive coherence nearly half a century earlier. In a variant on his study, he inserted a "confederate," an actor like the others but one who responded to the line test *accurately*. The number of actors who answered incorrectly far outnumbered the one confederate who answered correctly. Yet with just one confederate the percentage of study participants conforming to the incorrect majority view dropped by about 80 percent (Asch, 1956).

Taken together, the Asch experiment and the Rwandan radio program project suggest the power of conformity. It does not take all of society believing something is right; it only takes a minority, and often the rest will follow. In Rwanda, both the virtues and the vices of this instinct can be seen within the same one or two generations—genocide has been replaced today with nearly universal nonviolence.

Is the United States citizenry beholden to the same pattern of cultural conformity? If so, can the vices of the prevailing culture give way to the virtues of an altruistic alternative? It is true that the collectivism of the Rwandan people may have increased conformity, a point raised in the NPR episode (Vedantam, 2018). Yet the Asch and Milgram experiments both were conducted on American participants—a notoriously individualistic bunch—and conformity prevailed. As social psychologist Jonathan Haidt (2012) explains, all human societies are "groupish," and as a result they seek acceptance within their communities.

Consider the "door-in-the-face technique." As Arizona State University's Robert Cialdini writes of this well-validated theory, compliance to a request is increased "by preceding the request for a truly desired action with a more extreme request that is likely to get rejected" (Cialdini, Vincent, Lewis, Catalan, Wheeler, & Darby, 1975: 206). After rejecting the first unrealistic request, therefore, people are more likely to accept the next request to maintain harmony.

In one study, researchers conducted a field experiment in hopes of encouraging hotel guests to reuse their towels as part of an environmentally friendly agenda. The researchers left one set of hotel guests a note that read, in part, "The majority of hotel guests reuse their towels," but the note did not mention environmental or any other benefits of reuse. Another set of guests were informed of the environmental benefits of reusing towels, but the note did not mention other guests' behavior. Again, demonstrating the power of conformity, guests were more likely to reuse their towels when told that others had done the same than when told that doing so would benefit the environment (Goldstein, Cialdini, & Griskevicius, 2008).

This pressure to conform dates to humanity's earliest days. It belongs to the realm of evolutionary psychology in that conformity over time has given human societies—particularly complex societies—an advantage over societies with looser connections. The primatologist Frans de Waal explains, "Without a group, survival is hard, which is why belonging to a group is such a priority for all animals. They will do anything to fit in and not be ostracized, which is about as bad as getting killed" (Headlee, 2020: 140).

Generations of such evolutionary pressure contributed to a human biology that rewards conformity and punishes noncompliance. Conformity makes us humans more trustworthy and thus helps us to fit in. Research suggests that gaining acceptance within a group in turn brings increased self-esteem and self-worth (Cialdini & Trost, 1998; Goldstein, Cialdini, & Griskevicius, 2008). Research also suggests that being respected by others improves one's emotions by around 9 percent; conversely, feeling disrespected reduces emotional quality by about 3 percent (Tay & Diener, 2011). Our species is thus biologically programmed to care, sometimes quite deeply, about how others see us.

However, humans don't blindly conform; they conform especially to similar others. In a variant on the hotel towels study, hotel guests were even more likely to reuse their towels when told that the majority of guests who had stayed *in their room* reused their towels. Similarly, studies show that people experience particularly positive emotions when conforming to their culture's values and negative emotions when nonconforming (Diener & Biswas-Diener, 2002). As social scientist N. J. Goldstein wryly notes, "Adhering to provincial norms—the norms of one's local setting and circumstances—is typically both logical and effective. After all, the old adage tells us that we should do as the Romans do when we are in Rome—not when we are in Egypt" (Goldstein et al., 2008: 476). What, then, do we do when in the United States?

A Cultural Toolbox: Vertical Individualism and Collectivism

Cross-cultural researchers identify a number of cultural dimensions that tend to either separate or connect people around the world. The most well-researched of these are individualism and collectivism, with the United

States highly individualistic. Stubbornly individualistic, in fact. Americans continue referring to feet, pounds, and Fahrenheit degrees while much the rest of the world uses such mathematically friendly terms as meters, kilos, and Celsius. Meanwhile, the world beyond our shores reasonably refers to the sport that involves kicking a ball as football. "Nay," say Americans, "we shall call that soccer." American football is the sport that involves only a little kicking and an ovoid "ball." Americans are independent of other nations, and notorious for leaving the shores of their country less often—twice a decade on average—than the citizenry of most any other developed country (Kunkle, 2017). Even American government is among the world's least interventionist (Heritage Foundation, 2021).

The United States is a place where autonomy is valued and where self-interests and the interests of immediate family tend to take priority over the broader group. Collectivists, by contrast, concern themselves with their group's well-being, including, if required, at their own expense (House, Hanges, Javidan, Dorfman, & Gupta, 2004). Among individualists, self-definition involves the "I" or the "me" but rarely the "we." Collectivists tend to see their identities as interlinked with others. While an individualist might describe herself as smart or funny or athletic, or as a successful engineer or a rising lawyer, a collectivist is more likely to characterize himself as a father, brother, Google employee, or Nigerian.

Americans, in short, are perfectly willing to go it alone. On the individualism dimension, Americans have arguably gone further than any other nation, ranking on some measures as the *most* individualistic nation in the world (Oyserman, Coon, & Kemmelmeier, 2002).

This individualism is deeply rooted in American society. It is far more often a source of national pride than criticism, one of those cultural quirks that Americans have long seen as elevating the country above other nations. As the United Kingdom's ambassador to the United States James Bryce wrote in his 1888 polemic, *The American Commonwealth*, "Individualism, the love of enterprise, and the pride in personal freedom, have been deemed by Americans not only as their choicest, but their peculiar and exclusive possessions" (539). How did it get this way?

There are a variety of complex, intertwining factors, and any explanations here are necessarily incomplete—indeed, entire books are devoted to the subject of American individualism. Nonetheless, a brief overview may begin with Frenchman Alexis de Tocqueville's enchantment with the United States during his nine-month visit in 1831 that culminated with his 1835 publication *Democracy in America* (2004). In assessing the conditions that led to America's unique experiment with democracy, the nature of its robust civil society, and its capitalistic impulses, Tocqueville wrote that, "In a manner of speaking, the whole man already lies swaddled in his cradle. Something analogous happens with nations. Every people bears the mark of its origins" (31).

Tumbling further back in time, then, we can note that the country's individualistic origins began with revolution, a war for independence characterized in part by a desire for personal liberty (Grabb, Baer, & Curtis, 1999). Soon after, America's newest inhabitants found themselves moving from east to west across the continental expanse, often settling in remote, inhospitable regions. Societies across much the rest of the world had developed a communal ethos to survive hardship. In Japan, for instance, an unforgiving topography required an average of twenty farmers working closely to eke out a living (Ouchi, 1981). In such an environment, harmony and cooperation help explain Japan's national longevity.

By contrast, the United States offered more fecund yet also more spacious lands. Nutrient-rich soils allowed a single frontier family to independently farm their land (House, Hanges, Javidan, Dorfman, & Gupta, 2004), while those spacious territories separated neighbors from one another and required self-sufficiency among farmers working virgin lands in hostile environments. Thus, while collectivism arose in response to the conditions of many if not most societies, relentless individualism was one solution to early Americans' hardships (Curry & Valois, 1991).

America's individualism remains a defining cultural element, and in early America it fed into virtually every social, political, and economic system. Since these early days, Americans have embraced one system—market capitalism—that puts economic power and responsibility in each person's hands; and another—popular democracy—that places governmental power with the many rather than the aristocratic few. These were people, after all, intimately familiar with personal responsibility (Oyserman et al., 2002).

While undoubtedly correlated, some researchers argue that individualism spurs economic progress; others suggest that it is a consequence of prosperity (Ball, 2001). In truth, it's probably a little bit of both. For instance, American individualism deepened as the country amassed wealth, especially during the postwar boom years from around 1950 to at least the mid 1980s (Roberts & Helson, 1997). This wealth supported the belief in the cultural superiority of individualism and provided the bounty to make Americans less reliant on the collective unit, including family, friends, and neighbors (Helson, Mitchell, & Moane, 1984; Helson & Wink, 1992).

Individualism is in some ways, therefore, a happy by-product of American prosperity. Furthermore, newfound economic prosperity has led many other countries to grow more individualistic over the last century, as global economic growth far outstripped previous eras in human history. This helps explain why traditionally collective but economically prosperous societies like Japan and Hong Kong are now—surprisingly, to many—ranked as moderately individualistic (House et al., 2004).

Individualism and collectivism can at first blush appear as somewhat blunt conceptualizations, roughly cleaving the world in two. Yet collectivism and individualism are deeply layered theoretical constructs. For instance, a single person can—and often does—present elements of both individualism and collectivism. The United States is extremely individualistic, for instance, but Americans act collectivistically in areas ranging from religion to politics and sports.

Political scientists have identified collectivistic ideals that animated the America-first message of former president Donald Trump (Oliver & Rahn, 2016), for example, and the admonition to "buy American" reflects a collectivistic mindset. Researchers even demonstrated the collective orientation of Boston Red Sox baseball fans, who told researchers they would demand over $500 to root against their team—and *even more* to root for the New York Yankees (Grant, 2021).

Perhaps more important, individualism encompasses a wide variety of attitudes and behaviors. Denmark, for instance, like the United States rates as one of the world's most individualistic societies. Yet this hasn't stopped Denmark—nor many other individualistic nations of western and northern Europe—from offering its citizens a bevy of social programs that may appear repugnant to the individualistic identity (Marsh, 2021). By contrast, Georgetown psychologist Abigail Marsh (2021) writes in a *New York Times* opinion piece that "the United States is an outlier among wealthy, individualist countries in failing to guarantee its citizens health insurance, sick leave, parental care leave and child care."

Only by introducing nuance to the terms individualism and collectivism is a more complete understanding of these cultural differences possible. We can add layers to the vertical and horizontal axes by introducing vertical individualism, vertical collectivism, horizontal individualism, and horizontal collectivism.

As we've seen, individualism is briefly defined as concern for self, and collectivism as concern for others. Verticalism is in turn defined as competition with, or aggression toward others. Horizontalism is by contrast defined as noncompetitive and cooperative.

Combining these definitions, **vertical collectivists**—other-oriented yet competitive individuals—tend to cooperate with their in-groups, such as

TABLE 1.1   Horizontal/Vertical: Collectivism/Individualism

	Horizontal/Cooperative	Vertical/Competitive
Collectivism	Other-oriented and inclusive (noncompetitive)	Other-oriented but competitive ("us versus them")
Individualism	Self-reliant but inclusive (noncompetitive)	Self-interested and competitive ("me versus you")
Enlightened Self-Interest =	**Horizontal collectivism** + **Horizontal individualism**	

countrymen or co-religionists, but compete aggressively against out-groups. This is "us versus them." **Vertical individualists**, by contrast, tend to express concern for their own well-being and compete aggressively against others. This is "me versus you," and may help explain why vertically individualistic societies such as the United States prove resistant to social welfare programs (which, by definition, better everyone).

Like vertical collectivists, **horizontal collectivists** express concern for others. Unlike vertical collectivists, however, they tend to do so holistically without regard to in-groups and out-groups. They are more likely to see themselves as global citizens, to see all humans as connected, and to see everyone (and perhaps everything) as part of a universal in-group.

Horizontal individualists are, like vertical individualists, rather self-interested. Because they are horizontal in orientation, however, they non-competitively pursue their self-interests. If they do compete, it is against themselves—seeking to better last year's performance or attain new or different goals. They may lack the collectivistic impulse to better others but be willing to cooperate to help others attain their goals. In horizontally individualistic societies like Denmark, therefore, social programs that benefit one's neighbors are little threat to one's own position. Rather, such efforts may be seen to establish the stable foundations that allow all to prosper.

Before working through each of these terms in greater detail, we offer an admittedly simplistic shorthand to better recall each of these four terms. Every time you see "vertical," think of something equivalent to *competitive*, and every time you see "horizontal," think *cooperative*. In a sense, then, we have competitive individualists and competitive collectivists, in contrast to cooperative individualists and cooperative collectivists.

Vertical Collectivism

High rates of vertical collectivism are seen across the East, including in but not limited to China, Korea, and India (Singelis, Triandis, Bhawuk, & Gelfand, 1995; Triandis, Chen, & Chan, 1998). This cultural dimension is characterized by strong in-group conformity and strong out-group competition. A concern for the group is a decided advantage of vertical collectivism. As noted in chapters 8 and 9, this communal orientation leads vertical collectivists to use power more responsibly on behalf of other group members.

There are, however, concerns with the vertically collective orientation. First, studies show that vertical collectivists are more likely to punish nonconformity in order to compel cooperation (Kuwabara, Yu, Lee, & Galinsky, 2016). A variety of research similarly suggests that members of vertically collectivist societies submit to authority even when doing so requires behaviors repugnant to their sensibilities (House et al., 2004). A study by Rutgers University's Chao Chen found that vertically collectivistic Chinese are often willing to sacrifice self-interests to benefit the group (Chen, Meindl, & Hunt, 1997). Scholars attribute vertically collectivistic societies' willingness to sacrifice the one for the many to heightened economic and political inequalities (Kuwabara et al., 2016).

A second concern is the relative disregard for and even aggression toward outsiders. Management consultant Peter Drucker (1981) once reported that Japanese companies were so interested in harming their competition that they engaged in "ruthless" and "cutthroat" competition that harmed their own well-being. Similarly, vertical collectivists are more likely to wield power to disadvantage out-group members. Organizational research also shows that vertical collectivists collaborate effectively with in-group members by working harder together than when working alone. When teamed with out-group members, however, contributions decline (Earley, 1993).

This in-group preference carried a certain logic in the isolated nations of old, as a medieval Japanese peasant might never have encountered a Korean farmer. However, the downsides of this in-group/out-group dynamic are more pronounced in a connected world. As psychologist Joseph De Rivera and philosopher Harry A. Carson (2015) write of this disconnect: "On the one hand, human activity is increasingly occurring in a common environment in which all humanity and the planet itself is affected by the behavior of people who live in different localities throughout the entire globe. On the other hand, most humans are primarily identified with a particular local community, a family, tribe, nation, or religion. Since groups generally favor themselves above others, and some are more powerful than others, economic injustices and violent conflict prevail among different nations and ethnic groups" (310).

Vertical collectivism is thus characterized by in-group harmony, kindness, and compassion but also by potential "hostility and aggression" toward non-conformists and out-groups others (Schlösser et al., 2013). The vertical collectivist thereby reveals the benefits of the inclusive *collective* ideology along with the dangers of the provincial, *vertical* orientation.

Vertical Individualism

The United States, like much of the East, is vertical in orientation. Unlike those other mostly collectivistic societies, however, the US is also individualistic. Recall that with verticalism comes competition. Instead of group-level competition of the vertical collectivists, however, individualized competitions lead Americans to seek superiority in a battle of one against all. Groups may form in competition against others but, as in a business organization or sports team, these tend to be temporary alliances with a mercenary quality. Both individualistic and collectivistic verticalists thus direct their gazes outward, looking to advance themselves or their group by beating others (Markus & Kitayama, 1991).

Meanwhile, other individualistic nations such as Denmark, Australia, and the Netherlands are more horizontal in their cultural attitudes and behaviors (Triandis et al., 2001). The United States is in fact an outlier relative to much of the rest of the similarly wealthy and individualistic—but more horizontally structured—societies of the West.

There is some evidence that young American adults are resisting the vertically individualistic norms they've been taught (a topic explored more fully in chapter 15). Nonetheless, research also suggests the extent to which these vertical lessons embed early in life. American children in one study were more likely to compete for toys than their Mexican counterparts. The study authors found that American children took away another child's toy for "sheer spite" twice as often as the Mexican children did. They did so even when cooperation would have earned them more toys according to the established rules (Kohn, 1992). Research by cross-cultural scholar Shalom Schwartz also found that American students ranked considerably more hedonistic and power hungry—though also more achievement-oriented—than their global peers. Schwartz found these values, directed toward self-enhancement, operate in tension with so-called self-transcendence values that reflect concern for others (Schwartz & Bardi, 2001).

Consider that Amish societies, though probably vertically collectivistic (Cates, 2014), exemplify in-group cooperation and peacefulness. They revere the concept of "nonresistance" by refusing to use force in any context.

Military service, lawsuits, and other competitive practices are all prohibited (Bonta, 1997). In these communities, spread mostly across Pennsylvania, Ohio, and Indiana, schoolchildren are taught to improve their own scores and work cooperatively with others so that everyone succeeds. The lesson is that all suffer when any one is left behind.

By contrast, North American public schools are a microcosm of the broader culture, prioritizing individualized competition as mediated by grading and ranking systems (Bonta, 1997). Author Malcolm Gladwell (2018) has discussed his childhood in Canada, where elementary students were seated based on their latest examination scores: lowest scorers in the front right and highest scorers in the back left.

In the law school I attended, as in most throughout the United States, grades are ranked on a curve. Under this system, when one student succeeds, another by definition does worse. Haunting the halls were stories—perhaps apocryphal, but telling of the general mood—of anxious and competitive law students ripping out key pages of library textbooks to keep information from others.

Working-age Americans, too, seek victories over others—be it through higher salaries, promotions, or conspicuous consumption. When told that prices would remain unchanged, around half of participants to one study admitted to preferring a world in which they earned $50,000 and everyone else earned $25,000 than one where they earned $100,000 and everyone else earned $200,000 (Solnick & Hemenway, 1998). This illustrates the extent to which Americans value their own money in direct proportion to how much others have, and it is a recipe for the inequality under discussion here.

Social scientists have also shown that employed Americans have higher self-esteem than unemployed workers, not just due to greater financial well-being but because of their improved societal status. For instance, the well-being of low income but employed workers is higher than their economic positions alone would predict. Conversely, unemployed people are substantially less happy than their economic positions alone would predict (Lucas, Clark, Georgellis, & Diener, 2004; Clark & Oswald, 1994; Frey & Stuzer, 2000).

Designer Stefan Sagmeister (2014) gave a TED Talk about his decision to devote one year out of every seven to world travel. Naturally, in an achievement-oriented society, his talk and accompanying media coverage focused little on the lifestyle benefits of such a decision; rather, and "more importantly," in Sagmeister's words, it focused on how this made him a "more creative and successful artist." It is indeed only at the age of retirement that relaxing into the sunset is socially acceptable, with older people mostly immune to the malaise afflicting the unemployed, probably because retirement—unlike unemployment—is societally sanctioned as the just reward of a life of hard work (Diener & Biswas-Diener, 2002).

I spoke with neurosurgeon and Stanford professor James Doty (2021) to better understand vertical individualism in practice. Doty, a reformed vertical individualist, has a contented grandfatherly quality about him. He can often be found wearing colorful sweaters and is quick to flash a smile below his mop of graying hair. He spent much of our time speaking with energy about global poverty and inequality, only touching on the details of his eventful life when directly probed. His modesty came as something of a surprise, considering where Doty started. He said of his early life: "I wanted fame and fortune. I wanted to be someone that others looked up to. I wanted to be the best surgeon in the world." Even as a twelve-year-old, Doty writes in his bestselling book *Into the Magic Shop* (2017), "I knew I wanted money. Enough money so that people would be impressed with my success and would take me seriously" (111).

He got it, with investments in his company, Med-Tech, boosting his worth to a peak of around $75 million. "I lived on a bluff overlooking Newport Bay in a seventy-five-hundred-square-foot home," he explained. "My garage held not only the Porsche I had dreamed of as a boy but a Range Rover, a Ferrari, a BMW, and a Mercedes" (206).

Doty's roaring material success would not last, but neither would his materialism and competition, which are so emblematic of the vertical individualist. Instead, Doty today points to the promise of a horizontal ideology, at once cooperative and other-oriented. He writes: "I wish I had learned . . . to lead with a heart that's wide-open—to others and to the world. What pain could I have prevented? How different would my life lessons have been? What relationships might have worked out that ultimately didn't? Would I have been a better husband? A better father? A better physician?" (100).

Horizontal Individualism and Horizontal Collectivism

Horizontal individualism is characterized by independence, self-reliance, and self-actualization. While verticalists' sense of worth is contingent on their societal status, horizontals' self-worth is cooked up within, rather than without. Horizontal individualism is defined less as beating others and more as the right to independently pursue self-actualization and other goals (Singelis et al., 1995; Triandis et al., 2001; Triandis, McCusker, & Hui, 1990). Horizontalists, in contrast to verticalists, are therefore more interested in growth than wins. Consequently, horizontal individualism is in contradiction to and negatively correlates with vertical individualism and its competitive mentality (Triandis & Gelfand, 1998). Furthermore, horizontal individualists see themselves as independent from others but also neither better nor worse (Singelis et al., 1995). This perspective reduces inequalities, not because its adherents consistently seek to lift others but because they don't push others down the way that vertical types must in order to establish their own preeminence.

Horizontal individualism is common in many Western societies, though most prominently across Northern Europe. Some of these horizontal societies go so far as to actively restrain the vertical individualists among them. In Australia, for instance, researchers describe a societal tendency to bring those high in status down to size (Singelis et al., 1995), though there are warning signs that verticalism is on the rise in the continental country. Across Scandinavia, meanwhile, the ubiquitous sauna is an equalizing mechanism in which postal workers, barkeeps, home builders, and professionals rub shoulders, bereft of status-signaling trappings.

Horizontal collectivists attain their own goals in cooperation with others (Bonta, 1997). The horizontal collectivist—a rare but growing breed—transcends the self while striving for harmony and interconnectedness with others and with the planet (Singelis et al., 1995; Triandis, 1996). They thus move beyond a narrow sense of in-group harmony—displayed among vertical collectivists—and instead conceptualize the whole world as their in-group.

It is this mentality that leads philanthropists, aid workers, and so many others to devote their lives to strangers, to people from different countries with different-colored skin and speaking different languages. It is this mentality that led the late Archbishop Desmond Tutu to write a book titled *God Is Not a Christian* (2011). It is this mentality that led Melinda Gates (2019) to live and work in rural African villages on behalf of the Bill and Melinda Gates Foundation.

Horizontal collectivists can do all of this because the victories of others are no threat to their selves, as they are to vertical individualists. They similarly can hold a globally inclusive perspective because they are unrestrained by the provincial ideologies of the vertical collectivist. In result, horizontal cultures enhance socioeconomic equality and psychological well-being.

These horizontal ideologies, in which a distancing from the excesses of verticalism is advocated, are highlighted in the profiles described here. Such horizontal individualism and horizontal collectivism together may well represent the proper formula. When self and other interests are integrated through a horizontal lens, an individual may be said to act with enlightened self-interest.

There is a tension, well-documented in the research literature, between individual agency and collective concern (Eagly & Karau, 2002; Heilman & Parks-Stamm, 2007). An ESI's horizontal emphasis overcomes this divide. An ESI benefits from the individualist's agency while submitting to the collectivist's other-oriented concern. The ideology of enlightened self-interest therefore promotes at once the individual and the group. As the first-century BCE Jewish sage Hillel once asked, "If I am not for myself, who will be for me? If I am only for myself, who am I?" (Briggs, 2015: 1).

Horizontal individualism, rather than seeking to tear down and rebuild, thus represents an extension of American culture that offers it the chance to take root. In turn, horizontal individualism acts as a gateway to horizontal collectivism (Triandis & Gelfand, 1998), with the noncompetitive drive of the horizontal individualist making possible a more global identification.

Individuals acting with enlightened self-interest are already hiding in plain sight throughout the United States and across the globe. In part by sketching the portraits of these ESIs, we compare the vertical with the horizontal ideologies and give more texture to ESI. We see in the case studies presented here—including that of James Doty—that ESIs are rarely born; they are, rather, made. These stories offer hope that even the most vertically individualistic person need not remain eternally beholden to cultural norms. As Doty writes of his eventual transformation, "It informed my absolute belief that who we are today doesn't have to be who we are tomorrow" (Doty, 2017: 203).

Recalling his childhood, however, Doty explains the challenge that social norms present: "At twelve, you don't have wisdom or self-awareness, and even coming out of college oftentimes you don't have that. As a species, we learn by modeling our behavior off of those around us. So when you have a ruthless capitalistic society"—read: vertically individualistic—"that is the lens through which you look at the world" (2021).

This returns us to the topic of conformity, where we began. To oppose group norms is to face criticism and anxiety. People gain acceptance when conforming to societal norms (Kasser, Ryan, Couchman, & Sheldon, 2004). The dominant norm in the United States is vertical individualism (Singelis et al., 1995). In the past this individualism allowed Americans to survive and later flourish amid the challenges of frontier life. Indeed, today's societal norms are often tried-and-true methods that over time gave society a greater chance of survival. They are in this way an evolutionary, survival of the fittest, adaptation. In addition, conformity is valuable in and of itself, acting as a heuristic that allows large groups to quickly reach consensus without painstaking discussion and debate (Cialdini & Trost, 1998). From these perspectives, there is good reason to demand compliance and good reason for human biology—which seeks to survive and reproduce—to reward it.

Yet we have seen the dark side to such conformity. Societal norms to which we conform may be abused by the powerful (Cialdini & Trost, 1998)—such as occurred in 1990s Rwanda. The original purpose of norms may also, over time, grow irrelevant and outdated, even as conformists continue walking toward the cliff's edge (Cialdini & Trost, 1998). Consider the ongoing commitment to distinct gender roles—men at work and women in the house. While this was a logical division of labor for agrarian societies, the physical advantages of men are decidedly less useful when coding software or designing high-rise apartments. However, no society on earth yet exemplifies gender egalitarianism and the movement toward gender equality is a grudgingly slow one (House et al., 2004).

What is needed is something more than blind conformity. Yet to this end our minds deceive us, convincing us to defer to the wisdom of the masses and assume that if everyone is doing this or believing that, then it must be right (Imhoff & Erb, 2009). In the aforementioned Asch (1956) experiments, for instance, we might assume that study subjects conformed to the group even while inwardly knowing the majority assessment was wrong. After all, the correct answer was obvious to control group subjects 99 percent of the time. However, the conforming respondents did not just pretend to agree with their peers. Many decided that they could not trust the evidence of their own eyes and convinced themselves that their peers were in fact right.

We humans conform, at least in part, therefore, because we outsource our critical thinking and decision-making. As we are rewarded for conformity, both socially and biologically, those positive emotions may reinforce beliefs in the moral correctness of society's or the group's norms. Individualism is a source of pride for many Americans; a cultural idiosyncrasy enshrined in the country's laws, religions, families, and hobbies. However, generations of uncritical acceptance have left American society extreme in its ways: extremely individualistic and vertical and extremely lonely and competitive. It is therefore time to ask the tough questions about American culture. Has America's vertically individualistic culture outlived its utility? What are the consequences of adhering to these self-interested norms?

2

Lonely and Unequal

The Lose-Lose Consequences
of Unrestrained Vertical Individualism

The South American nation of Colombia is a case study in paradoxically exclusionary collectivism. I spoke with a hodgepodge of the country's locals while traveling across the Andean highlands near Medellin and Bogota and down to the coastal territory around the beautiful colonial town of Cartagena. Among the mostly African-descended residents of the country's coastal regions, many businesses, including restaurants, fruit stands, and shops, are family-run "cooperativos," or cooperative enterprises.

On the misleadingly named Isla Grande (Big island), a walk across the island takes no more than thirty minutes. I encountered a vendor selling decorative face masks and other tourist trinkets while sitting under a banyan tree on a typically hot and humid day. With tourist traffic virtually nonexistent, he patiently indulged my questions about business and life on the tiny island. "We are all friends here," he explained. "The community makes items, and I sell them on their behalf. The profits go to the creators and to the community as a whole."

Hardly a more communal environment could one conjure, and indeed Colombia ranks as one of the world's most collectivistic nations (House et al., 2004). Yet the Colombians I spoke with summarily rebuffed my efforts to identify the common bonds between the Colombian people. They did not deny that similarities exist among Colombians: Catholicism, for example, is a dominant cultural marker, as is Colombia's seemingly universal pride in its national "fútbol" team. However, Colombians expressed resistance to the idea that these and other similarities sufficed to establish a common identity. Instead, many seem preoccupied with the issues dividing them.

Joel, a US-educated businessman and co-owner of a high-end Bogota restaurant, said this: "If you go to Bogota and [then] you go to the coast, you feel like you're in a different country. Going from region to region, you feel like you're in a different country, from the way people talk to the way they eat, even the way they look. Someone in Bogota is very reserved, even if they have money; someone in Cartagena or Barranquilla on the coast, they show off money" (Anonymous interview, 2019).

I spoke too with a retired mechanical engineer now living comfortably in the lake resort town of Guatape. A genial, outspoken man with a heavy English accent, he criticized the political left of the country, from which, he argued, "no corporation has ever come" (Anonymous interview, 2019). As a study in contrast, just fifty miles away in Medellin is the state's largest university, its exterior walls unabashedly plastered with communist mottoes and signage celebrating Mao Zedong, Che Guevarra, and other communist leaders.

Although one might think of collectivists as more caring and empathic than the solitary individualist, Notre Dame professor David Lutz (2009) writes that in many collectivistic societies, as in Colombia, "love-of-neighbor is often limited to a relatively small circle of neighbors" (324). This describes vertical collectivism, in which compassion toward one's in-group is met with competition and even aggression toward out-groups. Such promotion of strict in-group/out-group dynamics marks the paradox of the vertical collectivism that characterizes much of the world.

By contrast, there is much to be said in favor of an individualistic society. Individualists are more open-minded to racial and religious differences, and individualism is associated with creativity, economic development, freedom, and individual initiative (Scott et al., 2004; Lutz, 2009). As was the case in 1990s Rwanda, by comparison, vertical collectivism is more strongly correlated with support for right-wing authoritarianism and rigid, restrictive conformity, which smothers individual initiative as well as intellectual and emotional freedoms (Triandis & Gelfand, 1998).

The problem with individualism is not one of quality, therefore, but of quantity. In *Psychology Today* journalist Carlin Flora (2017) recalls the Roman playwright Plautus in her article "Moderation Is the Key to Life." Noting that American culture "valorizes extremes," she writes that many experiences "are more and more positive until . . . the effects suddenly become more and more negative." This is American individualism as we know it. Recall that the United States is not merely vertically individualistic. It is "uniquely competitive" and among the most vertically individualistic *of any nation on earth* (House et al., 2004; Kohn, 1992).

Social scientists have highlighted innumerable examples of what is sometimes known as the Goldilocks rule of moderation. Personality researchers note the strong, positive correlation between conscientiousness and job satisfaction, job performance, and happiness in life (Judge, Heller, & Mount, 2002; Barrick & Mount, 1991; Kotov, Gamez, Schmidt, & Watson, 2010). Yet these too come with a boundary condition: those very high in conscientiousness are susceptible to perfectionism, obsessive compulsive disorder, and narcissism (Carter, Guan, Maples, Williamson, & Miller, 2016).

Similarly, University of Pennsylvania psychologist Angela Duckworth (2016) argues that perseverance—which she terms "grit"—is correlated with a high quality of life. Yet well before the research vindicated her fears, she fretted that people *too high* in perseverance may harmfully refuse to quit dead-end pursuits. Duckworth's colleague Adam Grant (2021), similarly, writes that gritty people perform worse in roulette, and are more likely to die while stubbornly marching to the top of mountain summits. So it goes with vertical individualism. The Goldilocks rule of moderation suggests there is a healthy limit to individualism which, once passed, leads a beneficial attribute to increasingly deleterious effects.

We chart more of James Doty's path as an illustration. Doty (2017) describes the unease that accompanied his vertically individualistic march toward a multimillionaire lifestyle: "I had wealth beyond my wildest imagination," he explains, "accomplishments that I would put up against anyone else's in medicine or business." But "I was single, having already been married and divorced by this time. The long hours of being a neurosurgeon and the pursuit of wealth and success hadn't made me a very good husband or a very good father to my daughter" (205).

Then the dotcom bubble stripped him of his home and fortune. "On the day I packed up my house in Newport Beach, I felt empty, lost, and more alone than ever. I had lost my marriage. I wasn't involved in my daughter's life. I couldn't think of a single person I could call and share how I was feeling. In the pursuit of things, I had neglected relationships. And when I needed someone the most, there was no one there" (180).

Doty was not an outlier, but a representative of a more general malaise among the vertically individualistic. Research confirms that people become more self-centered as their individualism increases, leading to shrinking and lower quality support networks (House et al., 2004; Scott et al., 2004; Triandis & Gelfand, 1998). Collectivists, by contrast, tend to have more and stronger social support (Triandis, Bontempo, Villareal, Asai, & Lucca, 1988).

Individualism is also correlated—perhaps due to a disregard for personal relationships—with higher rates of hopelessness, depression, and suicidal ideation (Scott et al., 2004). Psychology professor Greg Scott and colleagues detail this relationship, between weak social relationships and lower qualities of life. He summarizes his findings by writing, "As the collapse of communism shows the failure of extreme collectivism, so the American social recession shows the failure of *extreme individualism*" (143–44, emphasis added).

Meanwhile, each must work harder and longer in a competitive society. This may raise some boats, but it is for many others a draining experience. Perfectionism in America, defined as excessively high personal standards and overly critical self-evaluations, is indeed on the rise over a thirty-year period (Curran & Hill, 2019). Perfectionism is in turn associated with a hodgepodge of negative well-being indices, including high blood pressure, depression, and perceived insufficiency, even amid objective achievements.

Harvard Business Review's Bronwyn Fryer (2005) cites a study showing that "some 40 percent of workers today feel overworked, pressured, and squeezed to the point of anxiety, depression, and disease." Many are too busy to take vacation time—Americans left unused more than 768 million vacation days in 2018, up from 705 million the year before (US Travel Association, 2022). Author Celeste Headlee (2020) notes that this is consistent with a three-decade-long decline. And yet, "those who use all of their time off report being 20 percent happier in their relationships and 56 percent happier in general" (xvi).

Even more distressing is the effect of individualism on children. Studies show that when children living in individualistic societies like the United States are taught collectivistic values, they are more likely to build and maintain strong relationships than are individualistic peers (Scott et al., 2004). As society becomes more individualistic, however, the space for collectivistic norms shrinks.

Even in the face of all of this, it should be noted that individualists tend to have higher levels of subjective well-being, a fancy term for happiness (Diener, Suh, Smith, & Shao, 1995). This may seem counterintuitive, but there are at least two explanations. First, individualistic societies put great emphasis on personal happiness. As a result, social desirability bias may lead survey respondents from individualistic countries to overstate their happiness. Second, individualistic countries tend to be wealthier than collectivistic countries, wealth which up to a point positively influences overall well-being. This suggests that individualism may be correlated with but not the cause of happiness. If true, then wealthy collectivists ought to be somewhat happier than wealthy individualists, given these social advantages outlined earlier.

Though not conclusive in and of itself, at least one study offers preliminary support for this theory. Researchers have found collectivistic Chinese youth living in the individualistic (and prosperous) Netherlands reported higher rates of life satisfaction than did individualistic Dutch youth (Verkuyten & Lay, 1998).

Recall, however, that the term "individualism" paints with a broad brush. When researchers distinguish between horizontal and vertical individualists, they find that horizontally individualistic societies exhibit greater life satisfaction than do vertically individualistic societies (Arrindell et al., 1997). Here relationships are not weakened and destroyed, as among vertical individualists, but instead flourish. The difference? Here it is not one of quantity but of quality—of vertical competition vs. horizontal cooperation.

Extreme Verticalism

Consider Charles Darwin, notorious for his "survival of the fittest" theory. Advocates of America's competitive vertical individualism seek time and again to extend Darwin's work to the realm of modern-day societies: "It is a dog-eat-dog world," the thinking goes, and so all must fight for survival. Yet how likely that a species busy cannibalizing itself will succeed seems a question rarely contemplated. Darwin's "fitness" does not, in fact, require competition against other groups. Rather, fitness can describe the well-camouflaged, clever, thorny, spiny, poisonous, or anything that enhances survival rates (Le Page, 2008).

Many Americans nevertheless take for granted the idea that competition— a core element of verticalism—is essential for economic prosperity and achievement in a variety of areas, from sports and science to the arts and law (Abra, 1993). The US economic and legal system holds that competition between firms is essential for productive and efficient markets. The US political system is similarly defined by competition between parties, individual politicians, and other countries (van der Linden, 2015). US president Joe Biden, as one example among many, said in a February 2021 speech that he would "welcome the competition" between China and the United States to "win the 21st century" (Campbell, 2021).

By contrast, researcher Bruce Bonta (1997) reveals that some of the world's most peaceful societies presume that achievement leads to competition, rather than the other way around. Ranging from the Inuit in North America, to a Tibetan Buddhist group in India, to Native American societies in Mexico and Venezuela, and many others, countless societies are so certain of this relationship as to at times actively eschew individual achievement.

As the logic goes, personal achievement leads to self-aggrandizement, which leads to conflict which leads to societal harm.

Psychologists stake a middle ground, describing competition as a "double-edged sword," promoting achievement in some while reducing it in others (Tauer & Harackiewicz, 1999). DC Comics' chief creative officer, Jim Lee agreed to help sort through these conflicting results (Lee, 2021). An award-winning artist, writer, editor, publisher, and now executive, Lee has been front and center for some of DC Comics's biggest successes. Echoing Tauer and Harackiewicz's view of competition as a "double-edged sword," Lee recalls instances where there is a "weird battle of wills or egos that can push some amazing work." Outsiders may assume teams had been firing on all pistons to produce such work, Lee said, but in fact "there were a lot of conflicting ideas. It wasn't collaborative. But in that weird competition [for] the best idea, they produced the best work of their careers." Yet, Lee continued, this is, "more the exception than the norm."

What distinguishes healthy from harmful competition? William James (1983 [1899]) once noted, "There is a noble and generous kind of rivalry, as well as a spiteful and greedy kind." Lee would seem to agree, noting, "There is a form of competition that is maybe a healthy collaboration. [But] competition can be very debilitating if the dissention or agreement becomes full blown. It's a precarious line to walk, and a little too far leads everything to fall apart" (Lee, 2021).

MIT postdoctoral researcher Allison Thomas and colleagues showed that even toddlers understand this distinction in competitive quality. In their study, two- and three-year-old children observed puppets in mock battle. When one puppet "stood down," almost all children preferred to play with the winning puppet. When that puppet won by forcefully knocking down the other puppet, however, the children overwhelmingly preferred the "losing" puppet (Thomas, Thomsen, Lukowski, Abramyan, & Sarnecka, 2018).

While competition is "precarious," Lee (2021) recalls that some of the most successful teams he's worked with were also the most cooperative. "There are so many creative teams, where the writers and the artists are very much in sync," he explains, "almost knowing how to finish each other's sentences or concepts or ideas."

We will return to Jim Lee in chapter 8. Here, we continue exploring the cooperative ideal by introducing the Rwandan social entrepreneur Alice Mukashyaka. A child of the Rwandan genocide who came of age in abject poverty, Mukashyaka emanates a warmth that belies her earlier struggles. Mukashyaka today offers free science-based education to rural Rwandan high school students. Giver though she is, she is also the repeated *recipient* of free education—currently enrolled in a selective but tuition-free MBA program based in Washington, DC.

Perhaps cognizant that she was speaking to an American, she gently chided what she saw as an American culture emphasizing the good and ignoring the bad. Asked to elaborate, she explains: "Americans value this winning, winning, winning" (Mukashyaka, 2021). Mukashyaka, who spent a summer working for a tech firm in Oregon, explains, "I had a wonderful host family. I had great friends there." Yet in the workplace, "you feel like you're competing with someone. Everyone needs to be first. Of course, being first is good, money is good. But a sense of humanity is bigger. [At least] it should be bigger."

By contrast, Mukashyaka opened our interview by saying, without prompting, "I don't see life as a competition or as a game. I see it as a gift. I'm blessed to have this gift of life. It's just a miracle, and I have to bless others. I have to create opportunities for others, because it's all about everyone being happy. It's not about me winning and others failing. It's about our complementarities." She goes on: "When I was in high school, that's when I realized that I don't have this competitive mindset. I was among the top students. I was one of the top performers—and I had one of my friends and she was very competitive. She always wanted to be first in the class, and she was always anxious. And I said, 'So what if I am the first and you are the second, or I am the second and you are the first?' At the end of the day we all win."

She speaks of the virtuous cycle created by cooperation: "I celebrate the wins of others," a language counter to the vertical individualist emphasis on beating others. Celebrating others, she says, "allowed me to flourish. It tends to make many friends. People see me as friendly, and it's quite easy for them to recommend me, or to share opportunities." She continues, "You don't do it to get [something]. I don't expect reciprocal things, but it just happens naturally. I don't know how nature does it, but it happens."

Research may offer some indication of "how nature just does it" for cooperative types like Mukashyaka. As the tendency to conform attests, cooperative behavior is part of the human DNA. Just one example of this cooperative tendency is emotional contagion, where one person's behavior influences another's. For instance, one person's yawn may spur others' yawns (Platek, Mohamed, & Gallup, 2005).

Evolutionary psychologists posit that cooperative early humans were most likely to survive and pass on their genes to future generations. For early humans, cooperation facilitated essential activities, including "hunting, food sharing, defense and warfare" (Sosis & Bressler, 2003: 212).

For instance, cooperative early humans were more likely to help their kin survive; were more likely to receive reciprocal altruism; saw their group status improve as a result of altruism; and, relatedly, saw their reproductive fitness increase in the eyes of romantic suitors (the same might be said for modern humans, too). Oxford University's Dominic Johnson writes that, by contrast, uncooperative types face retaliation, including "social sanctions, seizure of property, physical harm, ostracism, imprisonment, punishment of kin, or death" (Johnson & Bering, 2006).

There is evidence as well that cooperation continues to motivate achievement in contemporary societies. In contrast to my own higher ed experience, for instance, cooperative US school environments typically see *higher* achievement than is found in competitive, individualistic settings. American students learn and retain principles better in cooperative environments. They display more intrinsic motivation to learn and greater appreciation for their teachers. They express stronger mental health. And they benefit socially, communicating and resolving conflicts more effectively, seeing their classmates more positively, and experiencing greater self-esteem (Bonta, 1997).

Most people, in fact, prefer to use cooperative rather than competitive strategies to attain goals (Bonta, 1997). Our passions are better sustained when helping and connecting with others (Duckworth, 2016). These deepening connections also lead to higher life satisfaction scores, which represents an ancillary but not insignificant benefit of cooperation (Van Hiel & Vansteenkiste, 2009).

Unsurprisingly, researchers find that as societal competition declines, self-reported happiness increases; and the reverse is also true, with competitive verticalists reporting lower happiness while controlling for other factors (Arrindell et al., 1997). Horizontal societies allow individuals to prioritize quality of life indicators such as strong interpersonal relationships, rather than relationship destroying competitions (Arrindell et al., 1997). Vertical societies, by contrast, demand strong, assertive behaviors from members— with particular pressure placed on males (Niederle & Vesterlund, 2011).

If competition has its place, then, cooperation clearly does too. Yet just as the United States is one of the world's most individualistic places, it is also one of its most vertically competitive. In embracing this cultural idiosyncrasy, the benefits of cooperation are reduced and the risks from competition are enhanced.

From Competitive to Hypercompetitive

Amid an ongoing global pandemic, it seems that the United States and many in the individualistic West botched their responses to the crisis. As of this writing, the United States has experienced around twice as many Covid infections and deaths as the next-closest country and, even adjusted for its sizable population, it is still one of the world's most afflicted nations (Pettersson, Manley, & Hernandez, 2022).

Meghan O'Rourke (2020) writes in *The Atlantic* that "America's individualistic framework is deeply unsuited to coping with an infectious pandemic," which requires that each of us defer our wants or comforts for a vague, deferred greater collective good. *Foreign Policy's* Ashish Kaushal (2021) writes in similar terms: "If there is one thing that the COVID-19 pandemic has shown us, it is that our survival depends on society putting the good of all above individual needs. It has also shown us, however, that we often fail to reach that ideal."

The United States ranks among the top ten most assertive countries (House et al., 2004). While assertive societies usefully value a "can-do" attitude, the theoretical construct is less helpfully associated with competitive rather than cooperative behaviors, dominant and tough behaviors, and support for the strong with lack of sympathy for the weak (House et al., 2004).

In a study comparing thirty-six countries, such assertive, competitive cultural attitudes are associated with lower life and job satisfaction and characterized by tense, stressful work environments (Arrindell et al., 1997). In the United States, rates of workplace stress are about 20 percent higher than the global average, with about half of Americans stressed nearly every workday (American Institute of Stress, 2019).

A psychiatrist specializing in high-performance competition, Steven Eickelberg tells the *Los Angeles Times*, "We define the American dream as people pulling themselves up by their bootstraps. But," he asked, "how many people do we walk over to be successful? When is this kind of competition admirable, and when is it pathological?" (Szegedy-Maszak, 2005).

Along with scholars like Bonta studying cooperative societies, scholars also seek to better understand this Goldilocks question of modulated competition by studying so-called hypercompetitive people. These people often seek external validation for winning socially sanctioned competitions (Ryckman, Libby, van den Borne, Gold, & Lindner, 1997). As University of St. Thomas psychologist John Taur says of hypercompetitives, "their self-worth is contingent on winning" (Szegedy-Maszak, 2005).

Hypercompetitive personalities tend to compete for money, power, and other status symbols, and they may even be more objectively successful than others. They are, after all, laser focused on winning at all costs (Szegedy-Maszak, 2005). The beneficial effects, however, are often short term. The result of hypercompetition is to take on too much work, expend too much effort, and undertake too many goals (Patock-Peckham et al., 2020). Hypercompetitive individuals often have lower-quality relationships with family and peers and weaker romantic relationships, and they exhibit markedly less concern for the welfare of others (Ryckman et al., 1997; Thornton, Ryckman, & Gold, 2011). Other studies find that hypercompetitive individuals have cynical Machiavellian attitudes, they exhibit narcissism, they use questionable ethics, and they engage in dishonest behaviors (Houston, Queen, Cruz, Vlahov, & Gosnell, 2015; Watson, Morris, & Miller, 1998).

Just as vertical societies tend to be unhappier than horizontal societies, so too do hypercompetitive individuals exhibit lower well-being than noncompetitive individuals (Van Hiel & Vansteenkiste, 2009). Workers who are subjected to hypercompetitive environments, too, present with higher stress levels, more work-life conflict, and less job engagement (Matos, O'Neill, & Lei, 2018). They are also at increased risk of sexual harassment, physical aggression, and extreme work hours (Berdahl, Cooper, Glick, Livingston, & Williams, 2018). As the University of British Columbia's Jennifer Berdahl and her colleagues (2018) write, these environments are "rife with toxic leadership, bullying, harassment [and] associated with poor individual outcomes for men as well as women" (422).

Uber, for instance, was featured in the *New York Times* in 2017 for creating a "Hobbesian environment . . . in which workers are pitted against one another" (Isaac, 2017). Then-CEO Travis Kalanick bragged of a tough corporate culture (Berdahl et al., 2018), though he was not quite so boasting of the company's people cheating regulators, threatening employees, or, in the words of the Federal Equal Employment Opportunity Commission, permitting a "culture of sexual harassment and retaliation" (Isaac, 2017).

If individualism and competition each offer potential attributes at moderate levels, each also increasingly veers into harmful territory at the extreme levels in which they are manifested in the United States. And if all of this is bad for vertical individualists, it is much the worse for the societies in which they exist.

A Tale of Two Cities

A surf competition is underway, though only some have volunteered to play. The waves are large and, as in any competition, some gain leads. Yet in this competition not everyone receives a board by which to surf. These other competitors tread water, a series of bobbing heads hoping to grab a board. Some find empty boards. Some surfers make space for them. Yet the surfers don't have space for everyone, so on they go.

The most competitive surfers knock these bobbing heads aside while thrusting forward; the more competitive surfer, the deeper the impact. Under the water goes the bobbing head. There in whose murky depths they join a mass that is invisible to everyone above. Some swim just below the surface, occasionally rising to gasp for air. Others are fully submerged, without hope of reaching the surface. They were not given a surfboard, not even taught to swim. Like in a nightmare they drown, again and again and again. So many of them.

Above the waters, the competition goes on.

If this description appears melodramatic, then let us inquire how it compares to reality. Economist John Kenneth Galbraith, writing decades ago, observed an America defined by private opulence and public squalor (Zakaria, 2020). The United States's Gini coefficient, a measure of inequality, puts it closer to the ranks of Brazil and other Latin American countries—long known for their race-based inequities—than to comparably wealthy nations (CIA World Factbook, 2022). By contrast, in more horizontal societies such as Denmark, Sweden, New Zealand, and Switzerland, society is prosperous while rates of inequality are considerably lower than in the United States (CIA World Factbook, 2022; House et al., 2004; Dalsky, 2010).

The American myth holds that competition is necessary to survival and prosperity in this dog-eat-dog world. Yet such dogma is a self-fulfilling prophecy, with inequality the inevitable result of unapologetic competition (House et al., 2004). Solitary individualists as they are, Americans also grow detached from the suffering of others in their communities. If anything, others' suffering serves as evidence of one's superiority. As the cross-cultural scholar Thao Le argues, the competitive, vertical individualist sees others through a self-serving and egoistic lens (Le & Levenson, 2005). James Doty (2021) told me similarly: "We have created this environment of ruthless capitalism, that benefits the few, and of course results in ever-increasing income inequality."

In consequence, vertical individualism not only fails to solve inequality, but fosters it (Frank, 1985; Michaelson, & Tosti-Kharas, 2020; Piketty, 2018). Research suggests, by contrast, that people living in horizontal societies, probably as a result of moderated competition, express higher levels of sympathy and concern for others—*especially the weak* (Arrindell et al., 1997, emphasis added). This is in sharp contrast to vertical societies, which express especial distaste for the weak. These autonomy-minded individualists thus live in societies with considerably less inequality—indeed, some of the lowest inequality rates in the world (Triandis & Gelfand, 1998).

The few wealthy countries ranking higher than the United States in inequality are all vertical in orientation, including Hong Kong and Singapore

(House et al., 2004). And yet, collectivism can moderate such within-nation inequities. Moderately collectivistic countries like Japan, for instance, exhibit lower inequality than the United States. This is easily explained by a collectivism—which, unlike Colombia—encompasses almost everyone in a highly heterogeneous country (House et al., 2004). Rather than spurring within-country inequality, therefore, highly homogeneous but vertical countries like Japan express relatively low concern with inequality beyond their borders. Indeed, Japan is notorious for its hostile immigration policies, despite needing foreign laborers to compensate for a rapidly aging workforce (Moschetti, 2019).

Then there's South Africa, which is one of the world's most unequal countries (CIA World Factbook, 2022). More than half its population lives in poverty, one in four experience food insecurity, and one in five exist in extreme poverty (World Bank, 2020b). Unlike Japan, South Africa is heterogeneous, with at least five ethnic groups (and many more subethnic groups) who speak eleven official languages. It is, furthermore, nearly as individualistic as the United States.

In South Africa, to paraphrase one Cape Town architect I spoke with, "Everyone is individualistic; we don't rely on the police or fire department. We each have our own security guards and security gates. We all go it alone." South Africa, like the United States, is a toxic combination of vertically competitive, individualistic, and heterogeneous citizens (House et al., 2004). Vertical individualism, as we have seen, is an ideology that expresses no substantial discomfort with inequality and sees inequality as a natural consequence of competition. Consistent with this view, economically dominant white South Africans surveyed by cross-cultural researchers not only exhibited very high levels of verticalism but also expressed little desire to reform a system that is clearly merciless to the drowning majority (House et al., 2004).

In South Africa's capital, Johannesburg, trendy inner suburbs like Rosebank boast chic shopping centers and abundant green spaces. Posh—though heavily secured—residential streets are lined with gnarling jacaranda trees budding a vibrant purple. The city center, by contrast, is gritty and hectic. But the outskirts—in Alexandria and Soweto townships, among others—is where the impacts of poverty are most visible. Nonetheless, a remnant of apartheid segregation means that trendy inner suburbs comprise a majority of the physical space housing a distinct minority—ethnic and numerical—of the population.

Yet more extreme is South Africa's second largest city, Cape Town. Nestled at the southern extremity of the country and the continent, a topographical quirk leaves a thin stretch of land resting between the ocean on one side and the lush greenery of Lion's Head and Table Mountain on the other.

Hundreds of thousands live along this verdant stretch in modernistic homes and high-end condominiums built into the sides of cliffs, which offer majestic mountain and sea views and act as tribute to human affluence. Bentleys, Porsches, and Ferraris all do their best to impersonate the streets of Monaco. The extensive seaside corniche is often full of families and family pets, well-trimmed joggers, adrenaline-seeking bikers, and young couples making the most of romantic evening walks.

On the other side of the mountains, just a stone's throw from this extravagant wealth, is a township, though in this case that's just a polite word for a slum. While the wealthy elite live amid semitropical splendor, during my summertime visit the township appeared like a low-grade dessert full of sand and sun. In place of elegantly cascading glass homes are tightly packed structures, which are "homes" perhaps emotionally but not physically; built of tin, looking ready to collapse under little more than a strong wind, and stretching across the flat expanse, endlessly it seems, as the millions submerged below the wave seek to make a life in this inhospitable landscape. Far from expressing remorse, however, during my short visit many of those on the prosperous side of the mountain expressed disdain of those on the other side, wishing them back to their sealed-off existence whenever they entered prosperous Cape Town for work or a brief escape from reality.

Yes, this is the tale of two cities in the world's most unequal place. Yet Cape Town is merely a microcosm of a broader phenomenon, a tale of two worlds in which those with the right education or connections rise, while everyone else sinks. For all the complexity of modern-day South Africa, it is possible to distill the inequality of the world down to this general truth: verticalism promotes it, and vertical individualism promotes it even more. Horizontalism, by contrast—whether individualistic or collectivistic—is an antidote to the world's townships, favelas, ghettos, and slums.

At best, therefore, competition is a double-edged sword: enriching but exhausting some, impoverishing and destroying others. This is true even in societies with moderate levels of competition. And the destructive American variant of competition suggests that it does not just exemplify the double-edge sword of competition, but instead wields that pointedly harmful variant: hypercompetition.

Extremism Rising

More bad news? Americans are growing more self-absorbed, that is to say, more vertically individualistic. In his book *The Road to Character*, David

Brooks (2015) of the *New York Times* writes, "It wasn't hard to find ... data" revealing an American "culture that encouraged people to see themselves as the center of the universe" (6). For example, between 1948 and 1954 psychologists asked more than 10,000 adolescents "if they considered themselves to be 'a very important person.' At that point, 12% said yes. The same question was revisited in 1989, and this time it wasn't 12% who considered themselves very important, it was 80% of boys and 77% of girls" (6).

Brooks continues: "The median narcissism score has risen 30% in the last two decades. ... The largest gains have been in the number of people who agree with the statements, 'I am an extraordinary person' and 'I like to look at my body'" (7). Similarly, as author Michael Battle notes, "one study found that American boys from the South were more sensitive about their own reputations than *anything* else" (2009: 11, emphasis added). While directly attributing this outcome to machismo and individualism, this reaction is also consistent with the vertically individualistic orientation in which societal status is prioritized as a matter essential to self-worth.

One of the more perplexing components of increased self-absorption is that as US women are increasingly seen as equal to men (despite continued inequities), they are also increasingly conforming to the traditionally masculine culture of competitive, vertical individualism (Roberts & Helson, 1997). As just one illustration of this change, rates of narcissism—characterized in part by self-absorption and a need for admiration—grew significantly among American women between 1958 and 1989. Scholars attribute this change to increasing individualism over the same time period (Roberts & Helson, 1997). Recent meta-analyses suggest that men remain slightly more narcissistic, as well as more likely to exploit others, more likely to see themselves as special, and more likely to believe they deserve special privileges. Nonetheless, rates of so-called vulnerable narcissism—which is characterized by low self-esteem and neuroticism—are now approximately equal in men and women, as are rates of vanity, self-absorption, and exhibitionism (Grijalva et al., 2015; Roberts & Helson, 1997).

Contrast Americans' ever-increasing rates of narcissism with the peace-loving, highly cooperative societies studied by scholar Bruce Bonta. Bonta (1997) details that in several horizontal societies, as babies become toddlers they experience a "dramatic plunge in status" in order to learn that "no one is special, stands out, or is above anyone else" (301). The infant learns that he or she "cannot dominate others," and nipped in the bud is the tendency to grow "egocentric, dominating, competitive, aggressive and perhaps even violent as an adult" (302).

In the United States, meanwhile, rising rates of vertical individualism are predictably worsening the epidemic of inequality. Inequality throughout much of the world has, mercifully, declined over decades. As the intellectual Fareed Zakaria (2020) writes, "Between 1993 and 2008, of the 91 countries analyzed by the World Bank, 42 saw rises in inequality, while 39 saw declines. And between 2008 and 2013, in those same countries the news got even better. For every country where inequality rose, in two it fell" (137).

Unfortunately, that good news is only part of the story. Zakaria continues: "The richest and most successful countries in the world are an exception to this trend. Inequality has risen sharply in many of them. That is especially true of the United States, where the Gini coefficient climbed to its highest levels since 1928." He writes, "The top 10% of America owns almost 70% of the total wealth of the country—from houses and cars to stocks and bonds—while the bottom 50% own just 1.5% of assets. Inequality in America looms worse than ever, the worst in the Western World" (147–48).

While this increasing inequality churned along, the average American worker's productivity increased by an average of 72 percent between the years 1973 and 2014. Yes, vertical individualism is achievement-oriented. Yet that same worker's pay rose only about 9 percent during those years, with the difference accruing to the vertical individualists dominating the competitive landscape (Giridharadas, 2019).

As Anand Giridharadas (2019) writes in his book *Winners Take All*, "A college graduate . . . on the safe assumption that she ended up in the top 10 percent of earners, would be making more than twice as much before taxes as a similarly situated person in 1980. If [she] entered the top 1 percent of earners, her income would be more than triple what a 1 percenter earned in her parents' day—an average of $1.3 million a year for that elite group versus $428,000 in 1980, adjusted for inflation. On the narrow chance that she entered the top 0.001 percent, her income would be more than seven times higher than in 1980, with a cohort average of $122 million." Continues Giridharadas, "The bottom half of Americans had over this same span seen their average pretax income rise from $16,000 to $16,200" (16).

Adding urgency to the situation, the Covid-19 pandemic reversed decades of global progress, and, Zakaria warns, "somewhere between 70 million and 430 million people will be pushed back into extreme poverty over the next few years. The most essential inequality, between the very richest and poorest humans on the planet, is now growing again, and at a rapid rate" (142).

Studies, meanwhile, shed insight on the psychological costs associated with inequality—of which just a few are detailed here. Lower wealth is, for instance, associated with rising cortisol levels—a stress chemical—in both adults and children, due to "more frequent exposure to daily stressors" (Van Vugt & Tybur, 2015). In one study published in the journal *Science*, low-income people were asked a hypothetical question about money, such as what might be needed to repair an imagined car. Researchers found that these questions could drop the respondent's intelligence quotient (IQ) rating by 13 points, representing "a plunge comparable to the effect of being an alcoholic or losing a night's sleep" (Giridharadas, 2019: 56).

Thomas Hobbes famously wrote of a solitary, poor, nasty, brutish, and short life. What is less well-known is Hobbes's addendum: that this unsavory life would arise in a world where everyone looked out only for themselves (Beauchamp, Bowie, & Gordon, 2004). As America's vertical individualism continues to rise, as its people grow evermore narcissistic and its civic life more inequitable, it must be asked whether Hobbes's mid-seventeenth century prediction has now come true. If it has, why is so little being done about it?

3

Rigging, R-Evolution, and Redemption

From Rationalizing to Rectifying Extreme Inequality

On the eve of the Great Depression, Secretary of Commerce and later thirty-first president of the United States Herbert Hoover published the book *American Individualism* (1922). In it Hoover wrote glowingly of individual initiative, of the "creative minds" on which progress "is almost solely dependent" (22).

Hoover was a product of and contributor to this progress. Born in 1874 to Quaker parents, both of whom would die before his tenth birthday, Hoover moved at age eleven from Iowa to the home of a hard-charging uncle in Oregon, traveling along a recently completed rail line that represented the progress so inspiring to the young Hoover. He earned average grades in Oregon but studied hard for the entrance exams to a newly opened university in Palo Alto, California.

Admitted to Stanford University's inaugural class as a geology major, Hoover graduated to become an internationally respected mining engineer, holding prominent positions in Australia, China, and London. Hoover later gained notoriety during World War I as an efficient administrator, responsible for evacuating Americans trapped in Europe while raising millions in aid to support the invaded Belgian people. Soon after the United States entered the war, President Woodrow Wilson tapped Hoover to head the US Food and Drug Administration, which marked the beginning of Hoover's meteoric rise in the nation's capital (Whyte, 2017).

Hoover, who "wrote the book" on American individualism, illustrates the balancing act for Americans who hold conflicting horizontal and vertical values. Portrayed in a profile by the *New Yorker* as self-absorbed and concerned with public approval, Hoover is also characterized as "genuinely devoted to what he construed as the public good" (Lemann, 2017). Describing his professional purpose, for instance, Hoover wrote of engineering as "a great profession. There is the fascination of watching a figment of the imagination emerge through the aid of science to a plan on paper. Then it moves to realization in stone or metal or energy. Then it brings jobs and homes to men. Then it elevates the standard of living and adds to the comforts of life" (Lemann, 2017).

Yet for all his individualistic hutzpah, Hoover warned that too much individualism could lead to injustice through the domination of the many by the powerful few. The key to protecting against this eventuality? "That firm and fixed ideal of American individualism—*equality of opportunity*" (Hoover, 2016 [1922]: 8–9).

Equality of opportunity—or meritocracy—is the bedrock upon which America's inequities are justified (Reynolds & Xian, 2014). Those who win the competitive games—meritocrats, rather than aristocrats—gain status, while those who lose seem to have only themselves to blame. Great inequality is acceptable, even desirable, so long as everyone has the *opportunity* to amass great wealth. Indeed, historian Robert Caro (2011) argues that Hoover, as US president, was ideologically incapable of aiding the needy during the Great Depression, the product of his individualistic ideology perhaps moderated by the pretense of equal opportunity.

The playing field in early American society never was, of course, equal for all. We can begin by seeing the playing field among those early Americans being limited to white men; more specifically, to property-owning white men; and still further to the elite cast of characters educated at Harvard, Yale, Princeton—or educated, period. It was this upper crust that most wanted to play the game, and of course they wanted to, because the game was rigged in their favor. Not so much the meritocrats of myth; rather more "nouveau aristocrats."

This verticalism has endured among a privileged "caste" of characters. Studies find that Americans of European descent even today remain more vertically individualistic than Hispanic and African-descended Americans, though there is some evidence of a cultural convergence underway (Marin & Triandis, 1985; Vargas & Kemmelmeier, 2013). Young, prosperous whites are more likely to view the United States as a meritocracy open to all, while minorities generally view society as nonmeritocratic (Reynolds & Xian, 2014).

So too are American men more vertical than women. They are, for instance, more likely to view money as a signal of achievement (Colquitt, Lepine, & Wesson, 2014). They also are more interested in money as a tool for gaining power and prestige (Falahati & Paim, 2011), which dovetails neatly with the discussion of vertical individualists' interlocking pursuits of money, power, and fame. Men are, furthermore, more motivated to compete than are women (Niederle & Vesterlund, 2011) and more likely to increase their contributions to the group when in competition with other groups (Van Vugt, De Cremer, & Janssen, 2007). Studies also suggest that women are significantly less interested than men in taking jobs that require making ethical compromises (Kennedy & Kray, 2014).

As mentioned earlier, men are also more narcissistic. This is unsurprising considering men's shrinking but ongoing social superiority, which tilts the playing field in their favor. Indeed, American society ranked thirty-third out of sixty-two societies in gender equity—well behind Russia, Mexico, Namibia, and Qatar (House et al., 2004). Regrettably, it is on this uneven playing field that Americans compete. Are you one of the lucky few—or, perhaps the better question is, just how lucky are you?

Life's Surfers

Imagine you are born a quadruplet but your parents decide they have resources to support only one child's education, for which you are randomly chosen over your three siblings. This one-in-four chance, incidentally, is similar to the percentage of the population that will ever enroll in higher educational institutions in South Asia, East Asia, and Latin America, and it far surpasses the 8.59 percent of enrolled sub-Saharan Africans (Roser & Ortiz-Ospina, 2013).

Surfing atop the waves of life, you are sent to private schools while your siblings try to stay afloat in overcrowded classrooms. You are tutored to excel on standardized tests and soon qualify for top universities. Just as the majority of the world's children drop out of school before finishing their secondary educations, one by one your siblings drop out of school, too exhausted by the burden of working to focus on their resource-scarce educations (UNICEF Data, 2021). They devote themselves to life on the farm, where they are subject to the vicissitudes of the season; to manufacturing facilities, where they work mind-numbing hours at mindless tasks, perhaps punctuated by moments of workplace danger; or to any variety of other demanding, dangerous, dead-end occupations.

You do well in university. Then your parents call in favors from their few contacts and soon you obtain your first job. Your modest starting salary still exceeds that of your siblings, who are doing the same work they will do for the rest of their lives. Within a few years you are promoted and now have a 401(k) retirement plan, annual bonuses, and the occasional corporate retreat in an exotic locale. Your siblings, meanwhile, have never left their home state and will work until their bodies fail. Now ask yourself: Do you as the sibling surfing atop the wave of life have a responsibility to your less fortunate siblings? And, if you believe you do, would you share your earnings with them?

We asked undergraduate business students at the University of Florida to imagine they were this lucky individual, and to decide to what extent (if any) they assumed responsibility to share with their less fortunate siblings. In fact, only one out of ninety participants refused to share any salary with their siblings, and the average participant opted to share 46 percent of their hypothetical salary.

The world operates much like what these quadruplets face, though few people are so generous to their unknown brothers and sisters around the world. In his book *Forty Chances* (2013), Howard Buffett—philanthropist, food insecurity expert, and farmer from Decatur, Illinois—quotes his father, Warren Buffett, as saying, "For literally billions of people, where they are born and who gives them birth, along with their gender and native intellect, largely determine the life they will experience. In this ovarian lottery, my children received some lucky tickets" (xiv). Howard Buffett continues: "[My father] believes that the opportunities available to a person with intelligence, drive, and spirit in the United States are different from what a person with the same profile, born into a Chad refugee camp or some remote village in El Salvador, could possibly hope to leverage" (69–70).

Even so, only 13 percent of American millionaires report feeling rich (Herron, 2019). James Doty (2021) explains: "They don't look down and say, 'You know, I'm so blessed. Half the world's population lives on $2 per day. Even in America I'm at the upper end. I need to do more [to help them].'" Instead, "They look at the person who has more than them and they say, 'I'm poor, relatively speaking.' Having spent years with extraordinarily wealthy people, I cannot tell you the number of people, whether they have $10 million, $50 million, $100 million, $250 million, a billion, who have told me, 'You know, Jim, I'm just not in a position to give, but I know a lot of rich friends who are.'"

For the ordinary masses, it is easy to look up and observe just how much more the Buffets of the world receive. But the real challenge is to ask yourself what this life has given you. No matter your background, you may have relatively more than it first seems. As a child, were you given electricity to complete homework by night? In the last year 13 percent of the world's population—nearly a billion people—had no electricity whatsoever; a much higher number experience regular and disruptive blackouts, including many of my own hardworking university students (Giattino, Ortiz-Ospina, & Roser, 2020). Did you have roads on which to get to school, a reliable form of transportation, and, for that matter, a school to go to? Nearly 300 million children globally are denied an education, period. Nearly one in five children will never complete elementary school, and the *majority* of girls will not finish secondary school (DW, 2017).

Many readers can go a step further, having arrived at school courtesy of a yellow bus and walking into a well-funded school full of teachers committed to their pupils' success. Many schools have counselors, teachers, and parents that normalize the idea of college or convince their young that they have what it takes to succeed. Contrast this with the millions of Americans, and billions around the globe, whose primary and secondary schools struggle to staff halls and fill library shelves (Smith & Smith, 2006). Countries throughout sub-Saharan Africa, for instance, are in the midst of dire teacher shortages (Coughlan, 2016). In Madagascar, as just one example, children who are "privileged" enough to attend school find themselves with about one teacher for every 250 or so classmates (Kazeem, 2016).

Consider, again, the implications of all of this. Imagine how you would feel if you woke up tomorrow and found that you could not send all your children to school; that the one or two able to attend have little expectation they might learn something of value; or that among your entire community, only a tiny percentage will beat the odds to get a college scholarship that might allow a life of modest means. In addition, for all the privilege of high-quality schools, electricity, medical care, and good ol'-fashioned plumbing, many of us are also the recipients of an even more substantial inheritance. It's called a college degree.

In the years of old, a young noble(man) could look forward to inheriting his father's properties. Perhaps a nice estate on one parcel, agricultural land on another (worked not by the inheritor but by the feudal peasants or slaves, also inherited). There might be some hunting lands to occupy the idle mind, harboring foxes, boars, deer, or buffalo. In the middle-class version, a father typically passed along his occupation to his sons. This occupational inheritance produced convenient British names such as Smith, Cooper, Tailor, and Carter, which would remain descriptive for generations.

Those days are mostly gone. Inheritances among the very rich today involve intangible properties such as stocks and bonds, even if the occasional family home is thrown in too. The middle-class version is much changed too. Instead of inheriting an occupation, many children inherit their educations, with American parents paying more than half of all college costs on behalf of their children (Abellard, 2021). These college degrees result in lifetime earnings that are estimated to be $1 million higher than what high school diplomas produce (APLU, 2022). Yet access to higher education is stratified by socioeconomic privilege, with only 7 percent of the world's population bearing a college degree (Barro & Lee, 2013). Fareed Zakaria (2020) writes that in the United States, "The top 1% of earners are 77 times more likely to have a child attend Ivy League or other elite schools compared to other children from families in the bottom 20% of earners" (149).

Other studies show that in the United States, both educational and economic outcomes are more closely tied to family connections than in other wealthy countries. As Purdue University sociologist Jeremy Reynolds writes, this socioeconomic stratification reveals the disconnect between stubborn Americans' belief in meritocracy and the very aristocratic reality (Reynolds & Xian, 2014).

Finally, many Americans leverage connections for that first job. Among my own suburban family, one brother was hired by my father's former business partner; he rose quickly and has excelled in that position to impressive heights. Nonetheless, that door opened through my father's connection as much as my brother's merit. Another brother got his start working for the accountant that serviced my father's business. He too has worked hard and distinguished himself—ultimately moving on to large and respected companies with whom he had no direct contacts. But it was getting that initial foot in the door that helped establish his legitimacy.

As for me? After graduation I was hired by a law firm that had a somewhat peripheral connection to my father. I recall, as I later transitioned into academia, my father's well-intentioned doubts about gaining admission to top institutions. He noted, without irony, that you have to "know the right people" to get into those elite realms. What he didn't say was that this was true in almost any profession, and I had chosen one into which his network did not extend.

What are the consequences of all these privileges—for me, for you, for all of us given a surfboard? Nearly all Americans are relatively privileged, with the median American income over $31,000 in 2019 and $47,000 for full-time workers, and life expectancy in 2020 ringing in at 77.2 years (Data Commons, 2020; Martin, 2019). Compare that to a global rate (purchasing power–adjusted) of $18,000 annual income and 72.6-year life expectancy (Alexander, 2012).

Any homeowner with a net worth of at least $93,000 is in the top 10 percent of the world's wealthy. A net worth of even $4,210 is enough to rank in the *top half* globally. A net worth of at least $871,320—claimed by around nineteen million Americans—ranks in the top 1 percent worldwide (Martin, 2019).

Yet total household earnings for Caucasian American and Asian American families average $76,000 and $100,000, respectively, compared to

$56,000 among Latino American families and $45,000 for African American families (Statista, 2021). The average earnings of American men, meanwhile, are higher than women's earnings at every age, peaking at around age sixty, at over $60,000 annually in comparison to around $45,000 for women at the same age (Martin, 2019).

Economic mobility in the United States is, to put it mildly, limited. Americans born into the bottom 20 percent of income distribution have just a 7.5 percent chance of making it into the top 20 percent. This contrasts with the 11.7 percent chance for Danes, and the 13.5 percent chance for Canadians (Zakaria, 2020). As Zakaria (2020) explains of economic immobility, "The studies on this topic are so numerous and convincing that even the staunchly conversative National Review published an essay that concluded: 'What is clear is that . . . American mobility is exceptional [for its] *limited* upward mobility from the bottom'" (68, emphasis added).

Upton Sinclair (1994) famously remarked, "It is difficult to get a man to understand something when his salary depends on not understanding it" (109). For most of us, even those atop the wave, life is still a choppy affair. Yet objectively assessing one's place in society is the first step to acknowledging the artificiality of a vertically individualistic system, which claims, without reason, that the competitions of life are games of equal opportunity. And perhaps we can more genuinely inquire what is to be done about it.

Peering into the Depths

Author Carolyn Han (2022) spoke to me from her home in Montenegro. She lives in a small village on the Adriatic Sea. A cursory glance at the village on Google images reveals an utterly beautiful wonderland, as indeed Han describes it. It is there the eighty-year-old currently calls home and a place from which to write.

A wandering, global citizen, Han spent four years in China—first arriving there in 1984 during the height of the Communist era. She would go on to spend eight years in Yemen, an adventure that she recounts in her book *Where the Paved Road Ends*. From there she and Zhara, her Yemeni cat, went to live in the oil rich kingdom of Oman, which she describes as "a bit tame" in comparison to the "raw" and "chaotic" world of Yemen. Leaving Oman, she and Zhara spent four and a half years in Cairo, Egypt, before departing the Middle East for the Balkans. In Kosovo, she recounts, the streets no longer ran red with blood, as they had done during the violent breakup of Yugoslavia. Metaphorically, however, the blood was still present. Finally, she moved to Montenegro, where she now lives by the sea in her writing retreat.

Han recalls the moment her international interest first bloomed, as a seven-year-old beholding the Chinese silk pajamas gifted to her by a doting aunt. Years later she would visit China on an eight-city, twenty-one-day cultural tour of the country that was then still a sleeping giant. Gray buildings, ramshackle roofs, hunched and skinny locals who seemed always in a hurry— these are the images that Han remembers most vividly. Yet while her fellow travelers expressed little regret when departing China's dreary landscape, Han started making plans to return to China as an English instructor before her flight home could take off.

Two years later she was back in China, at a university in what is now the mega-city of Chongqing. There she gained what she had not gained as a young woman in the United States: validation that she had something of value to offer to others, that she could write, speak, and teach in ways that could serve and benefit those around her.

What motivated Han to spend so much time abroad, first in China and then in the Middle East, is precisely that these were the last places many Americans ventured to live. That these societies, these people, had in many cases been categorized as utterly alien to Americans had led Han, a relentlessly curious individual even into her eighties, to explore and decide for herself whether they were as different as she might have been led to believe.

It is this curiosity that has led Han to epitomize the horizontal individual form, one in which societal conformity and cultural norms are to be observed with some distance, and perhaps even diffidence. This curiosity also has led Han to truly discover herself. For in looking upon countless others, across so many landscapes of this earth, Han says that she sees mirrors of herself. In each of them existed a piece of herself, a reflection gazing into which she was to learn and grown as an individual interdependent with the world around her.

What she also found, of course, is that love and joy, family and friends, are universal human values. She found suffering—immense and at times unbearable. Han claims to have experienced little suffering in her own life, a life, as she puts it, lived in the shoes of a privileged white Western woman. Yet she carries a profound awareness of others' suffering. She recounts, with her voice first straining and then breaking with emotion, drinking Turkish coffee with a woman in Kosovo. The woman explained to Han that the cup from which she was drinking once belonged to her husband—a man who had lost his life fleeing over the snowy mountains of the Balkans during the darkest days of that region's war. Stories like this, Han explains, are just one part of an endless well of suffering.

She contrasts this against an American culture that is, still, inexplicably competitive and harsh despite its outsized advantages. One that is driven by material consumption, and—this the inexplicable part to Han—doing so each to their own disadvantage. Why, in a society with such abundance and potential, is the trauma so distinct? Why, Han wonders, are depression, anxiety, drug abuse, and suicide at such extreme levels in American society? Han knows from her travels that humans are humans everywhere; it is not the people of this country who are flawed, but a toxic culture that is harmful and thus sickening to all.

Early in our interview Han spoke about the importance of nonjudgment toward others. She emphasized kindness as her guiding principle. Indeed, she speaks with kindness even when describing the sickness of American culture—a kindness underlined by compassion toward those in suffering.

Where, after all, did Han's sense of kindness come from? It was by her own admission not kindness nor love that first took her abroad. It was an overpowering sense of curiosity, and healthy though that it was, it was not the motivation of a typical horizontal collectivist. In fact, she distinctly recalls the judgment that, in her younger days, clouded her attitudes toward others. As she became overcome with emotion in describing the woman whose husband was lost in those Balkan mountains, it became clear that this deep entanglement with suffering is integral to the shaping of her person—a shaping which, as she put it, continues to this day.

If others were the mirror through which she saw her own reflection, then in some ways that suffering became hers to bear. For those living lives of plenty, therefore, we must do what our minds beg us not to do—we must look upon suffering, we must peer into those murky depths, we must see ourselves in the suffering others. Through this each of us may grow from the fiercely and even usefully self-interested individuals we are in our youth to the promise that we may one day live with the wisdom, the hope, the kindness, and yes, the ever-burning ember of curiosity, that is enlightened self-interest.

Let each of us now peer into the depths. Are you ready? It is, in the final analysis, the essential task before those of us who live with privilege and abundance. Yet, as Han broke down during our discussion, facing this reality is no easy task—and if you are not yet ready then please, without shame or judgment, skip to the next section.

For those ready to continue, again consider Howard Buffett. Buffett, as part of his work on global food insecurity, visited a severely malnourished young girl in Niger. He photographed that visibly suffering young girl and plastered her image in his book. He explained his decision to include her photo, his frustration palpable, as he wrote, "If we cave in to our own discomfort and look away, the pain of this little girl from Niger will continue for millions more" (Buffett, 2013: 98). An African proverb puts it perhaps more elegantly still: "Not to know is bad, not to wish to know is worse" (Woodson, 2012: 86).

Prosperous Americans too often respond to inequities less by trying to solve the problem than by trying to hide from it, like a toddler convinced that with eyes closed she remains invisible. Rationalizations are offered: that the playing field is open to all, that we work hard and deserve our privilege, and my personal favorite, that by buying a new car or new house we are doing our part to spur the economy.

We also separate ourselves physically, making it easier to forget what is happening sometimes just miles away. As is happening in Cape Town, South Africa, Americans live in communities segregated along racial and economic lines (Reardon et al., 2008). Gated and ungated suburbs and exurbs stretch far beyond city limits, fully stocked with shops and restaurants and business centers. Schools vary widely in funding and quality, ensuring that children also are separated along socioeconomic lines and that the vicious cycle of have vs. have-not continues into the next generation (Epstein, 2011). Jim Doty analogized this invisible barrier to socioeconomic tribalism and ruminated on the resulting loss of empathy. "This is why you see so many rich that are not generous," Doty said, arguing that these closed-off echo chambers create us-versus-them dynamics.

The research supports his view. In a groundbreaking study, UC Berkeley's Jennifer Stellar and Dacher Keltner found that participants raised in greater wealth, power, and prestige show fewer neurological signs of compassion when confronted with images of suffering, like cancer-stricken children. The scholars speculate that lower income individuals' time navigating the rigors of daily life leaves them more attune to others' suffering (Zakaria, 2020).

Of those living in these anesthetized oases, however, who could blame them? Privileged or not, most Americans work too many hours, live harried and hectic lives, and spend most of their workdays disengaged from their jobs (Gallup, 2013). At the same time, to look and to see one's own suffering and that of others is for many a distressing, even depressing experience. Avoidance is easier, just as an aging charlatan may avoid looking in the mirror. But we must do better. We must inquire what happened to that innocent little girl from Niger. The answer, as perhaps you suspected, is that she would survive Buffett's visit by only a few days.

A Buddhist proverb holds, "When the student is ready, the teacher appears." If you are ready, truly ready, to look below the murky surface on which you surf, begin with a simple but demanding task: conjure an image of that sweet girl's face, of her at play in happier times, and contrast that happy image with an image of her desperate mother in the end. Do this now. Feel the emotion that betrays your humanity, that reveals your own reflection in her face and in her eyes. Feel, as I do, the outrage of her short, painful life.

These emotions are not without value. Anger and sadness, painful as they are, can in fact serve as powerful change agents when targeted toward appropriate ends. Duke University's Mark Leary (2004), for instance, writes that anger is an evolutionary adaptation to help overcome threats, while sadness evokes our compassion. By undermining rationalizations, by removing the invisible barriers we have carefully constructed, by embracing just outrage, the world's privileged masses may finally work up the appetite to help implement the changes so dearly needed. Perhaps not as a revolution, but something more than simple evolution.

Radical Evolution

Japanese noodle consommé, Sri Lankan vegetable curry, Middle Eastern flatbread, and the perfectly named Buddha's Delight: these are just a few of the dishes that the Dalai Lama sampled while serving as guest judge on *Master Chef Australia* ("Dalai Lama on Masterchef," 2012). The Dalai Lama is open about his self-described "love" of food (Dalai Lama, Tutu, & Abrams, 2016). However, the illustrious religious leader refused to exercise judgment about the food he sampled. He explains: "As a Buddhist monk it is not right to prefer this food or that food" (O'Brien, 2011).

The Dalai Lama exemplified the Buddhist principle of nonjudgment, which holds that the human tendency to divide the world into likes and dislikes disrupts internal harmony and enhances suffering (Chodron, 2022). Far away in New York City, executive Mike Brady was implementing this same principle of nonjudgment. A business professional who is "traditional" in his early career thinking, Brady effectuates a radically inclusive business practice. With a sonorous voice, carefully chosen words, and close-trimmed hair atop a fit physique, Brady has a military precision that belies his Buddhist-inspired vision.

From 2012 to 2020 Brady served as CEO of Greyston Foundation, a company founded in 1982 by Zen Buddhist Bernie Glassman. The secular foundation assists over five thousand marginalized individuals annually with job readiness training and employment services. Greyston however, is a not-for-profit masquerading as a for-profit business: the foundation is funded, in part, through its wholly owned subsidiary, Greyston Bakery. As Brady explains of Greyston Bakery, "We don't hire people to bake brownies. We bake brownies to hire people" (Frederick, 2019). In fact, the term "bakery" is misleadingly humble. Greyston is a full-scale manufacturing facility, annually producing around eight million pounds of brownies. Ben & Jerry's, Whole Foods, Delta Airlines, and many other companies buy Greyston's product.

In addition to funding its not-for-profit parent company, the bakery exercises social responsibility through its "open-hiring" process. As Brady describes the system, "If you want a job at Greyston, all you need to do is come to the front door of the bakery, put your name on a list, and when we have a job available, we take the next person off the list and give them a chance. No questions asked, no background checks, no interviews, no references" (Frederick, 2019).

Incredible, perhaps, but Brady explains that this is the Buddhist ethic of nonjudgment exemplified by the acts of the Dalai Lama. Rather than judging applicants based on past experiences, "we are trusting in the power of people to be successful, so we give everyone an equal chance at that" (Frederick, 2019). As the *New York Times* reported, all seventy-one workers on the bakery's production line got there through open hiring (Rosenberg, 2019). This approach led Greyston to be named Fast Company's eighth most innovative company in 2019. And it is this approach that Brady continues to evangelize as a social justice consultant even after departing Greyston.

Brady claims that the average business spends about $4,200 to onboard a new employee, while Greyston spends about $1,900 (Frederick, 2019). This hiring system works ideally for filling positions requiring little experience or skills, which account for nearly one in five American jobs (Cagnassola, 2021). And any company, filling any position, can aim to hire with greater objectivity and less judgment.

Brady (2021) acknowledges the battle he faces, however, in saying, "I think over time, the win-lose models become mainstream, become acceptable. And it's not going to be something that changes quickly, by any means." But, the Wharton-educated Brady continues, "I'm a businessman. I'm not going to be suggesting models that are not good for your business. The things I believe in also have to drive business, but it is setting it up to be *win-win*, or to have multiple wins, that is critical" (emphasis added).

Med-tech executive Jim Doty (2021) puts it more cynically, telling me, "Never have I seen a situation where a corporation does something not out of self-interest. When you put the fox in control of the hen house, this is exactly what you see." Mike Brady argues that to tear down a system that creates such wealth and even opportunity is to throw out the baby with the bathwater. "I think capitalism is a great force," he said. "It can do wonderful things, it can motivate people in all the right ways" (Brady, 2021). But, he continues, *capitalists* must align their interests with others.

Indeed, for all the inequities spurred by a vertical interpretation of capitalism, the years beginning with the eighteenth century Industrial Revolution and continuing to the present day represent a period of remarkable and unprecedented progress. Our species' prosperity climbed in the last several hundred years to levels that infantilize the progress of previous millennia. In the years between 1800 and 1900, for instance, GDP per person doubled, representing an increase greater than what was seen in the previous eighteen hundred years. By 2016, global GDP per person increased twelvefold. Extreme poverty rates, meanwhile, declined from around 90 percent to 10 percent (Tupy, 2019).

Mike Brady, practically business royalty with his Wharton pedigree and senior executive experience, exemplifies the potential for a cultural, psychological, and ultimately political and economic system to be recalibrated to embrace enlightened self-interests. This recalibration can take the best that American culture has to offer—and there is much to recommend—while smoothing out its sharpest edges. This is the way of enlightened self-interest. It is a call for radical evolution, rather than revolution—to break the American status quo but not the back of America. It will begin with each of us.

Leveraging Your Debt

Philadelphia Eagles footballer Chris Long donated his entire 2017 salary to charity. In recognition, the league awarded Long the prestigious Walter Payton NFL Man of the Year Award. Explaining his decision, Long says, "In my tenth year, I want to celebrate the awesome opportunity I've had to play football by giving back to the communities that have given me that gift" (Busbee, 2017). Long viewed his success not as an isolated affair, even though no doubt much of his own blood and sweat went into his success. Instead, he saw his success as inextricably intertwined with that of the communities that supported him through schools and athletics.

Admittedly, Long's millions in career earnings may have oiled his philanthropic wheel, but the challenge to all of us now is to first admit our privilege and then, most important, do something to repay it. As Howard Buffett (2013) writes, "We *do* sit in the shade of trees planted by others. While enjoying the benefits dealt us, we should do a little planting ourselves" (xiv, emphasis in original).

Let us more fully consider the tale of Alice Mukashyaka, first introduced in the previous chapter. Mukashyaka is a graduate of the African Leadership University, but she came to my attention in a *Forbes* article featuring her work founding Starlight, a nonprofit initiative that encourages young people to embrace careers in STEM (science, technology, engineering, and math).

Mukashyaka and I met at a garden café in the center of Kigali, she dressed stylishly, with close cropped hair and a winning smile. When it comes to the lottery of life, however, Mukashyaka is no winner. She was born on the heels of the Rwandan genocide in 1995. Her family had recently returned to a shell-shocked Rwanda after fleeing to the Democratic Republic of Congo during the worst excesses of violence. As Mukashyaka explains, "It was really challenging, because even the country itself—it had nothing. No electricity, no water" (Mukashyaka, 2021). During this time, Mukashyaka told me, her family struggled to put enough food on the table while living in a rural wasteland. It is difficult to imagine entering this world with fewer opportunities at hand.

Yet Mukashyaka is an unlikely success story. Along with running Starlight and earning her undergraduate degree, she was at the time of our meeting concluding her MBA studies at the selective—but tuition-free—Quantic University. Expressing gratitude for her now-secure position, Mukashyaka, who exudes a calm evocative of a seasoned spiritual leader rather than the fresh university graduate that she is, said, "In my entire life I've been supported by so many people that don't know me. My family is not that connected. I'm not from a wealthy family. But now I've completed my degree, I'm about to [earn] my master's, and it's all about that supportive system that I have around me." Suffice it to say, most poor Rwandan children do not receive Mukashyaka's opportunities—even while most American children have far more opportunities than she. Mukashyaka echoes her inner Howard Buffett, saying simply, "I'm the luckiest person alive."

While many in her position would, quite understandably, take their success and run to wealthy countries abroad, to high-paying jobs in tech or finance, Mukashyaka sees the world differently. "All of these little things that happen in my life shape me to be more generous," she says. When she finished high school, she "had nothing," but still she chose to volunteer to teach at a nearby school. She began Starlight and volunteered at refugee camps. And she hopes her future impact is larger still. Far from seeking to spin her modest *Forbes* stardom into wealth, she says, "Being broke is not good, it's not fun. But it's not that I want to become a billionaire. No, that's not my main drive," she emphasizes. Instead, "money can help you make more of an impact and reach more people."

Mukashyaka, raised in a postgenocidal country with no running water, no electricity, and limited food, today exemplifies the cooperative, inclusive, and impactful ideal of enlightened self-interest. If she can do it, surely any of us can, too. There are, after all, hundreds of millions of Mukashyaka's still out there, awaiting the tiniest of opportunities—and asking the vertical individualists of this world to please, stop competing against them.

Part 1 Conclusion

You are not entitled to your privilege, nor are you guilty for having it. Your privilege is morally neutral. It is luck. What you do with that luck is very much morally tinted, however. Will you accept that luck and seek more for yourself? Or, when you leave this earth, will you leave it with more than—on the basis of a dice roll or a coin flip—you were given?

The United States has sanctioned the pursuit of personal growth at the expense of others. At the national level, similarly, growth is prioritized over equality. The decisions feeding this may have been logical in a world of scarcity, with some research suggesting that the competitive mentality may continue to benefit poor, developing countries. Yet that same research suggests that developed countries—now full of abundance, unequally shared—are harmed by such competitive practices (Arrindell et al., 1997).

It is, therefore, our very prosperity that animates the call for change. As Franklin Roosevelt said in his 1937 inaugural address, "I see one-third of a nation ill-housed, ill-clad, ill-nourished. The test of our progress is not whether we add more to the abundance of those who have much; it is whether we provide enough for those who have too little" (NPS, 2022). Too little has changed since Roosevelt spoke; indeed, the pace of decay is now at its most rapid in decades following Covid-19 disruptions.

No, this is not to advocate a return to Soviet-era communism, nor any particular political system. And not because there are no political systems that would respond to these issues, because there are. Yet to wait for a new political system is yet another excuse for the common citizens among us to do nothing. Instead, we focus on what each of *can* do, right now. We advocate that you and I and all of us begin chipping away at an inequitable system through simple if not easy actions: by changing our own attitudes and behaviors. In so doing we hold ourselves accountable for the world that we may not have created but which we do either feed or starve with our choices. What alternative do we present? It is the psychology of enlightened self-interest, an inclusive, noncompetitive mix of horizontal individualism and collectivism.

Vertical individualism contributes to extreme inequity and poverty within an overall wealthy society. It forces Americans who would much prefer cooperation to compete, to surpass rather than coexist, to look for outward favor instead of inner worth. Vertical individualism not only costs us psychologically but leads to particularly unhealthy forms of social comparison, unsatisfying materialism, and corrupting accumulations of power.

However, the cliches that money is evil, that power is corrupting, or that status-seeking is shameful are in many ways incomplete as well. Instead, a more nuanced perspective is needed to suggest that the problem is not status-seeking, nor money nor power, but rather our vertically individualistic approach to each of those. This nuanced logic, revealed in part 2, is that money, power, and fame can each serve good and bad ends.

Together we will see that money thoughtfully expended can support happiness, or just as easily diminish happiness if one is walking on a treadmill of hedonism. We will see that when power is used for self-enhancement, it does just that—enhancing selfishness and separateness along with it. Like Tolkien's ring, power is all-corrupting in the wrong hands. Crucially, however, it a source of good in the right hands, and the profiles to come distinguish the corrupted from the enlightened powerholder.

Finally, many find themselves ill at ease in this game of status-seeking, for the game never ends and no one is ever, finally, able to declare victory. Instead, there is a constant game of comparison: How do I compare to my neighbors? My friends? My family? My coworkers? How do I compare to the rich and famous on screen and in magazine? Because we are in a competition in which my win is another's loss and vice-versa, my heart sinks when I see others perform better but rises cheerfully with others' failures. This mentality perpetuates inequality and social isolation (Shavitt, Torelli, & Riemer, 2011). We will come instead to understand how we can convert schadenfreude to *mudita* and be able to take pleasure at others' successes.

In a world that remains half-built, the time is now to direct the achievement-oriented and individualistic American toward more harmonious and equitable pursuits. Let us see how money, power, and fame may be pursued with enlightened self-interest.

Part 2

Money, Power, and Fame

The Unholy Trinity of American Extremism

4

Status through Conformity

How to Fit In by Standing Out

Visiting Israel in 1984, Jerry White was a twenty-year-old college student studying geopolitics and Abrahamic religions. During an April holiday break, White went camping with two friends, a strapping Texan and a "maverick intellectual," in the hills outside Jerusalem. In his book *Getting Up When Life Knocks You Down*, White (2008) describes a "sunny day ... hiking the beautiful hills north of the Sea of Galilee" (20). Walking ahead, White recalls when "the quiet morning is punctured by a loud thud. The earth opens, and spits up at me, and I'm swallowed by dirt and rocks. The blast of soil in my face blinds me. I fall on my hands and knees" (21–22).

White had stepped on a land mine, a remnant of the 1967 Arab-Israeli War. His friends hazarded across an active minefield to his side. "As they roll me over, we see, for the first time, what landmines do. They maim. That's their job." His lower right leg was gone, and bleeding to death was a real possibility. White's friends signaled for help, and White was rushed to a well-equipped hospital for surgery. After an arduous recovery in Israel, he would once again walk with the help of a costly prosthetic leg.

For many, this is the stuff of nightmares. However, White today divides his life into "before accident" and "after accident." Far from bowing to loss, White instead came to view this as a transformative "Aha moment," an awakening to something bigger than himself and the launchpad for an award-winning, globe-spanning humanitarian career.

In 1997 White reached the pinnacle of humanitarian success. The coalition he founded in response to his loss, one devoted to the worldwide eradication of land mines, received the Nobel Peace Prize. With 164 national signatories, White and his team compelled nearly the entire world to commit to eliminating this efficient purveyor of death and misery. Now a Fordham University professor, he later served as US deputy secretary of state. While there he launched the Bureau of Conflict and Stabilization Operations, which seeks to reduce political instability, stabilize security, and counter extremism. He has testified before Congress and the United Nations and has won countless humanitarian and human rights awards.

White, as evidenced during an interview that covered a diverse array of topics, is outspoken and impatient for change. Foremost, he believes America faces three addictions that it must urgently overcome: to money, to power, and to fame. "I've run around the world with royals and celebrities and billionaires," White said, who collaborated with England's Princess Diana and Jordan's Queen Noor on his International Campaign to Ban Landmines. "There is," he explains, "the money crowd: which is the Wall Street version in which money and greed is the flavor of the city; the DC version, where they're motivated by proximity to power—who's in, who's out; and then there's the LA version, which is an addiction to fame. I need my hits, I need my likes, I need my fans, I need my Oscar, I need to be near celebrity" (White, 2020).

This is the unholy trinity of money, power, and fame, each of which grows and then sours under the direction of vertical individualism. These discrete yet regularly interlocking concepts are sources of status in the vertically indi-vidualistic United States. For a people who seek to beat others and display their victories, this is no small matter. To understand the crucial relationship between vertical individualism and the emphasis Americans place on money, power, and fame, therefore, it is incumbent to first understand status and why humans now and across history have valued it.

Status-Striving

Humans, like all mammals, are highly attuned to the little system of carrots and sticks that our biological systems generate to help keep us alive. Many people tend to avoid extreme heights, for instance, both to avoid the resulting pangs of anxiety and avoid the entailing risk. The pleasant sensation of sex, by contrast, leads humans to procreate without complaint.

Status is a particularly juicy carrot. Those high in status enjoy standing and privilege within their societal hierarchies, including, among early humans, greater access to life-sustaining resources such as food, shelter, and security (Magee & Galinsky, 2008; Van Vugt & Tybur, 2015). These privileges offered early humans such an advantage that researchers believe evolutionary pres-sures resulted in a "universal status striving tendency" (Van Vugt & Tybur, 2015: 3). So deeply is our species attuned to status that even very young chil-dren recognize status distinctions (Thomas et al., 2018).

Just as humans enjoy sex without much concern for populating the earth, however, we tend to pursue status for its material pleasure rather than any higher-order survival strategy. As University of Amsterdam evolutionary psychologists Mark Van Vugt and Joshua Tybur (2015) write, humans that compete in and win status competitions experience pride, happiness, and elation. No wonder, either, as those high in status are perceived as more intelligent, more competent, and more skilled (Cuddy, Fiske, & Glick, 2007). The pleasure of gaining status is, however, short-lived. A cruel but clever adaptation, this brevity prevents status-seekers from resting on their laurels. Instead, pride, happiness, and elation can be generated anew only by competing in and winning yet more status competitions.

Status is also a stick, the loss of which may entail anxiety, shame, depression, and rage, as well as a self-protective aversion to future status competitions (Van Vugt & Tybur, 2015). Low-status individuals are also more likely to behave more aggressively in a gamble for status and position (Fast, Halevy, & Galinsky, 2012; Kuwabara et al., 2016).

Status-striving is thus an evolutionary, biological process in which humans are psychologically (and often materially) rewarded for success. Though most everyone denies being as status-driven as others (Kim & Pettit, 2015), in fact all humans are status-striving to various degrees. How to gain status, however, depends largely on one's society.

Across time, status accrued to those achieving societally valued ends. The ancient Romans signaled a militant preference with elaborate triumphal processions. Successful military commanders felt honored to wear brightly colored and intricately embroidered togas that no others—usually not even emperors—were allowed to wear (Van Vugt & Tybur, 2015). Medieval Muslim societies in Baghdad, Cordoba, Persia, and elsewhere valued literary excellence and philosophical prowess, celebrating the immortal likes of Rumi, Avicenna, and Averroes. Contemporary East Asian cultures tend to reward in-group generosity, kindness, and communality, while also demanding strict obedience to group norms (Torelli, Leslie, Stoner, & Puente, 2014). Some societies bestow status on age, gender, religion, or any number of ascribed characteristics. The elders of Tasmania receive the choicest foods, the Kamba elderly of Kenya are given a monopoly to consume beer, and among the Ainu in northern Japan the aged have historically been the privileged few permitted to interact with foreigners (Henrich & Gil-White, 2001).

To lose status, one need only disregard societal priorities—for instance, living as a pacifist in Ancient Rome or as a nonmaterialist in contemporary America. Conversely, to gain status, join the Roman Legion, yes, but then rise to the rank of general and win a few battles.

This returns us once more to the concept of conformity introduced earlier, which may be seen as a prerequisite to status. The paradox of the vertically individualistic United States is that Americans, conformists by evolutionary design (like all other humans), conform in a rather unusual way: *they fit in by standing out.*

Consider a study in which highly individualistic American undergraduates chose one of four beers offered free of charge by research-lead Dan Ariely. In an article titled "Taking the Road Less Traveled and Less Enjoyed," Duke University's Ariely found that students chose to order differently from their compatriots, even if doing so meant ordering a less-desired beer. Signaling their distinctive individuality was more important than choosing their preferred intoxicant.

In a similar study, Hong Kong undergraduate students also did not select their top choice. This, however, is where the similarities ended. More collectivistic than their American peers despite rising levels of individualism, these students prioritized food orders that signaled their *similarity* to others at the table (Ariely, 2010).

Other studies return similar results. Collectivistic East Asians who were offered a selection of colored pens, for instance, tended to choose similar colors, while individualistic Americans sought more distinctive colors (Kim & Markus, 1999). East Asians are thus more likely to conform to situational norms, defer to others' decisions, and even mimic others' mannerisms and decisions. By contrast, individualists paradoxically gain social acceptance (*fit in*) by signaling their uniqueness from others (*standing out*) (Zhong, Magee, Maddux, & Galinsky, 2006). Americans do not simply act in aloof separateness, however. They play to win.

Status Symbols

Let us at last consider the remainder of James Doty's story, at one time a quintessential high-status American possessing loads of money and power. A doctor, good; a surgeon, better; a *brain* surgeon, best of all. Status? That's a check.

He was a Stanford professor. Status: check again. He was rich—very rich. As an entrepreneur of medical technology, Doty accumulated around $75 million by the early 2000s. Check, check, check. Doty was a product of his society. One might assume a West Coast elite like Doty is the product of generational wealth. In fact, Doty's story fits more snugly in the Horatio Alger rags-to-riches genre.

In his book *Into the Magic Shop*, Doty describes a tumultuous childhood. His alcoholic father regularly squandered the family's few resources at the local watering hole. Though always remorseful, he was occasionally violent. Doty relates departing for his first day of college with his father's blood on his shirt. A fight had broken out between the two after Doty's father attempted to attack Doty's mother.

Doty's family withered in this environment. Chronically depressed, his mother spent much of her life bedridden. Meanwhile, Doty lost both siblings at a young age—a sister who, as Doty says, was "very bright, but not able to live up to her full potential and died at an early age," and a brother who struggled with stigma and died young as well. Doty summarized all of this to say, "I have a personal and deep relationship with suffering. I understand it very, very well" (Doty, 2013).

Yet Doty was a rose in the desert. Through a combination of luck, pluck, and perseverance, Doty forced his way into medical school, then into a neuroscience residency, and later into the businesses that would earn him his fortune. Doty relates the story of his initial rejection from medical school, which came as a result of uninspiring undergraduate grades. Refusing to take no for an answer, Doty besieged an administrator until finally and reluctantly he was given a meeting with his university's pre-med committee, whose letter of recommendation was a virtual prerequisite. Facing down a skeptical and annoyed audience of senior professors and administrators, Doty argued his case, explaining his difficult family circumstances and his drive to succeed. Displaying a remarkable persuasiveness that helps explain his later success, he slowly turned each committee member to his favor. As Doty reports in typically understated language, "The premed committee ended up providing me with the highest recommendation possible."

Doty would build rapidly on these early successes. As an entrepreneur, he purchased a $5 million San Francisco apartment, with a 6,500-acre island in New Zealand and a Tuscan villa firmly in his sights. Doty was also flexing his philanthropic muscles during this time and donated $25 million in stock—one-third of his net worth—to the Stanford Department of Neurosurgery (Richter, 2007a). He recalls his lawyer telling him, "This is no small consideration for a man of your worth." Doty writes: "I absorbed his words. 'A man of my worth.' I took a deep breath and heard the voice in the back of my head wondering just who I was really trying to prove my worth to—myself or the world?"

"Who was I?" he continues. "Was I the guy Oscar Wilde described, the one 'who knew the cost of everything and the value of nothing'? My plan was to retire and spend part of my time donating my medical services in third world countries and the rest of my time traveling between San Francisco, Florence, and New Zealand. If it felt like something was missing, I didn't worry about it too much. Whatever it was, I would find it in my travels" (178).

Doty was soon forced to confront his anxieties, however. It was the new millennium and the dotcom bubble had burst. Over the course of six weeks all was lost. The San Francisco apartment, the island, the villa. Plus the $75 million fortune, even more, in fact. "I not only had lost the paper profits," Doty says, "but was $3 million in debt. I was worth absolutely nothing. Less than nothing" (Doty, 2017). If Doty's story had ended there, he might be nothing more than a cautionary tale. Instead, just as Jerry White's story began with tragedy, Doty's story begins with financial ruin.

One day not long after the crash, Doty received a call. It was his lawyer, sheepishly explaining that his donation to Stanford had not been finalized due to the firm's negligently filing incorrect paperwork. The upshot? Doty could legally rescind the donation. Though crashing stock values meant the gift was no longer valued at $25 million, Doty would again be a millionaire. Everyone assumed Doty would gratefully hang onto this not-insignificant remnant of his fortune. Instead, he told his lawyer, "I'm going to sign the trust paperwork and donate everything as planned. He said, 'You're kidding, right?.' 'No, I'm not kidding. Do it.' (228).

Stanford would eventually sell the stock for over $5 million, and by 2007 that same piece of stock would rise again to over $25 million (Richter, 2007a). Doty explains his unthinkable decision: "I felt an obligation to do what I said, and I went ahead and did it (Richter, 2007b). I didn't have millions of dollars, but I was still a neurosurgeon. I wasn't going to starve. I was still going to be wealthy by any normal standards, but I wasn't going to have a fortune. It was time to start over and truly become a person of worth and value that had nothing to do with any dollar amount" (Doty, 2017).

Doty was now in transition from vertical individualist to living an ideology of enlightened self-interest. After a service-driven stint with an impoverished hospital in Mississippi, Doty took his current position as director of the Center for Compassion and Altruism Research and Education at Stanford University's School of Medicine.

To fund the center, Doty landed a meeting with the Dalai Lama. From a Seattle hotel room, the Tibetan spiritual leader agreed to visit Stanford and use his renown to promote the new center. This was a major coup for Doty and the center, but the Dalai Lama was not done. Following a huddle with his translator, the Dalai Lama shocked the room by announcing an "extraordinary and unprecedented" donation to the center, which, as Doty explains, "turned out to be the largest sum he had ever given to a non-Tibetan cause" (Doty, 2017).

In addition to his work at Stanford, Doty is former chair of the Dalai Lama Foundation and remains a board member and advisor to a wide variety of philanthropic causes. In many ways Doty remains high status. His altruistic forays undoubtedly increased his status, while his career as a neurosurgeon allowed him to rebound from the dotcom crash (Doty, 2021).

Yet Doty also lost status with his fortune. Those around Doty could not imagine signing over the last of a still hefty estate numbering millions of dollars. Far from respecting the decision, Doty reported that more than one person told him he was a "complete fool" (Richter, 2007b). "It seemed that all of my friends disappeared almost as quickly as the zeros in my bank account," Doty relates (Doty, 2017).

Money, power, and fame are status symbols, each signaling that its possessor conformed by playing—and winning—the vertically individualistic game. The *famous* are well-known and thus successfully stand apart from the anonymous masses. The *powerful* hold their power over others. The *wealthy* beat others to accrue the limited resource that is money.

Wealth is perhaps the biggest of America's status signals. The economist Adam Smith (1822) anticipated by a couple of centuries Doty's "man of your status" moment, writing, "The rich man glories in his riches, because he feels that they naturally draw upon him the attention of the world. . . . At the thought of this, his heart seems to swell . . . within him, and he is fonder of his wealth, upon this account, than for all the other advantages it procures him" (2017: 110). To "draw the attention of the world," these vertically individualistic winners thus take to displaying their prize money—giving name to conspicuous consumption and recalling the Porsche, Ferrari, BMW, Mercedes, and Range Rover populating Doty's garage.

Even America's illustrious founding father, George Washington, regularly complained of the unforgiving debt motivated by the need to keep up appearances of wealth and success on the grounds of his Virginia estate (Chernow, 2010). Studies today show that those high in need for status tend to associate with "loud" consumer goods that signal wealth and privilege. The need for status among the less traditionally successful has also given rise to emulation of the rich (Han, Nunes, & Drèze, 2010) and the steady rise in the counterfeit luxury goods industry (OECD, 2019).

James Doty thus offers a sketch of the enlightened self-interested person, but also a warning of the costs associated with abandoning vertically individualistic norms; costs not only in money, but in status. Through the lens of

money, power, and fame, however, the costs of remaining vertically individualistic are far higher—for self and for others.

The Cost

In the second century AD, Plutarch writes of a Hellenistic Greek king,
Pyrrhus (Plutarch, 75 AD). Enthroned at age thirteen, Pyrrhus was a warrior-
king who spent much of his life picking battles throughout the Mediterranean
world. Plutarch's story picks up when Pyrrhus announces plans to attack the
rising power of the day, Rome. He asks his advisor Cineas, "a man of very
good sense," for counsel. Cineas, deploying the Socratic method of questioning, responds: "The Romans, sir, are reported to be great warriors and con-
querors of many warlike nations; if God permits us to overcome them, how
should we use our victory?" Pyrrhus boldly declares that if Rome topples,
the remaining powers will fall like dominos and leave them as "masters of all
Italy."

Cineas pauses, then asks, "And having subdued Italy, what shall we do
next?" Sicily, "a wealthy and populous island" near mainland Italy, will be
conquered next. "Will the possession of Sicily put an end to the war?" Cineas
asks. Of course not, Pyrrhus responds. "We will use these as forerunners of
greater things," taking next Libya, then Carthage in modern-day Tunisia, and
finally all of Greece. Pyrrhus would rule an empire. Cineas, far from denying
the logic of his king, asks, "And when all these are in our power, what shall
we do then?" Pyrrhus smiles and responds, "We will live at our ease, my dear
friend, and drink all day, and divert ourselves with pleasant conversation."
We might imagine a pregnant pause, before Cineas drops the hammer on his
liege. "And what sir, stops us from drinking and being merry now?"

"Troubled" by Cineas's counsel, Pyrrhus nonetheless proceeded to war.
He raised a vast army of over twenty-five thousand men, plus twenty war ele-
phants on loan from Ptolemaic Egypt. He fought for years, and he won. Yet
the victory proved costly. In the Battle of Heraclea, Pyrrhus's charging ele-
phants cleared the field but only after eleven thousand of his men had fallen.
A couple more "victories" like this and Pyrrhus soon found himself vulnerable to counterattack from the inexhaustible Romans.

Within five years the Romans reclaimed every inch of Pyrrhus's hard-
fought gains, with Pyrrhus forced to flee to his small capital. He died in
ambush three years later, during yet another failed power grab. And so this
Greek king's name is forever immortalized: King Pyrrhus of Epirus, the man
whose life inspired the term *pyrrhic victory* (Plutarch, 75 AD).

Historians in Plutarch's time sought to enunciate morality tales as much as precise histories. And it is clear that for Plutarch, it is more Cineas than Pyrrhus, that man of "very good sense," who merits attention. Cineas advised moderation, contentment, and cooperation. But the competitive, self-interested, and status-obsessed Pyrrhus was a vertical individualist, and he saw beating others as the only path to a life well lived. In seeking to add entire towns and cities to his estate, he sought to use his material gains to create a legacy surpassing that other more famous Greek, Alexander the Great. Alas, it was a pyrrhic victory.

The contemporary vertical individualist pursues a pyrrhic victory too, gaining wealth, power, or fame, but only at great cost. And, like Pyrrhus, many vertical individualists already have enough, if not to retire to a life of ease and pleasure, then at least to one featuring more of each. Or, like the playground builder Reza Marvasti, to retire from one life and construct a powerful other.

5

Materialism

Why Less Is More

"The first playground I built was in a South Sudanese refugee camp in Uganda. To go to the refugee camp you've got to be part of the UN [United Nations] or some other registered NGO [nongovernmental organization]. I start going to the Office of the Prime Minister in Uganda. The last thing they said was, 'Okay. We can do a favor for you. It's this many thousands of dollars for you to get a permit.'" Reza Marvasti shook his head and said dismissively, "No. I don't have time for this. I'm here to build playgrounds." I'm *not* here, went the unstated subtext, to pay bribes to government elites. "So," he explains in a matter-of-fact tone, "I had to get smuggled in" (Marvasti, 2021).

There is only one cliché applicable to Marvasti, and it is that he is one of a kind. Soft-spoken, even gentle, his dark eyes reveal an intensity that befit his fearless lifestyle. From a happy, play-filled childhood in the lush wilderness of northern Iran, Marvasti relocated to Vancouver, Canada, after war broke out with Iraq. During his college years a restless energy bounced him from major to major—four in total—before he became a luxury home builder in the shadows of Vancouver's glass high-rises and towering mountains.

Marvasti worked to live, and he lived on the edge. In the wilds outside Vancouver he sought one adrenaline rush after another, while flirting with death day after day. "I have broken so many bones." He ticks them off one after another. "I've broken my neck, I've broken my femur bone, I've broken my collarbone, my nose, so many fingers, my ankle, my wrist." For Marvasti, extreme sports represent a vertical competition not against others, but a relentless competition against himself, a symptom to which horizontal individualists are susceptible. He says, "It's something where I go and jump off this cliff, and then I want to do something higher. It's something I'm always pushing. I don't think it's a really healthy thing. It's not."

Marvasti was on a collision course and it was a hot summer day in the mountains sixty-five miles east of Vancouver when he at last made impact. Marvasti was speed flying, an adrenaline-lover's activity similar to paragliding but with a smaller wing, so that the rider is "coming down really fast. Except, usually, you have some control." On this day, Marvasti's wing malfunctioned.

Running down a cliffside perched hundreds of feet above the forest, Marvasti knew something was wrong even before he went airborne, but as his momentum carried him he also knew "there's no way of returning." He could only hope for the best and leap into the air. But Marvasti lost control almost immediately. "I turn to the right and am coming down really quick." Marvasti readies himself for a crash landing. "There's these huge pine trees. I pass by one of them, hit another on the shin, and then this third one just grab the tip of it. I hang on for a second, and it's like a cartoon. Things just stopped."

"And then the wings collapsed. The weight became too much, and, snap." The branch gives and Marvasti beelines to the earth below. "I fell down. A hundred, a hundred twenty feet." From a distance, Marvasti's friends watch in horror. Some begin running down the treacherous mountainside to reach Marvasti, but one friend warns the others to brace themselves. "Don't rush. We go slowly. Reza's dead." It seemed no one could have survived a fall of that distance. "They were certain I was dead," Marvasti explains. "But the reason I walked away is I fell on this one big dead tree that was rotting and it absorbed my fall." That, along with a built-in airbag of sorts, spared Marvasti's life.

Still reckoning with his own survival, just two days later Marvasti's close friend—one week away from the friend's daughter's birth—died in an accident eerily similar to his own. Marvasti was lost. "What was my purpose to walk away from this thing?"

Back in Vancouver, the last construction project Marvasti would work on was a half-million-dollar vacation home renovation. "We started putting in these Versace-designed tiles for this couple. And then they came and looked at the tile and said, 'Oh, I don't like this. Remove it.' Told that removing the tiles required smashing them to worthless bits, the husband responded, "I don't care. I don't want it."

"As we're removing this, I was kind of disgusted. This home is going to get used for a few months out of the year, and now thousands of dollars are going in the dump." In mourning and reeling from his own near-death experience, this marked the figurative breaking point for Marvasti, a man of so many broken bones. "I'm asking myself, what am I doing? How am I contributing to our planet? How is this making the world a better place? That was my last [construction] job. Within a few weeks I sold my business, most of my personal belongings, and everything that I could turn into cash, and left Canada."

Later that year, Marvasti is in the sun-baked wilds of northern Uganda, a region long terrorized by warlord Joseph Kony and his Lord's Resistance Army. Marvasti's destination is to a South Sudanese camp and a people that, if possible, are even more victimized and traumatized than the northern Ugandans among whom the refugees live.

There he decides to build a playground. A simple act to bring happiness to those with little. On a self-funded budget and in a region of ruthless corruption, Marvasti along with his partner, Sanya, must be smuggled in to hand deliver that big box of joy. In the ramshackle city of Gulu he hires a local driver. "Be ready before sunrise," he is told, "and wear something nice."

He puts on the nicest clothes in his suitcase, a collared shirt tucked into jeans. The driver arrives at 4:00 a.m. in an old beat-up Mercedes Benz. They avoid the main roads of the countryside, but soon hit a first military roadblock. With men in fatigues pointing machine guns through the windshield, Marvasti's story is that he is a diplomat on an official visit to the South Sudanese camp. He hopes the collared shirt and hired driver will lend him credibility, "And it worked." Marvasti is in.

Yet once inside, Marvasti explains, the real work began. "Once we got to the camp, it's like one hundred [degrees Fahrenheit]. Everyone lives in white tarp tents. There are long lines to pump water. Everyone is hiding in the shade. Everyone is so skinny. And then Sanya, my partner, got heatstroke. And all of a sudden she's like, 'Reza, what the fuck is happening? Three weeks ago we lived in Vancouver in this beautiful place. Right now we are in a South Sudan refugee camp. What the heck is happening?'"

With a team of mostly local workers, Marvasti and his recovered partner initially struggle to find a building location in the barren expanse, but eventually, in a relatively safe location near the church, they discover a single tree offering modest respite from the blistering sun. Already children were using this space to play, so Marvasti begins building. They work for eight trying weeks—scrambling for materials and adjusting to difficult conditions—but in the end Marvasti succeeds.

He explains that when the playground opened, the children—many of whom were orphans—were in a joyous uproar. "I was just sitting back and smiling. Then this guy came over to me and said, 'You did God's work. These kids, before they even got to cry, they had to run away. Some have had nothing to smile or laugh about for two years. Now look at them. They are all smiling and laughing.' Until then I wasn't sure if I was doing the right thing.

But at that moment it hit me: this is what I'm going to do for the rest of my life."

Marvasti is the founder and CEO of The Power of Play. He and his team have built playgrounds for thousands of children in Mexico and Iran, in India, in indigenous North American communities, and throughout Rwanda— where I first caught up with him. While traditional playground equipment materials are often unavailable, Marvasti explains, old car tires and other car parts are ubiquitous—and often difficult to dispose of in an environmentally friendly way. So Marvasti's team repurposes these materials into makeshift playground equipment, and in so doing "we clean up the world. More than fifty percent of the material we use is recycled." Trees are planted to replenish lost stocks, communities are taught about sustainable practices, and local leaders are trained into The Power of Play program so they may continue spreading play even after Marvasti and his team depart.

As of this writing, Marvasti is building playgrounds directly within South Sudanese territory—territory that is unstable at best and a war zone at worst. He is working out of a refugee camp for internally displaced persons and at a nearby orphanage overflowing with children victimized by decades of unremitting warfare. A ruggedly handsome thirty-eight-year-old, Marvasti exudes gentle confidence and boundless ambition while speaking about The Power of Play, or T-POP, as it's known. "I am so ambitious," he told me. "Anything that comes to children and making a difference for kids, I will go for it. I am *so* ambitious," he emphasized.

And yet, Marvasti's adrenaline-seeking days are over. "Since starting T-POP I've had no more accidents. I'm not pushing it anymore. My friends sometimes are going somewhere and say, "Reza, you want to go?' And I tell them no. I just have no desire to do that anymore."

The Science of Play

Marvasti is well-versed in the science of play. He knows that play is essential to childhood and healthy development. He recites studies showing that animals play to build physical skills but also to bond and develop their emotional repertoire. He explains that through play, animals—including humans—learn to take risks, control their emotions, and experience fear with equanimity.

Studies suggest that play is so important that it can extend animals' lives. One researcher spent fifteen years observing grizzly bears and concluded that the bears that played the most lived the longest (Brown, 2009). Another study found that rats deprived of play became emotionally crippled and unable to respond effectively to social signals.

While even rats need play, the larger the mammal's brain, the more play is needed. Children, consequently, play far, far more often than any other young mammals (Brown, 2009). As *Essentialism* author Greg McKeown (2020) explains, "Play expands our minds in ways that allow us to explore, to germinate new ideas or see old ideas in a new light. It makes us more inquisitive, more attune to novelty, more engaged. Play . . . fuels exploration. It helps us to see possibilities . . . and make connections" (86).

In newly independent South Sudan, families fight for survival. Children begin working almost as soon as they can walk—carrying a basket, watching over a younger sibling, digging a hole. In such an environment, play is not just an unaffordable luxury, it is actively stigmatized. Children at play are often taught they are "naughty," Marvasti says. The country—like many around the world—lacks not only playgrounds, but the view of childhood as a thing of whimsy and joy.

Surprisingly, the United States and South Sudan share something in common on this point. As Boston College psychologist Peter Gray (2014) explains, "Over the last 50 to 60 years, we've been continuously eroding children's freedom and opportunity to play freely." One large-scale poll found children spend less time outdoors than prison inmates (Bregman, 2020). Instead, Gray (2014) explains, children are spending more time in school, with summer breaks being reduced and school days lengthened. They also have more schoolwork—145 percent more, between the years 1981 and 1997, according to a separate study (Bregman, 2020).

Gray believes this decline in play helps explain Americans' higher rates of anxiety disorder and depression as well as a decline in creative thinking (Gray, 2014). It also may help explain children's declining sense of control over their environments, known as locus of control. Children in 2002, for instance, had a locus of control that was 80 percent lower than children in the 1960s (Bregman, 2020).

These studies reveal a time when play was more common and less structured. As Marvasti tells me, "Play by definition is a self-directed, voluntary activity. Our parents were climbing trees, playing with friends on the street. Play was a part of life" (Marvasti, 2021). Consistent with the vertically individualistic culture, however, today many parents structure their children's play. These are scheduled play dates, outings with adults, and organized sports. And they are often competitive.

Marvasti explains: "In sports you take a side. You are playing for losing or winning. And everybody is cheering for you, or yelling at you, telling you what to do. While you are competing you are screaming and cursing, you are not happy. Look at Olympic athletes: they are at the top of the top. They are 2 milliseconds behind the winner, they come in second, and they are *crying*. And they are already on top of billions of people, but they're sad because they're not number one. That is not play." Research even shows that watching and playing competitive sports such as football and basketball can fulfill individuals' desire to dominate or exert power over others (House et al., 2004). Structured play, therefore, may strengthen vertical individualists' already overdeveloped competitive instinct.

Self-directed play, by contrast, is cooperative. "It's a two-way thing," Marvasti explains. "It's not winning and losing. It's sitting on the see-saw and knowing that you're going to make it more fun for the other person by pushing harder." Think about it this way, Marvasti said: After the end of the game, the first thing the parents ask is "Did you win? Did you score any points?" With play, they only ask, "Was it fun? Did you have a good time?" As for kids at play, "A child's laughter is the most powerful human expression. Not only am I surrounded by it, I am *causing it*. This happiness of kids, it is the most contagious thing we have among humans. And [we] are creating an army of happy children. Now you tell me: is there any more powerful way to make our world a happy place? And just absorbing that, being a part of that, that's why it's the ultimate joy."

Jerry White, James Doty, and now Reza Marvasti: to a lifestyle of enlightened self-interest each converted, but only upon the altar of loss, misery, pain. Nonetheless, Marvasti says, "I can't even compare how much I've gained. What I gave up ... " He stopped, reconsidered. "No. There's nothing I gave up. I changed some materials, some *things*, for my ultimate joy."

A Material Conversion

In the year 1182 Francis was born in a fortified town near the Apennine mountains to a nouveau-riche Italian silk merchant. It was the high Middle Ages, the glittering Renaissance still centuries away. Francis came of age in a world in which boys and young men adored the semi-mythical action heroes Charlemagne, Roland, and Lancelot, each an Avenger or Schwarzenegger of his day. Francis got into the music scene, singing his own melodies to enliven a crowd. Not unlike today's prosperous youth, Francis took to fine clothing and spent lavishly on booze and bread at citywide parties known as "feasts" (Vauchez, 2012).

Yet amid it all were hints of discontentment foreshadowing a dramatic conversion. The existence of strict social classes excluded and grated on

Francis, who aspired to the nobility, but as a merchant's son possessed wealth with little political power. Soon he lacked wealth, too (Vauchez, 2012). While selling his wares in the market, a beggar approached. Initially ignoring the man to finish his sale, Francis belatedly ran after the needy man and offered him everything in his pockets. This altruistic impulse, Francis writes, marked his moment of clarity.

Not long after, it was Francis begging in the streets. He renounced his family's wealth, perhaps apocryphally stripping off his clothes to signal the completeness of his sacrifice. In return, his furious father publicly disowned him. Despite renouncing material things, however, Francis had not renounced his world. He soon founded the Franciscan Order, through which he and his followers would eventually restore chapels and nurse lepers—then considered the "dregs of society"—all while continuing to live a simple life. For these acts and countless others, Francis would thereafter be venerated as *Saint* Francis of Assisi (Vauchez, 2012).

Material renunciation is a minor theme among the spiritually inclined. The noble-born Buddha cut off his hair to symbolize a Francis-like renunciation of material goods. The Prophet Muhammed traded the prosperous commercial world of Mecca for an isolated cave in which divine revelations led him to reject the love of wealth.

These men of the cloth are accompanied by a long line of men of the mind. *Walden* author Henry David Thoreau, speaking to the "mass of men who are discontented," warned in the mid-nineteenth century against materialism, defined as the belief that money brings happiness (Campbell, 1987). Percy Bysse Shelley decades earlier had written *Ozymandias,* a poem mocking the immortal pretentions of an Egyptian pharaoh whose great works would—like all material things—eventually decay into rubble. Michel de Montaigne (2004) in sixteenth-century France wrote that virtues are measured "not in the worth of our horse or our weapons, but in our own." Dante Alighieri melodramatically doomed materialists of fourteenth-century Italy to the sixth circle of hell. And in the classical Greek era, Epicurus—rather unfairly condemned to Dante's sixth circle—argued that there is little to no correlation between improved well-being and material achievements (O'Neill, 2006). Finally, Aristotle considered the pursuit of pleasure and wealth no more than "a life suitable to beasts" (Keeling, 2017: 231).

Put more simply? Countless spiritual and intellectual leaders over the centuries assert that money doesn't buy happiness. It can, in fact, cause unhappiness. This is what Marvasti meant when he dismissively said he gave up only *things,* that is, nothing that really mattered. Similarly, Jerry White recalls materialists that had, like Doty, experienced bankruptcy, only to think, "I'm so glad that happened to me. I'm not wealthier than I was five minutes ago, but I'm richer" (White, 2020).

And yet Americans do love, even worship, the Almighty Dollar, the United States being among the world's most materialistic culture, and arguably—thanks to unequally distributed abundance—among the most materialistic *ever* (Ger & Belk, 1996). Americans are also unusually materialistic relative to their wealth, with studies finding that as wealth increases, materialism typically decreases—except, that is, in the United States and a small number of other culturally similar Anglo-American countries such as New Zealand, where materialism increases as the countries grow wealthier (Ger & Belk, 1996). As Doty (2017) says when explaining people's shock that he would give away the last of his fortune, "One of humanity's most enduring myths is that wealth will bring happiness and money is the solution to any problem" (227).

Yet a paradox is at play. In some instances money *can and does* buy happiness. But materialists, who believe that things will make them happy, are less happy than nonmaterialists (Richins & Dawson, 1992; Ryan & Dziurawiec, 2001). Like an accountant managing the books, let us attempt a reconciliation of these disparate ledgers.

The Purchase and the Price of Materialism

The father-son combo Ed Diener and Robert Biswas-Diener (2002) outline money's beneficial outcomes. They show that wealthier criminals receive lighter prison sentences, probably in part because they can afford stronger legal representation. The wealthy have better mental and physical health, they live longer, and they are less likely to experience violent crimes. Their childrens' infant mortality rates are lower and they experience less daily stress. All these things—poor health, infant mortality, violent crimes, life stressors—may obstruct happiness. True, the *absence* of unhappiness is not the same as the *presence* of happiness. Yet, like an oxygen-rich planet affords the possibility for life, wealth generates the conditions for, but not the guarantee of, a happy life.

It is true that on average, wealthier people and countries really are happier than poorer ones, thanks in part to increased security, improved health outcomes, and education and the financial wherewithal to overcome challenges. In addition, money tends to provide greater autonomy, which is one of the essential indices of life satisfaction (Killingsworth, 2021).

While work by Nobel Prize–winning economist Angus Deaton led to widely publicized claims that the benefits of income on happiness level off around US$75,000 (Kahneman & Deaton, 2010), more recent work by Wharton's Matthew Killingsworth (2021) suggests that the plateau may not be reached until attaining higher income levels—if at all. Killingsworth's study will have to withstand scrutiny in the years to come. However, at the very least it appears that as income rises, increases in happiness slow precipitously. As Deaton documents (2008), life satisfaction increases at a decreasing rate as GDP per capita reaches higher levels. His work suggests, for instance, that people of low-income Togo would see substantial increases in happiness with rather modest increases in wealth; but as people in the relatively wealthy countries of Norway, Finland, Denmark, or the United States grow wealthier, they are not likely to grow much happier.

Globally, the positive outcomes associated with income decrease dramatically as income rises above the modest sum of $10,000 per capita (in 2002 dollars) (Frey and Stutzer, 2002). In the United States, where expenses are higher than the global average, scholars debate the level at which positive benefits drop off. A 2006 Pew Research Center study showed that while 49 percent of people with an annual family income above $100,000 reported being "very happy," the same was true of only 24 percent of families earning less than $30,000 (Rubin, 2009).

If everyone were to grow equally wealthy, moreover, it is unlikely that happiness would skyrocket. Longitudinal studies—conducted over decades that saw vastly increasing wealth in the United States—support this interpretation. As Diener and Biswas-Diener (2002) write, "The increase in income was dramatic in the United States from World War II to 1995. For example, in 1988 the lowest fifth of the American population had per capita expenditures, adjusted for cost of living, higher than the median income in 1955! *Yet little or no change in* [happiness] *occurred during this period*" (139, emphasis added).

Japan saw even more dramatic rises in income with similar effects. In 1958, for instance, the average adjusted income of Japanese citizens was below today's poverty line. Japan today is one of the world's wealthiest nations. And yet, like the United States, Japan has seen but the tiniest of slivers of increased happiness during this period of remarkable growth (Diener & Biswas-Diener, 2002). In more recent decades, China has followed a similar trajectory, growing dramatically wealthier but not happier (Knight & Gunatilaka, 2011).

Diener and Biswas-Diener (2002) note that the data "implies that enormous increases in wealth in developed nations are required to produce tiny increments in happiness" (141). Or, as the scholar Leaf Van Boven (2005) puts it more simply: "The observation that material gains fail to produce lasting increases in happiness has become painfully salient in recent decades"

(133). To quote economist Robert H. Frank, "Bigger houses and faster cars, it seems, do not make us any happier" (2000: 6).

First, these results highlight the subjective benefits of money, as least as much as its objective benefits, namely, that the super-wealthy in the United States played the game and won. They thus fit in by standing out, gaining self-esteem and status, and thus increased satisfaction with life, from having *more than others*. Second, as Theodore Roosevelt highlighted in that 1937 inaugural address, the results suggest that the benefits of spreading wealth among the poor exceed the benefits of further enriching the upper echelon. And third, that aspiring for wealth above and beyond basic needs is to overvalue money. As *7 Habits of Highly Effective People* author Stephen Covey (2013) writes, "Sometimes there are apparently noble reasons given for making money, such as the desire to take care of one's family. And these things are important. But to focus on money-making as a center will bring about its own undoing" (120).

Covey, with his discussion of "noble reasons" for making money, hits on another important point. Reza Marvasti, after all, needed money from the sale of his business and possessions to fund that first playground in northern Uganda. He solicits donations still to keep going in a philanthropic life that he describes as the "ultimate happiness." Without money he would have no play-grounds to build, no joy to bring. Marvasti's narrative thus provides a crucial insight by emphasizing *when* money brings happiness. There is the vertically individualistic way, in which money fails to bring happiness. But for ESIs like Marvasti? Money pays.

6

From Status-Seeking
to Experience-Seeking

Spending Like a Horizontal Individualist

Three primary motives underpin materialism. The first is insecurity. Money is seen to protect against life's discomfiting uncertainties. Materialists see a world of scarcity and derive more satisfaction from accumulating money than spending it. The second category is pleasure: hedonists enjoy spending for the pleasures it brings. We do live in a world of abundance, but human biology still recalls the scarce days of early humankind. Triggered with each purchase is the release of pleasure chemicals, which, like a drug, keeps consumers coming back for more and more, at higher and higher doses. Consumption consequently *feels* good. The third is enhanced self-image: the materialists derive self-worth and status from the things they have and the money they make (Górnik-Durose & Jach, 2020).

Vertical individualism enhances all three motives. Financial insecurity is greater in the cutthroat economies of vertical individualists than in more communal societies. This legitimates to some extent the concerns of the Ebenezer Scrooge–like penny-pinchers. Hedonism, meanwhile, is consistent with the vertical individualistic framework in which self is valued above almost anything else.

Finally, vertical individualists are more status-oriented than horizontalists, with the latter better able to transcend self-interests (Roccas, 2003). Status-seeking materialism and a fragile ego are consequently by-products of a competitive, vertical society that elevates the rich and powerful and judges the less prosperous as less successful.

Jewish Israeli women considering the ideal partner, for instance, reported that wealth was a key consideration. Numerous studies show that American women, too, put a high value on the material wealth of prospective partners (Jonason, Li, & Madson, 2012). However, researchers asked women living in ultra-Orthodox communities about their priorities. These women told researchers that they cared very little about the wealth of ideal partners. Rather, they valued openly pious, religious partners.

The difference between women in the two communities? Both were status-seeking, which recall is a universal tendency. Yet among Israeli society in general, material wealth enhances status, just as it does in the United States. Among Ultra-Orthodox communities, however, men's status is determined less by wealth than by piety (Griskevicius & Kenrick, 2013; Yaffe, McDonald, Halperin, & Saguy, 2018).

American culture connects material accumulation with status, so materialists conspicuously consume to establish superiority over those with whom they imagine they compete (Braun & Wicklund, 1989; Mowen, 2004). As York University materialism scholar Russel Belk (2001) writes, "Materialism can result in ruthless competition to see who can consume the most conspicuously" (7). Conspicuous consumption makes material gains visible, so that vertical individualists fit in by standing out.

What are the effects of this consumption? Jim Doty (2021) told me that many people "falsely believe that the more stuff they get the more people will look up to them." Contrary to materialist beliefs, however, the effect of consumption is not to increase happiness. It is to diminish it—for self and for others (Scott, 2009). Neuroscientist V. S. Ramachandran and psychologist Baland Jalal (2017) offer insight into materialist priorities after asking participants, "Are you likely to envy the happiest person in the world, someone living like the Dalai Lama? Or are you more envious of someone who is not the happiest in the world, but living like Hugh Hefner?" The researchers report that males *unanimously* chose the latter, opting for status and wealth over happiness.

As Belk (2001) explains, "Materialistic people are not as happy and satisfied with their lives as less materialistic people" (4). This negative relationship, between materialism and well-being, is confirmed in a wide variety of studies—studies conducted on both the young and the old and among individuals living around the world (Dittmar, Bond, Hurst, & Kasser, 2014). This all leads to the inevitable conclusion that materialism, the belief that happiness lies in having more things, is a deeply flawed ideology.

Take the purchase of a new car. Neither the car itself, nor the effect of impressing others with the car (if indeed they are impressed) are likely to sustainably increase happiness (Scott, 2009). Instead, buyers quickly revert to baseline satisfaction. In addition, the time and effort involved in working to afford the car can crowd out other, more psychologically satisfying pursuits (Dittmar et al., 2014). This crowding-out effect leaves materialistic people less likely to experience self-actualization, less likely to feel a sense of vitality or joie de vivre, and—as with vertical individualists in general—more likely to experience depression and anxiety (Kasser & Ryan, 1993, 1996).

Also in common with the isolating tendencies of vertical individualism, materialism tends to separate one from others, diminishing social connections and in turn reducing well-being (Burroughs & Rindfleisch, 2002). In one study, materialistic working professionals were even more likely to overcharge customers, abuse expense accounts, and steal merchandise (Tang & Chiu, 2003). Doty (2021) speaks to this material-induced isolation: "As you get wealthier," he explains, "you don't need others to survive. Most of us need to ensure that we nurture relationships that allow us to survive and prosper." Yet, among the very rich, Doty argues, "everyone is replaceable. They [the rich] don't need to be kind to anybody."

The relationship between poverty and materialism is somewhat more complex. Consider a 1990 *Boston Globe* article titled "New Hampshire's New Homeless Belie the Stereotypes." The story centered on Lisa Labnon, "a 30-year-old New Hampshire woman [who had] become homeless when she lost her job and her condominium was repossessed. She refused to sell her Mercedes and mink coat, however, because the loss in image and self-esteem would be too great" (Gaines, 1990). Instead, she lived in her Mercedes and walked the street in mink, forgoing more basic needs in favor of status-striving.

In the United States, the poor and those without homes are stigmatized and regularly blamed for their situations (Phelan, Link, Moore, & Stueve, 1997). It is important, therefore, to distinguish between those who *seek* high status from those who—perhaps like Lisa Labnon—aim to *avoid* low status and its associated costs. The social sciences—not to mention millennia of human history—have shown that low status individuals are subject to heavy societal sanctions (Kellerman, 2010). Similarly, there is some evidence that status can help individuals meet basic needs for safety and sustenance (Kasser et al., 2004). Thus, researcher Judith Lichtenberg (1996) notes that status-seeking may at times be both rational and consistent with the pursuit of happiness.

In the past some researchers even speculated that materialism's negative effects might be reduced among the poor. The thinking went that a higher percentage of their earnings went to satisfying basic needs—housing, health, and security—which in fact increased well-being and happiness. Instead, however, researchers found that the poor are even *more* harmed by materialism. Whereas the wealthy materialist can afford that sports car or supersized TV, the poor materialist is more likely to sacrifice necessities in lieu of status-enhancing luxuries—thus doubling down on the unhappiness disadvantage (Belk, 2001).

Studies also show that societies in poorer countries as well as individuals raised in less-affluent environments place a higher value on materialism than wealthy countries and the general public, respectively (Ger & Belk, 1996; Kasser, Ryan, Zax, & Sameroff, 1995). Highly materialistic teens, for instance, are *more* likely to be socioeconomically disadvantaged, due to inadequate access to education, low parental income, or low neighborhood quality (Cohen & Cohen, 2013). Individuals who grow up experiencing insecurity and deprivation are more likely to grow into materialistic adults, as well (Ahuvia & Wong, 2002). One classic study from 1947 even found that poor children overestimated the size of coins, relative to wealthier children's perceptions (Bruner & Goodman, 1947). Adding insult to injury, materialists are, unsurprisingly, more likely to fall into debt (Van Boven, 2005).

What about successful materialists? Whereas the poor materialist may suffer in knowing he failed to achieve his goals, or may experience envy at others' successes, the successful materialist ought to bask in victory. And yet studies find that wealthy materialists are more dissatisfied than nonmaterialists (Dittmar et al., 2014). The problem may be that although people tend to grow wealthier with age, their rising material appetites outpace their growing wealth (Diener & Biswas-Diener, 2002).

Vertical individualists are, moreover, likely to pass down these materialistic values to their children (Twenge, 2010)—how could they not? Children as young as eight in one study understood the "status implications" of different brands, a finding that pointedly reveals the connection between materialism and status-seeking. Another study found American children recognized about a thousand corporate logos. They could, by contrast, identify fewer than ten native plants and animals (Belk, 2001).

The negative effects of materialism are, furthermore, exacerbated in young people. Psychologists Timothy Kasser and Richard Ryan (2001), for instance, find that materialistic teenagers report higher levels of alcohol, cigarette, and drug use than their less-materialistic peers. Other studies associate adolescent materialism with psychological disorders, including attention deficit disorder, conduct disorder, and narcissism (Cohen & Cohen, 2013). Yet the idea that money does not bring happiness is as widely accepted as it is ignored (Ger & Belk, 1999). In one 1999 study, research subjects in the United States, Turkey, Romania, and Western Europe overwhelmingly regarded materialism as something negative. Ironically, the study authors find, they almost all engaged in consumption practices that appear quite materialistic (Ger & Belk, 1999).

As Princeton sociologist Robert Wuthnow (1994) reports, "Materialism is a generalized symbol that stands for evil in our culture. . . . Sensing that something is wrong with society, people easily point their finger at material-ism" (177). Researchers at one time speculated that perhaps materialists fare so poorly precisely because they are so stigmatized. The scholars wondered if the negative effects would persist in cultures that celebrate materialism. Enter the typical MBA (master of business administration) students, a group that notoriously glamorizes materialism. Indeed, studies repeatedly show that MBA students—and here we acknowledge that two of our three authors hold MBAs—are on average more self-centered, more achievement-oriented, and more pleasure-seeking than their peers (Lan, Gowing, Rieger, McMahon, & King, 2010; Krishnan, 2008). Despite their materialism-friendly environment, however, a study involving Singaporean MBA students found that those highest in materialism were among their cohort's unhappiest (Kasser & Ahuvia, 2002).

It is not just stigma, then, that renders materialism an active and harmful practice. And yet, denials aside, materialism is widely practiced and even on the rise (Ger & Belk, 1999). Between 1987 to 1994, for instance, the income reported to be needed to "fulfill all your dreams" increased from $50,000 to $102,000. The number of Americans reporting that a vacation home was part and parcel of the good life increased 84 percent between 1975 and 1991. Of those earning over $100,000 as far back as 1995, nearly one in five suggested that they spent all of their money on basic necessities (Diener & Biswas-Diener, 2002). Meanwhile, the number of external storage units to hold all those "necessities" approximately doubled in just a ten-year period in the early 2000s (Rubin, 2009) and advertisements appealing less to utility and more to luxury increased consistently over a forty-year period in the late twentieth century (Belk & Pollay, 1985).

Charles Dickens wrote in his classic novel *David Copperfield,* "Annual income twenty pounds, annual expenditure nineteen six, result happiness. Annual income twenty pounds, annual expenditures twenty pounds ought and six, result misery" (1850, 259). Mislabeling necessities as luxuries has the result of leaving too many Americans in debt and, as Dickens opined, in "mis-ery." Misapprehending true needs also leaves fewer resources to use toward other, more-fulfilling ends. If Americans were to more accurately distinguish between necessities and unnecessary luxuries, for instance, how many more would balance compensation with more meaningful and satisfying work? Take the chance on a new business? Retire younger and pursue more mean-ingful pursuits? After all, the value of money lies in the freedom that it can bring (Killingsworth, 2021).

A similar rise in materialism is underway in other Western countries with whom the United States shares many cultural similarities. As Celeste Headlee (2020) reports, "The household savings rate in the European Union hovers at about 10 percent. That's close to what it was in 1960 in the United

States. Now it's fallen to about 2 percent for Americans, and the American approach to spending may be spreading. In 2017, for the first time in three decades, British citizens spent more than they made. Australia has seen a similar change: Savings fell from nearly 10 percent in 1959 to just over 2 percent in 2018" (69).

Poorer countries, too, are quickly signing up for the materialistic ideal. Materialism and conspicuous consumption are on the rise among the Chinese, a people who have gone from poverty to relative wealth in just one or two generations (Podoshen, Li, & Zhang, 2011). In Ghana the prosperity gospel has taken hold, with pastors recklessly promising that through faith— read: donations—prosperity will come (McCauley, 2013). With overflowing coffers, more and more spiritual leaders are local "big men." They challenge traditional government and business leaders with their wealth and power— wealth and power for which, as with the rich and famous of the United States, they are idolized (McCauley, 2013).

Materialism is very much present in American society, indeed in increasing swaths of the world, and most of us are probably more materialistic than we'd like to admit. There is, however, one ray of light amid this darkness: those who have long possessed relative wealth are moving in the opposite direction, often quite vocally. For instance, as Americans have grown dramatically more materialistic over the last twenty-five years, more-horizontal Europeans have become less materialistic (Bartolini & Sarracino, 2017).

One explanation for this change is that wealth is more widely shared in Europe and a broader subset of its population experiences the dissipating pleasures of the materialistic lifestyle. Dissatisfied materialists may thus respond by reducing materialistic impulses. In similar terms, older individuals— disgruntled at last by their material pursuits—tend to exhibit less materialism despite greater wealth (Diener & Biswas-Diener, 2002). Unlike in Europe, however, in the vastly unequal United States there is a steady flow of disenfranchised poor ready to take the place of disenchanted materialists.

Cineas, counselor to the ill-fated Pyrrhus, understood that money, put to proper ends, is helpful to bring about the truly fine things in life. If he were still around today, how might Cineas advise the use of money to achieve these more hopeful ends?

Money Matters: From Vertical to Horizontal

If materialism is the misguided belief that money brings happiness, then how is it possible to explain data showing that the wealthy tend to be happier? If not coming from materialistic ends, what drives this well-being? Part of the explanation may be the status and power it brings, which renders the affluent happier only so long as others remain worse off. This, of course, is not a particularly hopeful solution.

However, the wealthy may also use their money to sustainable benefit—and regardless of others' wealth. As Diener and Biswas-Diener (2002) found, wealth instrumentally used may generate health and security, and by increasing autonomy or locus of control it may also lower stress. Sixteenth-century polymath Francis Bacon intuited that "money is a great servant but a bad master" (Wei, 2021). Aristotle, writing nearly two thousand years before Bacon, held that "wealth is clearly not the good we are seeking, since it is merely useful, for getting something else" (Crisp, 2000: 7).

In the late twentieth century, Mihaly Csikszentmihalyi and Eugene Rochberg-Halton (1981) were among the first psychologists to scientifically describe the principles relating to healthy and harmful uses of money. Csikszentmihalyi, one of the world's leading happiness researchers, articulated with Rochberg-Halton the views of nonmaterialists who, like Bacon and Aristotle, see material things as useful instruments. That is, how a new car may be an *instrument* for weekend visits to waterfalls or night classes at the local college.

Scholars balked, however, noting that materialists also see their cars as instruments. Yet instead of viewing access to nature or higher learning as the goal, it may be status-seeking or hedonic drive that ignite a materialist's engines. Researchers such as Marsha Richins and Scott Dawson (1992) thus criticized the pair for arbitrarily declaring some ends "better" than others.

Richins and Dawson argue, essentially, that the researchers were applying their own ideas of good and bad without any empirical support for distinguishing good from bad. At the time, scholars basically agreed that materialism leads adherents astray, and they also agreed that money sometimes serves valued ends. They struggled, nevertheless, to articulate a distinction between healthy and harmful uses of money (Scott, 2009).

Enter self-determination theory, a paradigm changer in the field of psychology, and an "I told you so" moment for Csikszentmihalyi and Halton. Developed over decades by Edward Deci and Richard Ryan and popularized under the steady hand of author Daniel Pink (2011) in his book *Drive*, self-determination theory now stands as one of social science's most well-validated theories.

Self-determination theory holds that autonomy, competence, and relatedness tend to maximize individual happiness (Deci & Ryan, 2013; Pink, 2011). Autonomous individuals experience independence and the freedom to choose what to do or not to do. Competence measures one's ability to complete challenging tasks, with mastery representing the desired pinnacle of achievement. Finally, relatedness measures the strength of relationships with family, friends, and coworkers. These are all viewed as intrinsic goals, which are "desires congruent with actualizing and growth tendencies natural to humans" (Kasser & Ryan, 1996: 280). In plain English, these three variables tend to satisfy deep human needs. By contrast, extrinsic goals "depend on the contingent reactions of others" and are generally less satisfying objects of attention (280).

Years earlier, with Deci and Ryan's research not yet fully available, Csikszentmihalyi argued that material values enhance well-being when money is used to support personal growth, self-actualization, and strong relationships. Bolstered by this new theory of self-determination, researchers could finally empirically test Csikszentmihalyi and Rochberg-Halton's results.

Contemporary researchers found that using money in pursuit of extrinsic goals—such as status—is indeed associated with lower well-being indices. For instance, those reporting financial success as a central motive show lower levels of self-actualization (Kasser & Ryan, 1996). They are less likely to enter the so-called flow state, that desirable place where work is deeply satisfying, fully absorbing, and productivity is at its highest potential (Kasser, 2002; Kasser & Ryan, 1993). Materialists also value financial security more highly than close relationships (Richins & Dawson, 1992). Unsurprisingly, materialists experience lower-quality relationships and stronger feelings of insecurity and societal alienation (Kasser, 2002).

Researchers also have found that when used in service of intrinsic goals, money serves as an instrument of happiness (Howell & Hill, 2009) And yet, Kasser and Ryan (1993), applying their self-determination theory to the question of materialism, find that extrinsic motivation reduces the capacity to fulfill these value-adding intrinsic goals. Furthermore, research suggests that when materialists exhibit simultaneously materialistic (extrinsic) and communal (intrinsic) values, their sense of well-being declines yet further. Scholars suspect this result is because materialism and communalism are conflicting values and they create psychological tension for people struggling to meet the demands of both (Burroughs & Rindfleisch, 2002; La Barbera & Gürhan, 1997).

Using money for intrinsic purposes doesn't simply put the brakes on this long list of negative consequences, however. In fact, it reverses the direction and leads to positive outcomes. Thus, money *does* bring happiness, at least when expenditures expedite intrinsic goals. As one study put it, "It may be that income earned after basic needs are satisfied can increase [happiness] *only when* it satisfies high-order"—read: intrinsic—"psychological needs" (Howell & Hill, 2009: 518).

This link was soon replicated in studies among Americans, Germans, Russians, and respondents from a variety of other nationalities (Burroughs & Rindfleisch, 2002; Kasser & Ryan, 1996; Ryan, Chirkov, Little, Sheldon, Timoshina, & Deci, 1999; Schmuck, Kasser, & Ryan, 2000). The research had caught up to Csikszentmihalyi and Rochberg-Halton, not to mention Pyrrhus, Bacon, and Aristotle.

This contrast between intrinsic and extrinsic motives neatly aligns with vertical and horizontal cultural values. Vertical individualists are extrinsically motivated—recall that they seek their welfare through competition and social acceptance. Horizontal individualists are, by contrast, intrinsically motivated. They look within, seeking self- rather than social validation.

The Gautama Buddha famously asserted that desire is the root of all suffering. His contemporary messenger, the Dalai Lama, speaks of *chisoku*, or contentment (Dessì, 2017). The Dalai Lama says, "Certain desires are positive: a desire for happiness, for peace, for a friendlier world. These are very useful. But at some point, desires can become unreasonable. . . . Greed is an exaggerated form of desire, and that leads to trouble. Although the underlying motive of greed is to seek satisfaction, *the irony is that even after obtaining the object of your desire, you are still not satisfied.* The true antidote to greed is contentment. If you have a strong sense of contentment, it doesn't matter whether you obtain the object or not; either way, you are still content" (Dalai Lama & Cutler, 2010: 46–47, emphasis added).

To understand why the materialist is so rarely satisfied, we return briefly to the story of Lisa Labnon. The materialist Labnon, who perhaps understandably held onto her Mercedes Benz and mink coat even as she lost her home, was stuck in an extrinsic mindset (Kasser & Ryan, 1993). The satisfaction the fur coat brought to Labnon was "contingent"—to use the language of self-determination theory—on others' positive reactions. Perhaps one sees a fur coat as alluring, another as animal abuse; some as trendy, others as passee. This uncertainty increases the anxiety and stress of extrinsically motivated people like Labnon, who nervously hope to measure up to external expectations (Burroughs & Rindfleisch, 2002; Kasser & Ryan, 1993; Kasser, 2002). Material objects, the presumed source of happiness, are thus unable to satiate their possessors (Holt, 1995).

Intrinsic motivations, by contrast, are more easily satisfied and subject only to self-assessments. Consider Peter Buffett, a horizontal individualist standing in contrast to the vertical Labnon. Wild child of Warren and carefree brother of farmer-philanthropist Howard, Peter Buffett dramatically altered his life trajectory at just nineteen years of age. With his family's blessing, he dropped out of Stanford University and sold his inherited Berkshire Hathaway stock. He pocketed $90,000 from the sale and asked his father to help him budget the money to last. He figured he would need to stretch it out since he'd just jilted Stanford to become a musician.

Today that stock would be worth about $90 million. Ninety. Million. Dollars. Astoundingly, Buffett claims to have no regrets about selling his stock. Is that plausible? Consider that for a relatively trivial $90,000, Buffett purchased a bank vault overflowing with intrinsic satisfaction. He rented a small apartment in San Francisco, bought a "funky car," and used his inheritance to "buy the time needed to explore" his new career. "My sole extravagance," Buffett (2011) writes, "was in updating and expanding my recording equipment" (113).

A few years later he was asked to write a ten-second advertisement for a little-known start-up channel on cable television called MTV Music Television. MTV blew up, Buffett gained popularity, and before long work flooded in (Buffett, 2011). Over the years Buffett released sixteen musical albums while writing musical scores for television and movies, including the crescendo to Kevin Costner's epic film *Dances with Wolves*. He collaborated with Grammy-nominated musician Akan and Grammy-winner Angelique Kidjo, and even won an Emmy for his musical number on the CBS Miniseries *500 Nations* (GDA Speakers, 2022). He has, in his words, lived a life worth living—one that even $90 million could not purchase.

Buffett used his money to purchase intrinsic satisfaction: competence as a musician and the autonomy to pursue a passion unhindered by other responsibilities. While acknowledging his privilege, in a chapter titled "Buying time" he ponders why more privileged young people aren't taking advantage of the "luxury of time" that money can buy. He notes sardonically, "I've never known anyone to have been hurt by living for a while on cottage cheese and apples" (119).

In centuries past, social philosophers, economists, and politicians blithely assumed that should the progress of technological revolution make possible wealth such as we now have, we would be a most contented people, working just a few hours each week. As late as 1965, a US Senate subcommittee predicted that by the year 2000, Americans would work around twenty hours per week and take nearly two months of vacation time (De Graaf & Batker, 2011). John Maynard Keynes famously predicted in 1930 that one hundred years later we would all be working fifteen hours each week. Georgetown economist Karl Widerquist (2006) says of Keynes's theory: "It didn't seem logical to people in 1930 that the economy could continue to grow without freeing us from the struggle for survival" (85).

In fact, work hours declined throughout the nineteenth and early twentieth centuries. Yet this downward trend soon reversed. Today's American works 199 hours per year *more* than did an American in 1973 (Hunnicutt, 2013). The "overwork" scholar Benjamin Hunnicutt (2013) argues that Americans value work more than any other society, current or past. Furthermore, the average American today gets less than ten paid vacation days annually, while around one-quarter receive no paid time off (Hess, 2018). And, as noted already, for decades Americans have left unused more and more of these scarce vacation days (US Travel Association, 2022).

Two factors explain why Americans continue to work even as wealth surpasses basic needs: a rise in materialism and a rise in inequality (Headlee, 2020). Both materialism and inequality are driven by verticalism. Thus, some work long hours because the benefits of prosperity never reach them; others who could afford to work less, or who could work to ensure that *others* gain the benefit of prosperity—such as Reza Marvasti and Mike Brady—have instead increased their spending on nonessential luxury goods.

For this prosperous group of materialists, researchers coined a new term: "overearners" who earn more than they need rather than taking the opportunity to "work less and enjoy more" (Hsee, Zhang, Cai, & Zhang, 2013). Researchers describe a process of "mindless accumulation," of working until tired rather than until material needs are satisfied. This over-accumulation comes at the expense of happiness. As author Celeste Headlee (2020) writes, "If your goal is less stress and more happiness, years of scientific research have proven that rather than trading your time for money, it's best to trade your money for time" (198). In this way, autonomy is purchased.

Competence and relatedness are also for sale. Close personal relationships—or relatedness—are considerably more important than money, once basic needs are met. Money can facilitate close personal relationships, such as affording a family vacation or a night out with a budding romantic partner. Similarly, spending money to afford Italian lessons at the local college may purchase a sense of competence.

It bears noting, however, that a little money may go a long way. Costa Rica, for example, is ranked the thirteenth-happiest country (BER, 2018), despite a GDP per capita of just over $12,000 (World Bank, 2020a). The *World Happiness Report* finds that high levels of social support boost Central Americans far beyond what its middling income alone would predict (BER, 2018). Similarly, the happiest workers tend to be those working in socially rich even if modestly paid occupations, such as hairdressers (BBC News, 2005).

To buy competence, relatedness, and autonomy is to choose experiences over things. Experiences may satisfy intrinsic needs and thus increase happiness more effectively than do material purchases (Van Boven & Gilovich, 2003). Like Peter Buffett, a price may be paid—even if not a $90 million price—to gain mastery over a new tool or trade. One may also purchase experiences with loved ones; with autonomy one can buy time to enjoy those experiences. There is another psychological benefit to these experiential purchases as well, and it has to do with how experiential and material purchases are distinctly recalled.

Horizontal Individualism and Paying for Experience

Money brings happiness when used to meet *basic* needs, such as housing, food, water, safety, and security. And yet what is considered a basic need is often a questionable proposition. Ever more Americans claim that a second home or a six-figure salary are necessities rather than luxuries.

To be fair, one might argue that owning a villa by the sea is necessary if for no other reason than to achieve solitude and relaxation. But how many of us have seen (or been) the person on vacation who is unable to detach from work or release stress? How many monks, conversely, retreat to distant caves to live in utter tranquility? The point? Gaining tranquility is cheap. Or as the ancient Roman poet Horace put it around the time of Christ: "Reason and sense remove anxiety, / Not Villas that look upon the sea."

Consider the value derived from spending on experiences such as the proverbial dinner and a movie, or mountain climb, or vacation. Each of these may validate intrinsic motives for growth (Howell & Hill, 2009). Traveling is to learn about the world beyond. When climbing mountains, inner resilience—and perhaps limits, too—become better understood. Even dinner and a movie may satisfy intrinsic motives to experience life's little pleasures. In addition, the intellect is most satisfied when mindfully focused on a particular object of attention. As psychologist Daniel Gilbert and colleagues write, "A wandering mind is an unhappy mind, and one of the benefits of experiences is that they keep us focused on the here and now" (Dunn, Gilbert, & Wilson, 2011: 7). It is this ability for experiences to satisfy growth needs that leads to a surprising finding: that experiences can bring satisfaction *even when they aren't particularly enjoyed.*

A mountain trek may have brought great pain from battling the elements or aging knees. A vacation may have featured long airport security lines and perhaps a couple of screaming kids. Looking back, however, we see such challenges as part of our personal growth, and as a result we recall positively experiential purchases, whether good or bad in the moment (Van Boven & Gilovich, 2003).

By contrast, people seem to experience no such reevaluative capacity from material purchases (Van Boven & Gilovich, 2003). If the picture on a purchased TV is not quite as crisp as hoped, we are not likely to think back years later and decide that it was, after all, a kaleidoscope of beauty. In fact, even if first impressions are positive, even the most beautiful of possessions quickly lose their luster in a process known as hedonic adaptation (see chapter 7).

Humans consequently tend to view their experiences, rather than their things, as more integral to their sense of self, a finding which one study's authors attribute to the increased value derived from experiences (Carter & Gilovich, 2012). This cognitive mechanism also helps explain why in one study of over a thousand American participants, 57 percent reported greater satisfaction with their experiential purchases, while just 34 percent preferred their material ones (Van Boven & Gilovich, 2003). In another study, participants similarly indicated that experiential purchases brought greater satisfaction while reporting fewer regrets (Van Boven, 2005).

Another reason experiences tend to increase happiness is that, unlike material purchases, experiences tend to occur in conjunction with other people. We may go to dinner by ourselves, for instance, but we're more likely to go with a friend or loved one. Experiences are therefore more likely to draw on the intrinsic motivation for relatedness (Van Boven & Gilovich, 2003). This helps explain why even experiences that reek of luxury and status-seeking—such as visits to high-end hotels—may nonetheless bring a degree of happiness superior to objects (Holt, 1995). Research suggests a benefit to prioritizing experiences, especially experiences enjoyed with others, over objects (Caprariello & Reis, 2013; Van Boven & Gilovich, 2003). In the same vein, the memory of an experience—even one that occurred in isolation—often has a social connection. You may recall talking to friends about that lake vacation. Your friends listened intently, living vicariously through you and perhaps thinking about their recent trip to the Rocky Mountains.

Are we as likely to share memories of our purchases? If we do, will our friends listen as intently? The University of Colorado–Boulder's Leaf Van Boven and Cornell's Thomas Gilovich (2003) randomly assigned participants to discuss with a partner either an experiential or a material purchase. Afterward, participant listeners who discussed experiential purchases reported their partners as more likable and interesting, and the conversation more enjoyable, than those who discussed material purchases. Van Boven and

Gilovich speculate that the stigma associated with materialism may subject to judgment people who speak of their possessions. By contrast, those who live an experiential existence may be seen in positive, even romantic terms. And, because people tend to value their experiences more highly than their things, they are probably more engaged when others share their own experiences. Thus, merely reminiscing about experiences facilitates and strengthens social connections, while discussing material purchases may weaken them.

Meanwhile, the desire to fit in by standing out leads to social comparisons, which in competitive cultures such as the United States tends to result in envy, jealousy, and greed for more. Importantly, however, experiential purchases are less susceptible to social comparison than are material purchases (Van Boven & Gilovich, 2003). It is easy to compare my car to yours, for instance, but somewhat harder to compare my trip to Paris with your Tuscan vacation. Recall that researchers asked participants whether they would prefer to earn a salary of $50,000 when others earned $25,000, or $100,000 when others earned $200,000. Approximately half—presumably the more vertically individualistic of the group—preferred the $50,000 (Solnick & Hemenway, 1998). This seemingly irrational decision—after all, participants were told to assume that prices would remain the same in both scenarios— was motivated by social comparison and a desire to financially "beat" others.

Yet that wasn't the end of the study. Participants were also asked whether they would prefer two weeks of annual vacation while other people were given one week off, or if instead they would prefer four weeks of vacation when others enjoyed eight weeks annual leave. Here 85 percent of respondents indicated that they would prefer four weeks of vacation, even though this would put them in a relatively worse position than others (Solnick & Hemenway, 1998). This result illustrates how personal experiences such as vacations are less susceptible to social comparison than are experiential purchases or income.

If, diehard individualists that we are, personal happiness is top of the agenda, we are well-advised to pursue intrinsic satisfaction, including closer relationships and experiential purchases. To blend these experiential and social expenditures with somewhat more horizontal and inclusive practices, what must we sacrifice? Perhaps, little more than time on the treadmill.

7

From Hedonism to Collectivism

Spending Like a Horizontal Collectivist

The late South African archbishop and Nobel Prize winner Desmond Tutu attends a meeting at the home of a well-heeled supporter near Sin City, USA. Tutu's biographer describes it as "a beautiful home, actually more like a Persian estate, with multiple buildings with fountains and flowing channels of water. It was reminiscent of the great structures of Islamic civilization" (Dalai Lama et al., 2016: 68). Tutu's existence could hardly have presented a sharper contrast. Known for an ascetic taste, he lived much of his life in a modest home in the hardscrabble township of Soweto, forgoing the mansions in affluent parts of Cape Town and Johannesburg offered by virtue of his position. Tutu also did not hesitate to raise awkward questions with politicians, officially chastising the governing elite of South Africa for their ostentatious lifestyles (Euronews, 2013).

He steps to the podium of the Las Vegas estate then eyes the gleaming surroundings. Perhaps the crowd has a moment to wonder whether they—like many a South African politician—might be in for a Tutu tongue lashing. Instead, he smiles to the assembled crowd and declares, in that booming voice that once shook the foundations of apartheid, "I was wrong—I do want to be rich" (Dalai Lama et al., 2016: 68).

The archbishop teased, but the jest is a revelation: materialism, unlike intrinsic pursuits, reduces happiness, and most claim they know this already. Yet materialism continues to flourish. Why?

Status-seeking is part of the answer. As the archbishop's faux rapture suggests, however, nice things also feel good—literally. Like a drug, pleasure chemicals are released into the blood when getting a raise or buying a shiny new thing. Not just "like a drug," in fact; studies show that when experiencing monetary gains, the brain lights up in the same areas as when using cocaine (Breiter, Aharon, Kahneman, Dale, & Shizgal, 2001).

Yet there is a yin to every yang, an equal and opposite reaction to every force. And, like a drug, there is a crash that results after the temporary lift enjoyed when acquiring things, leaving us, like rats on the wheel, no further along than before. Consequently, while monetary gains induce temporary euphoria, craving money induces its opposite: a neural reaction equivalent to the cravings of a cocaine addict (Breiter et al., 2001). As sixteenth-century Frenchman Michel de Montaigne wrote, "The sages teach us often enough to beware of the treachery of our appetites, and to distinguish true and entire pleasures from pleasures that are mixed and streaked with a preponderance of pain" (Montaigne, 2004: 181).

In quipping that he *did* want to be rich, Tutu may have been remarking on the good feelings induced by an ultra-luxe mansion but, if so, acknowledging that those feelings would quickly dissipate. The owners of that house were likely less enthusiastic still—having long ago adapted to the pleasures of their palace. This is the hedonic treadmill, which, not for nothing, is interchangeably known as hedonic *adaptation*. As materialist scholar Ed Diener writes, "According to the hedonic treadmill model, good and bad events temporarily affect happiness, but people quickly adapt back to [their starting point]" (Diener et al., 2009: 305).

The archbishop's close friend and one-time coauthor the Dalai Lama explains: "People think about money or fame or power. From the point of view of one's own personal happiness, these are shortsighted" (Dalai Lama et al., 2016: 68). My own feelings toward money are usually not far off from this perspective: money and things sound nice, occasionally even tempting, but still, I live a modest lifestyle with a rather airy unconcern for the finer things in life. I recall in high school when my teenage brothers worked at a plant nursery for an hourly wage that sounded like a fortune. Not having the responsibilities of adults, they used this money on luxury items—one buying (then stylish) Boston-brand stereo equipment for his bedroom and car, the other purchasing a Fossil watch and Oakley sunglasses.

I distinctly recall envying their purchases, but then considering the cost—hours pulling weeds and heaving sacks of soil under the hot and humid summer sun. No, I decided resolutely (if lazily), I would rather have my day free for other diversions. I took a job, for fewer hours and less pay, but with scheduling flexibility, air-conditioning, and precisely zero physical labor.

As Celeste Headlee (2020) recommends, explaining what Howard Buffett had done, I had traded money for freedom. Somehow I have never fully stopped that. Indeed, this book is the product of prioritizing work that offers greater life balance than do more-traditional positions in corporate America. My favorite job of all? A $1,000-per-month teaching job I held in Central

Asia. I used chunks of time off each summer to pursue a rather aggressive brand of travel across dozens of countries.

I am not free of hedonistic impulses, however. Where money failed to motivate, intensive globe-trotting drew my attention. From studying in Madrid by week and taking trips to Europe's capitals by weekend, to a summer in which I visited sixty-one cities in sixty hectic days, I caught the proverbial travel bug while young and never lost it. By my late twenties I had designed a life in which travel predominated. I lived light, which was all the better for traveling at every—and I mean *every*—opportunity.

It was invigorating. While ticking off countries, I put little colored pins on a framed world map, at least on the rare occasions when I had stable enough accommodations to have the map on hand. Eventually I was traveling even when work or life ought to have precluded it. I recall organizing a conference in Kyrgyzstan while hiking across northern Spain—taking and making calls as I walked—and a virtual meeting conducted beneath the arches of an ancient Roman theater in Bulgaria, the snow falling thickly around me. I blush to admit that I even traveled while millions were dying as the Covid pandemic raged across the world, rationalizing that I would limit my interactions with others by renting my own car and taking private accommodations. The trip, full of anxious moments, guilt, and a legitimate fear of a national lockdown, was not particularly enjoyable.

Suffice it to say, the pendulum was shifting from excitement to stress in my life of travel, and a recalibration of my travel-life balance was needed. I had developed and then fed a mild addiction, one that operated on the same hedonic treadmill as for every other materialist. I needed more and more travel, to more and more exotic places, in order to experience the same feelings of unadulterated joy I had felt during my younger years of carefree travel.

Reza Marvasti (2021), too, spoke of the hedonic treadmill when describing the "drug" that motivated his extreme sports. The "joy of that drug," he explains, "lasted for like five minutes. And then it's gone. And it's like, 'What's next? What's the bigger one that I should do?'" He went on to explain that when he arrived in Canada as a young man he dreamed of owning a camera and a bicycle. "I thought, I'll be the happiest man, just riding around taking pictures." Eventually Marvasti owned not just a bicycle but a car, too. "Now I say, 'Once I have a house, I'm going to be the happiest man.' And I'm never the happiest man. There's always something new."

While my hedonic treadmill took the form of travel, and for others it is food, alcohol, illegal drugs, or adrenaline-seeking, for many Americans money and the material things that money buys are the rat wheels along which they race. Why did the human mind evolve in a way that allows such addictions to take root? As with most things, the hedonic treadmill, when moderated, is a valuable evolutionary adaptation.

Thanks to the hedonic treadmill, we humans can carry on even amid terrible tragedy. Hedonic adaptation allows us to mourn the loss of loved ones, for instance, but regain the will to live ourselves. Psychologist Dan Ariely similarly reveals how hedonic adaptation allows people to adapt to even extreme levels of pain. In one study Ariely (2011) created one group consisting of hospital patients who had experienced severe injuries and another group of patients who had suffered minor injuries. He wanted to know whether the experience of severe pain had changed patients' threshold and tolerance for pain. Ariely explains:

> The participants who had been mildly injured reported that the hot water became painful (pain threshold) after about 4.5 seconds, while those who had been severely injured started feeling pain after 10 seconds. More interestingly, those in the mildly injured group removed their hands from the hot water (pain tolerance) after about 27 seconds, while the severely injured individuals kept their hands in the hot water for about 58 seconds. This difference particularly impressed us since, in order to make sure that no one really got burned, we did not allow participants to keep their hands in the hot water for more than sixty seconds. We did not tell them in advance about the sixty-second rule, but if they reached the sixty-second mark we asked them to take their hands out. We did not need to enforce this rule for any participant in the mildly injured group, but we had to tell all but one of the severely injured participants to take their hands out of the hot water. (110–11)

Ariely thus reveals that exposure to pain increases pain tolerance. The same adaptation occurs for positive experiences. The more positive emotion experienced, the less positive the effect from the next good thing—whether a vacation or a purchase. More is needed.

In fact, this quick reversion to baseline is "much more powerful" when dealing with positive rather than negative outcomes, according to distinguished psychologist Sonja Lyubomirsky (Walsh, 2020). The hedonic treadmill thereby ensures we aren't satisfied for long, but instead try, try again. Among early humans, this insatiability increased; in Darwinian parlance, this is "fitness" and survivability. Compared to humans that were easily satisfied, those that hunted down a bison and promptly started thinking about finding the *next* bison were more likely to survive.

Useful though this was in a world of scarcity, Americans today live amid abundance. Most *do* have enough to celebrate successes with a week's rest. And yet, the premodern mind persists. As neurosurgeon Jim Doty (2013) explains, "Our DNA has not changed for the last two hundred thousand years. We are the same as we were then, in this modern world of science and technology, which has evolved far faster than our evolution. And as a result, we have evolutionary baggage which stands in the way, oftentimes, of us being happy." This is the hedonic treadmill on which runs the materialist, making little progress while seeking happiness.

Within the workplace, the hedonic treadmill leads to people caring less about their salaries and more about how their salaries might change. One might initially see a starting salary as a hefty chunk of change, for instance, but if not continually increasing, adaptation and diminished excitement quickly set in. Thus, job satisfaction is more strongly correlated with actual or expected *changes* in pay rather than the pay itself (Clark, 1999; Lévy-Garboua & Montmarquette, 2004).

We also see this effect when zooming out to the United States as a whole, which has grown considerably wealthier in recent decades. As the hedonic treadmill might predict, wealthier Americans have come to need more and more to declare themselves satisfied. In fact, when given a raise or winning the lottery, the hedonic treadmill is thought to gobble up the emotional benefits of about eighty cents of every dollar banked—meaning that the benefits of only around 20 percent of those increased earnings are felt (Diener & Biswas-Diener, 2002). Research reveals that after one year even lottery winners are only slightly happier than their less lucky peers (Brickman, Coates, & Janoff-Bulmann, 1978).

All of this—the hedonic treadmill and the unrewarding pursuit of things, status, and social acceptance—suggest that the hyper-competition of the vertical individualist is a rigged contest. In this game there are no winners. Or, rather, the winners are those who learn to give up the quickest.

Yet most Americans are still trying to run quicker, and getting nowhere fast. This is the hedonic treadmill on which society races. As Alexis de Tocqueville wrote in 1835, Americans' "minds are universally preoccupied with meeting the body's every need and attending to life's little comforts" (2004: 617). Nearly two hundred years later Tocqueville's analysis remains relevant: while the hedonic treadmill may be based in biology, a vertically individualistic culture continues to subject Americans to its worst excesses.

The famed values researcher Shalom Schwartz, for instance, asked people around the world to rank ten values in order of importance. Globally, respondents ranked hedonism or pleasure-seeking as their seventh-most-important value; Americans ranked it third, well ahead of security (sixth) and universal concern for others (seventh), even ahead of self-direction/autonomy (Schwartz & Bardi, 2001). This is consistent with other research findings, that vertical individualists share an outsized emphasis on satisfying hedonistic values (Triandis & Gelfand, 1998). The risk, as author Stephen Covey (2013) explains, is that "a person in this state becomes almost entirely narcissistic, interpreting all of life in terms of the pleasure it provides to the self here and now" (122).

Unfortunately for vertically individualistic materialists, the temptations of consumption—even if intuited as hollow—are higher and harder to resist than for nonmaterialists (Hudders & Pandelaere, 2012). University of Virginia psychologist Shigehiro Oishi found that the verticalist's interest in holding power over others is correlated with greater satisfaction when buying expensive clothing (Oishi, Diener, Suh, & Lucas, 1999). These are short-term pleasures but, as Ghent University's Liselot Hudders and Virginia Tech's Mario Pandelaere (2012) note, the short-term pleasure may "'lock in' materialists to their lifestyle, irrespective of the long-term adverse consequences for self and society" (411).

What can we do? Apply to material consumption the Goldilocks rule of moderation. As Russel Belk (2001) writes, "This echoes discussions of the golden or harmonic mean. The idea is that there is a happy medium between the desire to spend and consume (materialism) on one hand, and the desire to deny ourselves material gratification (asceticism) on the other hand" (6).

James Hong, the prosperous founder of a dating website, spoke to the *New York Times* about trading a sporty Porsche Boxster for a modest Toyota Prius: "I don't want to live the life of a Boxster," he explains, "because when you get a Boxster you wish you had a 911, and you know what people who have 911s wish they had? They wish they had a Ferrari" (Hafner, 2006).

Similarly, Reza Marvasti recalls traveling to Peru after selling his home renovation business. With an overflowing backpack, he worried constantly about theft and became tired of lugging the hefty bag. "[But] as I traveled more, my backpack is getting smaller with less and less things [as I give things away]. I am light. I can go anywhere, and I'm not worried about my things getting stolen." Marvasti, who eventually sold nearly all his possessions to fund The Power of Play, concluded, "My lessons in Peru apply to all of life. We don't need all this baggage. It is not about more. We can live with so little."

As for me? I now limit myself to a more modest travel schedule, prioritizing travel in the company of family and friends over novelty and exoticism. I am putting down roots, establishing myself in a community, and developing a nest that I call home. In this way I too am contentedly living with less.

Money but Not Materialism: The Way of Enlightened Self-Interest

"When you have more than you need at a material level, what's next? Where do we go from here? Where do our gifts connect with a need in the world? How do we use our lives to build up our larger human family?" So asked Melinda Gates (2019: 212–13) in *The Moment of Lift*. Perhaps inadvertently Gates touches on a key point when referring to the "larger human family." Humans are in fact "unusual as a species in the extent to which they form longstanding, non-reproductive unions with unrelated individuals—namely, we have friends" (Apicella et al., 2012: 1). It is this capacity to cooperate even with strangers that provides humanity some of its greatest evolutionary advantages.

Cooperation is intrinsically—that word again—satisfying (Dunn et al., 2011). Yet to *serve* others is to go further. These altruistic actions do much to satisfy the need for relatedness and the deep-seated desire to connect with others (Diener & Seligman, 2002). Giving wealth to friends or family may strengthen those relationships. Giving wealth to charity may strengthen one's connection to "our larger human family" or something bigger than oneself. Givers tend to believe that others see them in more positive terms, which further enhances well-being for us hypersocial humans (Dunn, Biesanz, Human, & Finn, 2007). The upshot? There may be no better way to use money than to use it on or for others. Jim Doty (2017) spoke of his ideological transition to enlightened self-interest, recalling his "false belief that money would make me happy, that money would give me control. I learned that there's only one way for wealth to bring happiness—and that's by giving it away. I was free" (229).

Consider the study in which participants from a nationwide sample reported that money gifted or donated brought them more happiness than money spent on themselves (Dunn, Aknin, & Norton, 2008). In another study, scholars handed college students a small sum of money and randomly assigned them to either spend the money on themselves, or on others. Those assigned to spend on others reported greater satisfaction than those spending on themselves (Dunn et al., 2008).

There are even physiological benefits one can get, as older individuals with hypertension saw decreased blood pressure when assigned to donate money (Dunn et al., 2008). Harvard's Dan Gilbert reports that giving to others also stimulates a biological response, with MRIs showing that *giving* money away activates parts of the brain associated with *receiving* (Harbaugh, Mayr, & Burghart, 2007). As Archbishop Tutu intuited, "We receive when we give" (Dalai Lama et al., 2016: 156).

These studies suggest that it matters little how much one spends on others; as long as others are recipients, then the giver's happiness (not to mention the recipient's) tends to increase. Cross-cultural studies involving 136 countries—nearly two-thirds of the world's nations—replicate these findings (Aknin et al., 2013). It seems the benefits of giving are not culturally contingent but rather go to the very essence of our humanity.

Despite this evidence, few have learned the lessons articulated by Reza Marvasti, who speaks of the immense joy he felt when giving nearly everything he owned to others. He recalled one birthday in which he received charitable donations rather than personal gifts. He explains: "We helped five hundred children that year, and I'll be able to tell you about this gift until I am ninety. I will never forget this birthday. But you ask me about another year's birthday? I will tell you I don't know, maybe I got a bottle of wine" (2021). Marvasti concludes by challenging others to give. You will see, he explains, that "there is so much more joy in giving than getting."

Yet most people continue to believe that spending on themselves will make them happier than spending on others (Dunn et al., 2008). This fallacy leads to the embrace of materialism, which, as we have seen, acts in opposition to intrinsic satisfaction and well-being. In fact, studies show that while people who place high importance on money have lower life satisfaction, among the happiest people are those ranking love as the highest of values (Diener & Biswas-Diener, 2002).

Recall that materialism reduces connections with others, as materialists value relationships less than do nonmaterialists (Burroughs & Rindfleisch, 2002). The reason is simple: vertical individualists are in zero-sum *competition* with others. Another's successes are their failures. Far from drawing closer to others, money thus comes between vertical individualists as they compete for material standing (Mowen, 2004). Yet the need for relatedness is nested within. Materialists unsurprisingly report feeling disconnected from others in society (Kasser, 2002), a disconnect that points to a longing for deeper connections.

The costs of American vertical individualism and the allure of a collectivistic mindset are apparent. Marsha Richins and Scott Dawson (1992) conducted a study in which participants were asked to imagine unexpectedly receiving $20,000. They were given options for how they might spend the money, including on self and others. The authors found that respondents high in materialism chose to spend three times as much on themselves as did respondents low in materialism. They also contributed half as much to charities or church organizations and gave less than half as much to friends and family.

In the same study, Richins and Dawson asked participants to complete a "nongenerosity" survey. This asked participants to indicate their level of agreement with questions such as "I don't like to lend things, even to good friends" and "I enjoy having guests stay in my home." Again, materialists rated more selfish than those low in materialism. The authors write, "Materialistic people are self-centered. . . . An overriding concern with possessions and acquisition for oneself is inherently incompatible with sharing and giving to others" (1992, 308). Materialism researcher Russell Belk (2001) similarly notes that "religions have long opposed materialism on the grounds that avarice and greed oppose altruism and charity" (7). In vertically collectivist societies in the Far East, modesty, humility, and other communal values serve to combat selfish vertical tendencies—at least among in-groups (Wong & Ahuvia, 1998). The vertically individualistic West, by contrast, sees the ill effects of materialism fester and metastasize nearly without bounds.

These studies and others lift the gilded lid of American materialism and reveal the rot beneath. This materialism is a cultural value incompatible with the intrinsic needs of relatedness and competence. It is not hyperbole to say that materialism brings out our worst, the natural consequence of which is a more selfish society. It leads to a situation, described by Holocaust survivor and psychologist Viktor Frankl (1985), in which "people have enough to live by but nothing to live for; they have the means but no meaning" (165).

And yet pervasive materialism is socially sanctioned, with American culture cheering its people into the deep, dark gully through a seemingly endless and growing appeal for luxury and material accumulation. For ourselves, for our increasingly materialistic children, let us strip away vertical individualism—characterized in part by status competitions and overconsumption—and see money as a means to intrinsic ends. What might follow in the American context is the horizontal individualist. The horizontal individualist competes against himself, not others. To run faster than yesterday, not faster than others. In so doing, the needs for competence and autonomy are more fully realized and the opportunity for connection is created.

Space is needed for the horizontal collectivist to rise, as well. She seeks not only to better herself, but others too. The horizontal collectivist, overflowing with social relatedness, knows that the key to gaining more from money is by giving more to, and enjoying more experiences with, others.

A long line of antimaterialistic philosophers and spiritual leaders were introduced earlier (see chapter 5). In proposing that money be used for intrinsic purposes, however, it is not proposed that happiness comes only through the cave of the ascetic. When prioritizing the intrinsic needs of competence, autonomy, and relatedness over material accumulation, one can genuinely benefit self and others. As Doty says, "If you can authentically remain compassionate, it's okay to do well. I don't believe you have to be a pauper to be of service" (2021). This all-encompassing concern represents horizontal individualism and horizontal collectivism combined toward enlightened self-interest.

Next considered is the second of the unholy trinity of money, power, and fame. Is power, as the old saying goes, truly all-corrupting, or is that just another contingency of the vertically individualistic West?

8

Power Plays and Pays

When Power Is Corrupting

"Power tends to corrupt, and absolute power corrupts absolutely," according to nineteenth-century British historian and politician Lord Acton, who added, in his letter to Bishop Creighton: "Great men are almost always bad men, even when they exercise influence and not authority, still more when you superadd the tendency or the certainty of corruption by authority. There is no worse heresy than that the office sanctifies the holder of it" (Acton, 1887). William Shakespeare provides one of the most memorable (albeit fictional) illustrations of this same phenomenon in his play *Macbeth,* in which King Lear loses empathy in direct proportion to his rising power.

For those who follow the enduring drama that has long surrounded the competition between DC Comics/DC Entertainment (a subsidiary of Warner Brothers Discovery) and Marvel Comics/Marvel Studios (a subsidiary of the Walt Disney Company), the corrupting influence of power seems to some observers to be on display in the furor over the movie *Justice League* and its two directors. Joss Whedon's *Justice League* (2017) is a lighthearted and reasonably bloodless PG-13 affair. Zack Snyder's R-rated version is darker, considerably bloodier, and with deeper character development and origin stories. The difference between the two versions of the film can be said to derive, at least in part, from the industry veterans' respective directing styles.

Snyder's departure from the production of the film came following the unexpected death of his daughter, Autumn, though lackluster reviews of Snyder's earlier theatrical releases for the DC Comic franchise may have contributed to his exit from that film (Raheja, 2021). Whedon, who had achieved enormous success as director of *Iron Man,* took over for Snydér well into the film's production and was given the mandate to lighten the tone of Snyder's flick. The result was mixed at best, with Whedon's product an imperfect mash-up ignominiously situated somewhere between Snyder's somber tone and Whedon's more lighthearted variant. In the process, Whedon's widely panned release lost parent company Warner Brothers somewhere north of $60 million (Aten, 2021), which coincidentally or not preceded the exit of several senior executives from the company (Masters, 2021).

There ensued a fair amount of public grumbling on the part of the film's actors about Whedon's alleged on-set treatment of them (Masters, 2021). Whedon has denied the allegations. In the meantime, Snyder came across as a deeply sympathetic figure in a misty-eyed *Vanity Fair* piece covering the sudden loss of his twenty-year-old daughter (Breznican, 2021). Amid the torrent of complaints against Whedon, Snyder publicly expressed support for the *Justice League* cast and crew and was reported to "genuinely care for those he works with" (LaBonte, 2021). *Forbes* reported, "In an age of hostile and abusive creatives, everyone speaks highly of Snyder, even executives that have clashed with him, as an incredibly nice guy who cares deeply about his cast and crew and tries to create great working environments for them" (Tassi, 2021).

Facing a seemingly interminable outcry to resurrect Snyder's perfor-mance, Warner Brothers took the unusual step of releasing Snyder's version of *Justice League* on HBO Max—in all its unedited four-hour glory. As of this writing it appears well on its way to cult classic status and is widely seen as superior to the Whedon version (Rotten Tomato and IMDB both offer quick comparisons).

Snyder and Whedon, two decorated and sought-after Hollywood direc-tors, exemplify opposing sides of the coin of power. Whedon is accused of failing to dialogue with his own cast, dismissing their concerns and using his power to threaten careers. Snyder is portrayed as caring, compassionate, and genuinely interested in subordinates' well-being. To label Joss Whedon a vertical individualist and Snyder as motivated by enlightened self-interest is perhaps superficial, but it seems that in Whedon's alleged dismissal of others, and in Snyder's compassion, the core elements of each cultural dimension are present.

Jim Lee (2021), the chief creative officer of DC (first introduced in chap-ter 2), understandably declines to add fuel to the Whedon-Snyder fire. He was willing, however, to speak extensively about power generally. Lee, who was born in South Korea and moved to St. Louis, Missouri, as a child, earned a psychology degree from Princeton University before accepting a position with DC Comics as an artist tasked to the X-Men comic series. Monthly sales of his renderings broke records that still stand today, and decades later Lee started his own production company, WildStorm Production. Six years later,

DC Entertainment bought WildStorm, and Lee left another company he had founded, Image Comics, to join DC Entertainment.

Lee, who lives with his wife and nine children in Los Angeles, leveraged his substantial successes to reach a position of power and influence within the DC universe. Yet even before these achievements, he exemplified the horizontal individualist, motivated by inner drive more than external incentives. Following his Princeton graduation, Lee clashed with his Korea-born parents over his decision to forgo a career in medicine. Lee spoke of this "cultural pressure to be the obedient son that brings glory to the family. But their plan didn't recognize so much about the individual and about free will." Lee explains that his time at Princeton gave him the horizontal individualist's "inner strength, or resolve, to do something different." Self-expression, Lee continued, is essential.

Lee is deeply intrinsically motivated. "That's part of the journey," he explains enthusiastically, "knowing what motivated you and how you work best." Lee had a "creativity and yearning to create and express through work. It's a calling," he said, and "it's hard to avoid that kind of destiny. It may seem courageous" to have gone against the wishes of one's parents, "but it doesn't feel like there was ever a choice. You see this in the lawyers that drop out and become Lego artists, or that are now writers."

Today Lee continues to avoid the pitfalls of vertical individualism. He is a self-described family man who has managed to avoid material traps, despite the fact that he lives in a multimillion-dollar compound he calls a "fortress of solitude," a world away from the stress and fast pace of Hollywood. He explains: "You get all the creature comforts, you have home and car, X-box, all your stuff—but the thing that you cherish is your time. Just to read a book or paint a landscape—things that recharge the soul and inspire you. You have to make time, because success and money can be an enemy to time."

Lee exercises power in a similarly horizontal, egalitarian style, emphasizing the importance of "dialogue with the whole team. Of asking, How are we doing? What could be done better? Are we working in this environment where you feel encouraged to express your point of view?" He continues: "Creativity isn't linked to your title in the org chart. It can come from anywhere, [and] it's about engaging with people that give you the widest set of ideas." Sometimes, Lee says, the bigger-than-life figures on the studio floor need to step aside and give oxygen for others' ideas. And yet, received wisdom holds that the powerful are constitutionally unable to practice modesty and collaboration. After all, all power is all-corrupting, right? If that old trope holds true, then how do we explain Lee's soft touch? Or, for that matter, the collaborative nature of a Zack Snyder? As it happens, power is not all-corrupting. Not all-corrupting, except for vertical individualists.

Perks of Power

Power is in part a consequence of wealth—consider the many rich who bankroll their own political careers. Power is also a means for accumulating wealth, as when politicians turn into high-priced lobbyists, consultants, or law partners (Magee & Galinsky, 2008). Victor Frankl (1985) spotlighted this link between wealth and power, writing, "Sometimes the frustrated will to meaning is vicariously compensated for by a will to power, including the most primitive form of the will to power, the will to money" (129).

The wealthy may purchase scarce resources, like diamonds and land, or intangibles such as access to rare talent or influence over others. It is this asymmetrical influence over that which is valuable and limited that is the essence of power. Our friend Jim Doty understood this from a young age. He explained that even as a child he saw money as a solution to his problems. Through money, he told me, he could get anything he wanted. This was control. This was, in his own words, "power" (Doty, 2017: 216).

Power also generates material bounty. Thomas Hobbes—he of "life is short and brutal" fame—feared a world of self-interested vertical individualists. He advocated gaining power in order to protect oneself and one's things from vicious others. Only through power, Hobbes argued, may one enjoy the pleasures of life (Allport, Clark, & Pettigrew, 1954). In contemporary terms, the powerful can demand higher salaries or take a harder line in negotiations. They may receive preferential treatment—a nicer office, a better seat at the restaurant. Doty recalled that as his fortune dwindled, he lost access to "free drinks, free meals, VIP seating in the best restaurants"—all perquisites of the powerful (Doty, 2017: 216).

Also recall that though money holds objective relevance, it also contains an important comparative and subjective element (Cheung & Lucas, 2016). For instance, studies show that happiness declines as neighbors' wealth increases, with those left behind seeing themselves in degraded terms. This rank-ordering comparison is used when evaluating power as well. You may control millions of dollars of resources, for instance, but if everyone else controls billions of dollars worth, then your power is diminished (and, Hobbes would argue, your resources are threatened).

Thus, the materialist may pursue power and the power-hungry may pursue material wealth. What about the vertical individualist who seeks fame and status? He is interested in both power *and* wealth. In a materialistic and competitive world, power, like money, is held up as one more measure of success. It is something over which many Americans compete and which, once obtained, is flaunted so that victories may bring to powerholders status, esteem, and yet more influence.

This is the contemporary, culturally contingent power motive. Yet vertical individualism only moderates the preexisting biological motive of *all* humans to seek power. Power may lead to status (and status may lead to power) (Thye, 2000)—and, as we have seen already, status is psychologically and tangibly beneficial. Moreover, the propensity for power to generate additional resources was indeed a mighty advantage in early humans' resource-scarce environments. These survival advantages unleashed over generations a cornucopia of biological rewards for achieving power, which exacerbate the vertically individualistic American's power-hungry tendencies.

The approach-inhibition theory holds that power activates the reward-sensing part of the mind, while disempowerment activates the threat-sensitive part (Keltner, Gruenfeld, & Anderson, 2003). As material successes ignite pleasure receptors, therefore, so too does increasing power enhance moods and emotions. Former secretary of state Henry Kissinger did not need a degree in neuroscience to understand this. He learned from decades roaming the halls of power that "power is the ultimate aphrodisiac" (Zakaria, 2020: 89). Conversely, reductions dampen mood and incentivize clinging to power (Keltner et al., 2003)—something the aged but still working Kissinger may also recognize.

Speaking of aphrodisiacs: power promotes reproductive odds for both humans and nonhumans. The powerful, thanks to all those resources at their disposal, have increased capacity to care for their young. In return, power-holders attract a variety of desirable mates (Maner & Mead, 2010; Van Vugt & Tybur, 2015). A 1989 landmark study by the University of Texas's David Buss showed that women particularly value romantic partners who acquire or had the capacity to acquire control over valued resources. Wealthier partners, ambitious partners, and those atop power's proverbial pecking order are all, Buss found, at a premium.

Stress levels thus decline as power increases, with the subconscious mind intuiting that influence and authority reduce risk exposure. Power researchers Adam Galinsky and colleagues note in a review article that powerful individuals exhibit lower heart rates when speaking publicly (Galinsky, Rucker, & Magee, 2015). Similarly, powerholders expend less effort to gain status and its associated privileges and protections, which helps explain why a middling real estate broker might flaunt a Gucci suit while Mark Zuckerberg and his billionaire ilk sport hoodie sweatshirts. We know, however, that rewards are temporary pleasures, and the rewards initiated by the approach-inhibition pathway lead right back to the hedonic treadmill. A reward may satiate us today, but by tomorrow powerholders are (power) hungry for more.

And how is power arrived upon? The next section introduces two power plays, beginning with the oldest and best known. To illustrate this path to power, we need look no further than the common chicken.

Playing with Fire

The *Oxford Reference Dictionary* defines a pecking order as a "hierarchy of status seen among members of a group or animals." It is a phenomenon "originally seen among hens." Yes, the pecking order, so familiar to corporate America, is in fact a natural occurrence in which chickens establish supremacy by pecking their way to the top.

These bullies of the poultry world flap their feathers, confidently strut, and threateningly squawk, pecking any unfortunates that do not get the message about who reigns supreme (Barth, 2016). Evolutionary psychologists Mark Van Vugt and Joshua Tybur (2015) write that after a short time together, chickens develop a "simple linear hierarchy" in which every hen in the group knows its place: "A pecks B, B pecks C . . . and so on, and the pecking order determines which hens get preferential access to food" (3). Sound familiar?

This and similar bullying approaches are the *only* known way to gain dominance in the animal kingdom (Henrich & Gil-White, 2001). Canines and primates, felines, and bovine—all battle if not peck their way to the top of hierarchies, sometimes inflicting serious injury or even death to others along the way.

Using force to reach the hierarchy's top exists among humans, too. Harvard University evolutionary biologist Joseph Henrich and colleague Francisco Gil-White (2001) characterize the leaders that emerge from these power plays as individuals "who maintain their position through fear, threat, and compulsion" (167) Even today, physically stronger men are more likely to self-servingly endorse norms benefiting the strong—essentially advocating human pecking orders and their resultant hierarchies. Furthermore, the strong are more comfortable with status inequities, believing at some primordial level that they are the deserving beneficiaries of such differences. These attitudes are the likely genetic consequence of generation after generation in which the strongest rose the highest (Van Vugt & Tybur, 2015).

Not only do the powerful embrace status inequities; society in general is more likely to view them as natural leaders. Because height is a proxy for strength, taller individuals similarly tend to rise in the hierarchy. Taller men, in particular, are seen as more dominant, intelligent, and healthy, whereas taller women are seen as more intelligent but no more dominant or healthy. Evolutionary biologists suggest that this gender difference exists because men have traditionally risen to power, so their physical advantages remain biologically salient (Blaker et al., 2013). Taller men, more so than taller women, also tend to see themselves as natural leaders and thus claim leadership positions (Murray & Schmitz, 2011).

More attractive individuals also rise quickly, at least partly because attractiveness also correlates with physical fitness and strength (Blaker et al., 2013; Van Vugt & Tybur, 2015). As with height, attractive men are more likely to gain status, whereas attractive women are more likely to gain the notice of prospective mates (Buss, 1989).

These biological adaptations to the violent world of old (and to today, to a lesser extent) manifests in other ways, too. The force of a handshake is a measure of social dominance (Van Vugt & Tybur, 2015). Individuals acting in "subtly rude and norm-violating" ways are seen as strong and powerful—otherwise, the mostly subconscious reasoning goes, they would not dare to misbehave so (Van Kleef, Homan, Finkenauer, Gundemir, & Stamkou, 2011; Van Vugt & Tybur, 2015). Finally, just as the dominant member of an ape clan may view extended eye contact as an implicit threat, so too are dominant individuals more likely to hold a "firmer gaze"; like peacocks, they "stand at full height with an expanded chest," and like an intimidating dog, "they speak in a low[er]-pitched voice" (Van Vugt & Tybur, 2015: 15).

Boxer Mike Tyson seems to have understood this correlation between pitch and prowess, as even a cursory comparison of audio clips reveals a vocal pitch that lowered markedly over the course of his career. Amazingly, one study found salaries increased by $187,000 as pitch of voice lowered by 25 percent among CEOs at publicly traded companies (Mayew, Parsons, & Venkatachalam, 2013). Some studies also suggest a disproportionate number of business and political leaders exhibit the so-called dark triad: a combination of Machiavellian, narcissistic, and psychopathic tendencies that promote the power via force pathway (Van Vugt & Tybur, 2015).

As just one example of forceful shows of power, the *New Yorker* reports that Henry Kissinger—quoted earlier for his understanding of power's intoxicating effects—signaled strength to the Soviet Union by supporting a genocidal campaign in eastern Pakistan. The same report suggested that Kissinger negotiated peace with North Vietnam not at the point of a gun but with the fuse of the bomb—mercilessly bombing the enemy until reaching terms of agreement. Meanwhile, Kissinger and then-president Richard Nixon allegedly supported the coup (and eventual assassination) of democratically elected but socialist-leaning Chilean president Salvador Allende (Meaney, 2020).

We could go on—about Kissinger, about politicians generally—but perhaps political force is low hanging fruit. Consider instead legendary basketball player Michael Jordan, a retired Chicago Bulls star and notorious bully, considered by one former teammate "the most viciously competitive player I've ever seen" (Wu, 2014). Well documented are Jordan's threatening tactics on and off the court, which included intimidating and belittling competitors and teammates alike as he strove to earn the title "best ever."

Former teammate Steve Kerr recalls getting a fist to the face when disagreeing with Jordan in a practice session; another teammate recalls Jordan screaming "You're a loser, you've always been a loser" (Wu, 2014). To paraphrase comedian Joey Adam, with teammates like this, who needs opponents? After Jordan retired and ascended to the executive suite as Washington Wizards general manager, he continued exercising the only power tactics he knew: by demeaning his own players. This included subjecting star Kwame Brown to a range of demeaning and homophobic remarks.

It should be acknowledged that the likes of Jordan, Kissinger, not to mention Joss Whedon, possess knowledge and skills that helped them attain power. Teammates of Jordan, for instance, may have experienced belittlement or embarrassment, but they also won rings—and this, because Jordan's interests aligned with those of the team.

As will be seen, however, self-interested powerholders are all too ready to sacrifice their followers in the event of conflicting interests. For instance, Mexican drug cartels—exemplifying the animalistic power-via-force route as much as any organization anywhere—do indeed offer many of their prey the chance to gain enormous wealth in return for cooptation. Of course, to refuse an offer of *plato* (silver, or cash), is to instead receive *plomo*—the lead of a bullet.

Notwithstanding the benevolent dictator who believes his forceful acquisition and maintenance of power is ultimately for the good of his infantilized peoples, those who use force, coercion, or manipulation to gain power tend to have their own best interests in mind. How could they not, considering the pain inflicted on followers? These are our vertical individualists, and they are in turn most susceptible to the Shakespearean archetype of power as a corrupting force.

University of Amsterdam psychologists Van Vugt and Tybur (2015) write, "In non-human primate groups such as gorillas and chimpanzees . . . dominant males (alphas) appear to be feared and, at the risk of anthropomorphizing internal states, loathed by lower ranking individuals" (22). There is little difference in human populations, with powerholders inciting subordinates' disdain and opposition (Yukl & Chavez, 2002). Recall director Joss Whedon's coercive methods incited a minor revolt among his cast of characters. A former coach of Michael Jordan recalled that Jordan "alienated" teammates, diminished morale, and caused a seething resentment. Former teammate Jud Buechler said that Jordan "made it so guys were rushing to their agents saying, 'You have to move me'" (Anderson, 2020).

This sense of danger and antipathy toward coercive power-seekers has led most every human society to attempt to rein in the power-hungry. Consider the English Magna Carta of 1215, or the American Constitution proclaiming a balance of powers in response to King George III's tyranny. Or contemporary political and corporate term limits aimed at preventing the aggrandizement of power.

This practice is at work even high in the Andes Mountains. There, a Peruvian community two-thousand-strong lives on hundreds of artificial reed-islands bobbing atop the frigid waters of Lake Titicaca. Leaders boat from island to island, resolving disputes and managing crises that threaten their environment or income. Yet no matter how effective the leader, the community holds annual elections with no possibility of reelection. As one elected leader explained to me, one thousand years of accrued experience taught the community to fear the effects of concentrated power. The robust term limits, he explained, prevent corruption; or, in a different turn of phrase, prevents the corrupting influences of power.

Aside from small and highly egalitarian societies such as this one on Lake Titicaca, societies with strong middle classes are typically most successful at restraining powerholders. Low-income groups hold relatively little power and are more susceptible to the whims of disproportionately powerful elites. By contrast, the middle class everywhere tends to hold values that prioritize their own development, providing them with aspirations for development and consequently diminishing their willingness to subjugate themselves. They therefore have both the desire and the power to organize—to boycott and to derail economies, to harm the powerful, and to negotiate or win their way.

However, culture—by normalizing some behaviors and sanctioning others—can say a lot about *how* societies hold powerholders to account (Chiu & Hong, 2013). Powerholders may in some places be made strong but accountable, while in others they are left weak and unaccountable. Deciding which pathway is taken depends largely on the alternatively benevolent or malevolent intentions of societal powerholders.

9

From Predatory to Prestigious

When Power Is Purifying

The Wharton School's business ethicist Thomas Donaldson (1989) writes, "Great power enhances the possibility of effecting great evil, but similarly enhances the possibility of effecting great good." Donaldson remarks that "power itself is morally neutral" (32). What distinguishes these good and bad uses of power, and do intentions matter? Sometimes, but not always. Intent has an idiosyncratic component, dependent on personality traits and individual upbringing. Yet culture also strongly influences the norms pertaining to appropriate uses of power. When cultures fail to expect communally responsible actions from powerholders, more powerholders *intend* to use power selfishly. University of Southern California scholar Leigh Plunkett Tost (2015) writes of this "dual nature of power," explaining that when power is seen primarily to serve one's own ends, "we can expect a negative effect on. . . responsiveness to others' needs (i.e., communal behaviors); however, when responsibility is evoked, we can expect just the opposite" (45–46).

Recall from chapter 4 that Westerners fit in by standing out. Consistent with this, powerholders are able to pursue superiority "without social interference or serious social consequences" (Gruenfeld, Keltner, & Anderson, 2003: 240–41). By contrast, in the East, one better fits in by blending in—and power thus enhances Tost's "communal behaviors."

Confucian and Buddhist ideologies undergird an Eastern value system that is at once both hierarchical and collective. Supporting a hierarchy implies that these societies welcome power differences, but collectivism demands that powerholders exercise communal responsibility. As noted in *Shaping the Global Leader*, for instance, Confucianism requires those high in power to care for subordinates. In return, juniors are expected to show loyalty and respect to seniors, thereby effectuating an unwritten contract with mutual obligations (Biggs, Bussen, & Ramsey, 2019).

Buddhism similarly blends hierarchy and collectivism by holding that rulers provide for all citizens' basic needs while maintaining a fair and equitable legal system. Selfish powerholders in breach of these communal expectations face loss of position, while the communally minded gain in prestige and rank. The incentives, therefore, are clear: even the power-hungry must act communally to maintain their positions of power.

In the West, alternatively, a competitive environment in which power is often gained by force, views powerholders as victors over defeated subordinates. Far from demanding responsibility to the "losing" party, hyper-competitive types are sanctioned to leverage power to dominate others (Szegedy-Maszak, 2005). Writes University of Maine psychologist Richard Ryckman, "The gist of this kind of competition is self-aggrandizement at the expense of others" (Szegedy-Maszak, 2005).

In similar terms, Chinese University of Hong Kong scholar Chen-Bo Zhong and colleagues write, "Power [in the West] often is part and parcel of the ability to do what one wants to do and to take action to satisfy one's desires and goals" (Zhong et al., 2006: 54). Westerners thus tend to use power to stand out—grabbing a corner office and a higher salary, for instance, rather than getting ergonomic chairs for staff or giving office-wide holiday bonuses.

This self-interested motive is driven by individualism and egalitarianism, which flourish in place of Eastern collectivism and hierarchy. Westerners, for instance, tend to prefer competition and autonomy over cooperation and subordination. Protestants across Europe and the United States have a long history of bucking powerholders' reigns. This dates back to German priest Martin Luther's obstinately nailing his ninety-five theses to a Wittenberg church wall; it continues to the present day with countries like France seeing years of sporadic "yellow jacket" protests (Haddad, 2021).

These differences between Western and Eastern views of power shape powerholders' intentions. The resulting consequences of power are dramatic, yet little known: *in the East, power is not all-corrupting. It is scarcely at all corrupting.* Instead, power promotes altruistic and harmonious interactions, and powerholders of the East are more likely to use power to benefit their groups, signal their connectedness with others, and perhaps gain the social approval to hang onto power a bit longer. But in the West? Study after study reveals that *power is corrupting*—harmful to self and others (Galinsky et al., 2015).

As power and status researcher Adam Galinsky (2015) notes, power fundamentally changes an individual's thoughts and behaviors. Admittedly, some of these cognitive changes are beneficial. On the positive ledger, the powerful tend to think more abstractly and creatively. They exhibit an improved ability to plan and pursue goals, see improved oral and written skills—recall that the powerful exhibit lower heart rates when publicly speaking—and benefit from higher levels of self-confidence and optimism. Finally, full points to University of Kent's Pascal Burgmer, who creatively highlighted the impact of power on motor skills by asking high- and low-power subjects to putt golf balls and throw darts. Those primed for power in Burgmer's study consistently outperformed low-power participants by landing more putts and bull's-eyes (Burgmer & Englich, 2013).

However, the cognitive downsides of power are at least as significant as the upsides—and are even worse for those further down the pecking order. As Durham University's Barbara Wisse and colleague Diana Rus (2012) write, "Empirical research has conclusively linked leader self-interested behavior to a host of detrimental consequences for all those involved" (40).

Once power is obtained, the hedonic treadmill gets moving and the powerholder feels a hunger for power that is nearly insatiable. The result is a virtual obsession with retaining and acquiring power (Galinsky, Magee, Inesi, & Gruenfeld, 2006). There is perhaps no more prototypical image of the corrupting influences of power than the aging, shrunken leader clinging desperately to power (Galinsky et al., 2006). Consider how Tootsie Roll company's stock jumped 7 percent after CEO Melvin Gordon's fifty-three-year "iron grip" over the company finally came to an end—due only to his passing at ninety-five years of age (Della Cava & Jones, 2016; Strom, 2015).

Furthermore, rising self-confidence can lead even powerholders in their prime to make irresponsible decisions harmful to themselves and subordinates (Zhong et al., 2006). Power also promotes an inflated self-view, and thereby inhibits the ability of the powerful to consider alternative viewpoints. In negotiations, as just one example, the more powerful self-sabotage by seeking out less information than do the less powerful (Galinsky et al., 2015).

Recall, furthermore, that the C-suite is disproportionately occupied by narcissists seeing themselves in inflated terms (Cragun, Olsen, & Wright, 2020). While the self-serving advantages bestowed by power in vertically individualistic societies *attracts* narcissists, its corrupting tendencies also *increases* individual rates of narcissism (Mead, Baumeister, Stuppy, & Vohs, 2018). Consider the company Enron. Led by an astoundingly successful (and powerful) team of executives, the company began to crumble in late 2001 amid a spectacular display of fraud and ego. Postmortem studies of the now-expired company reveal an environment of groupthink, in which Ivy League executives trumped up on the certainty of their own brilliance failed to question one another's reckless (not to mention unethical and illegal) decisions (O'Connor, 2002).

In addition to reckless behaviors and unchecked egos, the powerful also withdraw physically and psychologically—in essence becoming *more* self-interested vertical individualists. They exhibit a stronger desire to work in solitary conditions. Worse still, they are less attentive to subordinates and recall less-distinguishing information about them (Overbeck & Park, 2006). They also give lower performance evaluations than do the less powerful (Georgesen & Harris, 1998, 2000). And just as in Shakespeare's *MacBeth*, higher power reduces empathy and distress when others suffer (Magee & Galinsky, 2008; Van Kleef, Oveis, Van De Löwe, LuoKogan, Goetz, & Keltner, 2008).

Indeed, the powerful are more likely to *cause* suffering. This reduced concern for others heightens stereotyping, sexual harassment, corruption, and abusive behaviors—both verbal and physical—toward subordinates (Fiske, 1993; Galinsky & Moskowitz, 2000; Georgesen & Harris, 1998, 2000; Goodwin, Gubin, Fiske, & Yzerbyt, 2000; Magee & Galinsky, 2008; Wong & Ahuvia, 1998).

In one study, researchers observed study participants approaching a pedestrian crossing while driving either a rundown Mitsubishi or an old Ford Pinto. Each participant duly yielded to pedestrians. Next, the researchers swapped the clunkers for the classy, with participants now driving Mercedes and BMWs. Fancy wheels alone were enough such that 45 percent of Mercedes drivers and an even higher percentage of BMW drivers failed to yield to pedestrians (Coughenour, Abelar, Pharr, Chien, & Singh, 2020). It seems that the worst of people is brought out in the nicest of cars.

Both the powerful and the powerless may be tempted to cheat. The difference is that if the powerless cheat, they are more likely to do so to help others—admittedly a mixed virtue. The powerful, however, unvirtuously cheat for their own advantage (Galinsky et al., 2015). Other studies have shown that the self-interest of powerholders may be neutralized by aligning powerholders' goals with those of their followers. It's no surprise that if those interests diverge, however, the self-interested prioritize their own interests (Galinsky, Gruenfeld, & Magee, 2003).

Finally, consider a study coauthored by UC Berkeley's social psychologist Dacher Keltner, in which Keltner and colleagues revealed both the psychologically isolating and greed-enhancing effects of power. Keltner first found that adult participants raised in environments of wealth and power experience less compassion when shown images of children suffering from serious illnesses (Stellar, Manzo, Kraus, & Keltner, 2012). In a subsequent experiment, Keltner sought to understand how quickly these adverse effects arise. Keltner's team randomly appointed one of three study participants as group leader. In an apparently unrelated move (never trust psychologists), the researchers put out a plate of four cookies. After each participant snagged a cookie, they found that the randomly selected leader took the fourth and final cookie twice as often as did the other study participants. One of Keltner's graduate students also hypothesized that these randomly assigned leaders even ate their cookies differently. Keltner, initially skeptical, explains that after reviewing the video, "Lo and behold, our high-power person is more likely to eat with their mouth open, lips smacking, crumbs... falling onto their sweater. It's ridiculous" (Dahl, 2015).

Power, therefore, does not simply change the mind of the powerholder; like a heat-seeking missile, it causes the powerholder to lock onto tactics that ignite self-interest. But does all this self-enhancing behavior pay off? It seems not. The irony is that Western culture promotes self-interested leadership but fails to promote those same leaders' interests. As France's Jean Jacque Rousseau (2018) infamously lamented, "Man is born free, and everywhere he is in chains" (43). But, he continued (to somewhat less notoriety), "one believes himself the others' master, and yet is more a slave than they."

Westerners that use the self-interested tactic of force to gain and maintain power, for instance, are among the least successful of leaders. Reluctant followers are disloyal and uninterested in the goals of their leader, and they may actively sabotage the leader's interests and seek greener pastures elsewhere (Yukl & Chavez, 2002).

Researchers also have failed to find a positive correlation between holding power and increased career satisfaction (Martins, Eddleston, & Veiga, 2002). And among those who seek power as a matter of conformity to societal norms—rather than out of a personal desire—power-seeking reduces life satisfaction (Oishi et al., 1999).

In response to powerholders' selfish intentions, Western society has over time chosen to marginalize the powerful and limit their scope of action. In these environments, even the most self-interested of powerholders can only cause so much damage. Thus, we see in the American democratic system— and in Anglo-America generally—a variety of checks and balances to restrain politicians who are widely viewed as untrustworthy and self-interested.

In horizontally individualistic nations such as Scandinavia and the Netherlands, similarly, power differences are among the world's smallest. In these egalitarian societies, each person is expected to act in his or her own best interests, without treading on others. The late Wharton cross-cultural scholar Robert J. House, for instance, reported Dutch children were reluctant to admit that their fathers were managers (House et al., 1999).

We saw in the nether regions of Peru an example of this restrained power, too, with political leaders' one-year term limits. Among the horizontally individualistic Tristan Islanders of the South Atlantic, the most respected figures are those who invade little on others' privacy. The !Kung people, meanwhile, bestow respect, but little authority, upon the wise and skillful. The book *Eating Christmas in the Kalahari* documents the !Kung custom to ceremonially belittle hunters returning with a catch for the community's benefit, in order to forestall any bubbling pride (Lee, 1969).

Bruce Bonta (1997) writes that even when authority figures were appointed in the highly egalitarian societies he studied, they rarely were accorded any particular "power, prestige or privileges that would distinguish them from others" (305). These societies seem to understand that power is indeed corrupting within the individualistic context (House et al., 2004). The result is that powerholders in the East are kept strong but are expected to support the community with that power, while powerholders in the West are left comparatively weak and expected to act selfishly.

Within the United States, the relative weakness of a leader is undermined by, you guessed it, vertical individualism: inequalities are welcomed in a way they are not in more horizontally individualistic cultures (Schwartz, 2012). Americans are rather egalitarian in their personal lives, keeping it casual with the mailcarrier and neighbors, for instance. In fact, the United States is ranked the thirteenth most egalitarian society (of sixty-two surveyed). Professionally, Americans are positively hierarchical, however, with US and other Anglo-American countries' workplaces ranking second most *hierarchical*, ahead of countries in East Asia and after only South Asian societies (House et al., 2004).

Indeed, cross-cultural researcher Geert Hofstede notes that US management theories historically stand out for their emphasis on the individual over the group and for prioritizing managers over workers (Hofstede, 1984). For instance, the so-called father of scientific management theory, Frederick Taylor, saw workers as little more than sheep in dire need of a shepherd (Bregman, 2020). The result is that in the socially egalitarian but professionally hierarchical United States, many organizational leaders are given vast reservoirs of power and permission to use that power to selfish ends. Understandably then, many Americans seek power in a Hobbesian move to protect self and loved ones from powerful antagonists.

In contrasting West with East, it is important to reiterate that culture is not destiny but merely a proxy. Culture establishes norms, either sanctioning or rewarding self-interested and other-oriented behaviors. Crucially, then, an other-oriented powerholder in the West acting with enlightened self-interest is no more corrupted by power than one in the East. Similarly, a vertically individualistic powerholder residing in the East is subject to the same corrupting pathologies as a Westerner.

Thus societies like the United States, which see power as corrupting and expect little of their leaders, tend to get what they expect—with the result that forceful, self-interested individuals seem to rise to positions of leadership. Yet what of those who act for the communal benefit? Among these other-oriented powerholders, there is a distinct pathway to power. We term it the Stephen Hawking approach.

How Stephen Hawking Became King of the Jungle

We have seen how power may be attained through sheer force. We have seen, too, that when power is selfishly claimed, it is corrupting. Yet ESIs tend to see power as a responsibility and service opportunity.

This view of power as responsibility stands in sharp contrast to the ancient laws of nature. The lion is king of the jungle for the simple reason that his strength dominates all others. Humans are modern-day jungle kings. Our species has spent millennia building strength, with early hunters on the African savannah gaining dominance over nonhuman species; with the ancestors of those dominant hunters suppressing other clans; with dangerous warlords compelling compliance among weary populaces; and with overlords from medieval London to Imperial Russia and samurai Japan riding roughshod over peasant serfs. A simple Nietzschean formula has long applied: might makes right. But attaining power via force is only one formula for power—and it is a formula that is particularly attuned to the self-interested vertical individualist. There is another formula readily used by the horizontalist and exemplifying it is a man who spent much of his life in a wheelchair.

Stephen Hawking was born in 1942—the three hundredth anniversary of Galileo's death, as he liked to remind people—and by his twenty-first birthday had been diagnosed with the nervous system disease ALS. Hawking was given just a few years to live (Kaiser, 2018). Instead, he flourished, and he did so in a way that would have been impossible in the long, violent age of early humans. By the twentieth century Hawking was positioned to succeed by brain and not brawn, and with his 1988 publication, A Brief History of Time, he claimed his stake to history while also rewriting the rules of theoretical physics.

Hawking epitomizes what social scientists call the *power via prestige* pathway. Under this approach, "People attain influence because they garner respect and use valuable skills or knowledge to help the group achieve its goals" (Maner & Mead, 2010: 483). It is unsurprising, then, that even children intuit that prestige-based leaders are preferable to force-based leaders (Thomas et al., 2018).

Hawking's illness decimated his physical strength, but he retained his mental capacity to the end—reputedly possessing a "remarkable ability to do complex calculations in his head," according to Hawking's former doctoral student, Marika Taylor (Kaiser, 2018). As anthropologist Helene Mialet writes, Hawking's diminished condition led him to become something of a "brain in a vat" (Kaiser, 2018). And yet, with brainpower alone Hawking amassed incredible power and influence. By the time of his death in 2018 he had worked as Cambridge University's Lucasian Professor of Mathematics for thirty years, earned a baker's dozen honorary degrees and a Presidential Medal of Freedom, written numerous best-selling books, and—not least—established himself as the most important theoretical physician of his time (Marcos, 2019).

While power is *taken* by force, prestige-based power is freely given by followers. In return, the power via prestige pathway requires that leaders offer something to followers (Van Vugt & Tybur, 2015). In Hawking's case, this included offering followers the scientific theories that would provide a springboard to advance their own scientific studies, including Hawking's landmark formula to measure the temperature of a blackhole (Marcos, 2019).

Others thus allowed Hawking to accrue power and influence because they benefited from his rise. This includes the dozens of graduate students that Hawking advised, as well as countless collaborators, many of whom spoke on the occasion of his death to highlight his far-reaching contributions to their successful careers (*inter alia* Taylor, 2018). Like Easterners who use their power for others, Hawking's prestige-based career presented an unwritten contract in which his power accrued in direct proportion to the value he offered followers. As Harvard's Joseph Henrich and colleague Francisco Gil-White (2001) write of the power via prestige pathway, leaders gain willing followers who hope that they may, like Hawking's students, benefit from proximity to the prestigious individual's rare skills.

It is true that not all leaders deemed prestigious offer value. Ivy League professors engage in research misconduct, for instance, while CEOs, like wanted fugitive and former auto executive Carlos Ghosn, are accused of fraud and other wrongdoing. While such actors may for a time have prestige, they do not meet the definition of a "prestige-based leader"—that is, using knowledge or skills to help the group achieve its goals. They instead better fit the definition of the forceful powerholder who, recall, gains power by force but also by coercion or manipulation.

Power via force is the only known route to power in the animal kingdom, and it remains ubiquitous among humans as well. Hawking is far from alone, however. Has Bill Gates ever won a fight—or even been in one? Did Oprah Winfrey physically claw her way to the top?

It is this capacity to *earn,* as opposed simply to take, power that separates humans from every other known species (Henrich & Gil-White, 2001). As the University of Zurich's Ernst Fehr and the University of Konstanz's Urs Fischbacher write, the human capacity to choose cooperation over cooptation "represent[s] a huge anomaly in the animal world" (Fehr & Fischbacher, 2003: 785).

Prestige-based leaders benefit in ways unbeknownst to forceful power-holders. It's true that in both cases powerholders tend to receive preferential access to valued resources (Hill & Kaplan, 1988). Anthropologist Gregory Bateson, ex-husband to famed anthropologist Margaret Mead, offers a colorful example. One Iatmul man, Bateson explains (1958), derived significant prestige from his role as a fighter, debater, and sorcerer. This veritable polymath "had sufficient standing" to marry the mother of his own, alive-and-kicking, wife. The community's response? "It was nobody's business to say him nay" (91).

Closer to home, studies show that people less often attempt to deceive individuals wearing business suits (Bickman, 1971). They are also given more leeway to make excuses, "even though nobody is fooled about who is to blame" (Henrich & Gil-White, 2001: 183). Furthermore, prestige-based leaders accrue considerably more status than do force-based leaders. For instance, lab studies show that participants' status increases when they are ready and able to benefit their group (Anderson & Kilduff, 2009; Hardy & Van Vugt, 2006; Willer, 2009).

This is unsurprising. Force-based leaders seek their own benefit, while genuine prestige-based leaders seek benefit for the group (Maner & Mead, 2010). Followers consequently avoid forceful leaders but ingratiate and flatter prestigious leaders (Henrich & Gil-White, 2001). As Henrich and Gil-White (2001) note, "Someone with prestige is *listened to,* their opinions are heavily weighed (not obeyed) because the person enjoys credit, estimation, or standing in general opinion" (168).

However, it can be difficult to disentangle which of a prestige-based leader's skills are most developed. If Stephen Hawking clearly possessed skill as a physicist, then what about in other areas of science? What about subjects unrelated to science—as a car repairman, an interior designer, or a football coach? Where is the line drawn at which followers no longer listen?

Given the uncertainty surrounding all of these questions, followers tend to defer widely, with prestige-based leaders gaining influence in areas sometimes far beyond their immediate areas of expertise. Henrich writes of turtle hunters among the Meriam people of Melanesia who "are permitted to speak and are listened to more than others, despite the fact that their skill in hunting turtles gives no direct indication of their skill in public affairs or politics" (Henrich & Gil-White, 2001: 184). This may backfire on leaders who begin operating in alien subject matters—think athletes tinkering in business ventures or actors running for political office—but it is one more example of the extensive status that prestige-based leaders enjoy.

What happens once power is attained via prestige, you may ask? Do these leaders come to be corrupted by power, even power virtuously gained? Some research suggests cause for concern in this area, especially among prestige-based leaders in the vertically individualistic West. "As leaders accumulate power over time," University of Amsterdam's Van Vugt and coauthor Joshua Tybur (2015) write, "their positions in status hierarchies can transition from prestige based to [force] based as they can start to monopolize resources" (23). These leaders may thus rise on prestige only to rule with force.

This is by no means inevitable, however. Studies—including those with Western participants—show that power leads to more other-oriented behaviors when held by those who are "communally disposed" (Tost, 2015). It is, in turn, reasonable to assume that prestige-based leaders are more communally disposed; they, after all, offer value to their followers. Similarly, a new study by the University of Maryland's Trevor Foulk and colleagues (2021) reveals that when power is gained by empowering followers—exactly as prestige-based leaders do—"some of the negative and antisocial patterns associated with power do not emerge, but rather a more prosocial type of power is exhibited" (Foulk, Chighizola, Gencay, & Chen, 2021). Power, reframed from opportunity to communal responsibility, can thus lead to *greater*—not lesser—sensitivity, attention, and generosity toward others (Tost, 2015).

In addition, altruistic powerholders "serve as a beacon of pro-social behavior" and enhance philanthropic giving among their followers (Zhong et al., 2006: 61). Their followers are also likely to engage in more self-sacrificial behaviors, for instance, by contributing more to the group even at their own expense (De Cremer, 2002). Relatedly, other-oriented behaviors by a powerholder can concentrate followers on the successful achievement of group goals, thus improving performance (Van Knippenberg & Van Knippenberg, 2005). In addition, these leaders are likely to be seen as more charismatic, higher in status, and more trusted, while their followers show higher levels of satisfaction, cooperation, motivation, and commitment (Choi & Mai-Dalton, 1998, 1999).

As Wharton's Donaldson was quoted at the start of this chapter, power is neither corrupting nor uncorrupting. It is merely a means to accomplish the goals of the powerholder, whether self-interested or other-oriented. Thus, those already corrupted by self-interest are further corrupted by power—power that they tend to claim by force. By contrast, people purified by communal concerns seek power via prestige and rise to yet higher levels when empowered by grateful followers.

The East Asian way, of course, is defined largely by *vertical* collectivism, and thus is limited by a perspective that extends communal concern to some but not all. Thankfully, while East Asians may have the market cornered on other-oriented leadership, they do not hold a monopoly. A communal orientation can grow and develop among other individuals and societies. In addition, there is a sizable population in the United States already operating with heightened communality.

Western women—in common with East Asians—remain less interested in power than Western men (Flynn, Gruenfeld, Molm, & Polzer, 2011). They are more likely to see power as a responsibility than are men, and consequently they seek power less enthusiastically than those seeking power's benefits (Tost, 2015). More generally, women report valuing prosocial and prestige-based actions more than do men, while men are more accepting of selfish, egotistical, and dominant behaviors (Van Vugt & Tybur, 2015).

Why are women more communal? Perhaps it is in part genetic. Evolutionary psychologists posit that women generally are more concerned about their offspring than are men, and that this may unlock an other-oriented tendency (Buss, 1989). Undoubtedly part of the explanation is also that women are still held to higher ethical standards (Foschi, 2000). In general women thus conform by seeking to live up to these standards, just as much as men conform by living up to their more self-interested standards. It consequently bears monitoring whether this heightened communality continues as America's just march toward greater gender equality arguably increases conformity to vertical, masculine norms.

There is cause for a more general optimism, however. Studies shedding light on the motivations of self-interested people reveal that actions may at times be worse than attitudes. As organizational behavioralist Katherine DeCelles and colleagues report, many self-interested leaders are wholly unaware of the damage they cause to others; they are simply too self-absorbed to see their impact. DeCelles's team's work offers hope that self-interested behaviors are not as deeply ingrained as they appear. They write: "Our findings go beyond imply-ing that bad people do bad things when they feel powerful or that good people do good things when they feel powerful. . . . [Rather,] this self-interested behavior is a result of [people] being less aware of the moral implications of their behavior, not necessarily because they are bad people" (DeCelles, DeRue, Margolis, & Ceranic, 2012: 686). The key, DeCelles argues, is to have a well-developed moral compass, a north star upon which self-interested actions are made to shine in all their blinding light.

There is the possibility, consequently, that by intentionally becoming more aware of one's at times deleterious impact upon others, Westerners may move from an environment in which all power is all-corrupting to one in which power purifies. And, ironically, it may be by acting in this other-oriented way that one could benefit personally—gaining status and prestige without inducing fear and aversion in followers. Having seen how acting with enlightened self-interest may spin money and power from harmful to benefi-cial, the final piece of the interlocking money-power-fame triumvirate to be explored is the desire to keep up with the Kardashians.

10

Social Comparison, Superiority Complex, and Schadenfreude

When My Reputation Comes at Your Expense

"Somewhat by accident I was on a luxury yacht in the Mediterranean," Jim Doty (2021) began, almost apologetically. "The owner and his wife of course were there. And a much larger yacht goes by. You know, a *significantly* larger yacht," Doty emphasized. "The woman comes to me and says, 'I'm so embarrassed. Our new yacht is being built and it's not going to be ready for another year. So, I hope this is okay.'"

While introducing the world to social comparison theory, renowned psychologist Leon Festinger (1954) wrote of a "drive" to evaluate how one measures up to others. Scholars refer to social comparisons as an automatic impulse (Wood, 1996), while University of Connecticut psychologist Frederick Gibbons writes with Abraham Buunk (1999), "Virtually everyone engages in social comparison from time to time" (129). The tendency to look to others and automatically assess whether they are better or worse, stronger or weaker, is a key survival tool (Gilbert, Price, & Allan, 1995). The lion prowling the prehistoric African savannah? Stronger, so run away. Your autocratic but aging chieftain? Weaker, perhaps an uprising will succeed.

Social comparisons may also be used to look upon superior performers and learn something from them or, alternatively, to aid those in comparatively worse positions. Of course, not all is quite so innocent in a vertically individualistic West, which sees another's gains as one's own losses in a zero-sum race to the bottom. Social comparisons are in this context evolutionarily ancient tools repurposed to track money, power, and anything else that helps vertically individualistic Americans fit in (conform) by standing out (status-striving).

With the goal of such comparisons being to have more than the other— more money, more power, more prestige—rare and difficult-to-imitate items take on an outsized value. A case in point is the rare tulip lily imported from Turkey to the Netherlands in the seventeenth century. As the item became a status symbol, its value rapidly increased. York University's materialism scholar Richard Belk (2001) explains: "The mania got to the point that in order to acquire a single rare bulb, one farmer traded 'two *last* of wheat and four of rye, four fat oxen, eight pigs, a dozen sheep, two oxheads of wine, four tons of butter, a thousand pounds of cheese, a bed, some clothing, and a silver beaker'" (3–4). Lest we judge our ancestors too harshly, we might acknowledge the Turkish tulip lilies of contemporary society. Everything, from electricity to telephones, television to cellphones, computers to the internet, were once rare status objects that lost their luster as mass production rendered them available to millions and then billions. The almost proverbial corner office, by contrast, is a status symbol still, its value exceeding its inherent worth by virtue of scarcity.

Thus, economic "success" is not an objective measure, but attains meaning by indicating gain *in comparison to* others—like the Jones' with whom we are perpetually keeping up (Easterlin, 1973). In pre-genocidal Rwanda and Burundi, for instance, the Tutsi and Hutu people were both desperately poor. However, the Tutsis possessed more capital in the form of cows and were favored with priority access to schools and universities (Kidder, 2010). As a result, the equally impoverished Tutsis were a high-status elite.

By contrast, a middle-class American today is among the wealthiest human to ever live. As the term "middle class" implies, however, she is probably not particularly high status. Status-seeking verticalists, therefore, view life in much the same way as professional sports teams: they prefer winning a low-scoring game to losing a high-scoring game. Billionaire Reid Hoffman, as quoted in the *New York Times*, offers a case in point.

The Randian Problem of Contingent Self-Esteem

A *New York Times* article about Silicon Valley, "The Rich Now Envy the Superrich," quotes Reid Hoffman, who earned $1.5 billion for his involvement with PayPal, who said, "It's kind of embarrassing. You started a year or two earlier, and they start after you and then this thing zips right past you and gets the golden results." Hoffman acknowledges some level of "implicit envy" at the successes of these lucky others who "happened to pick the right time" (Hafner, 2006).

Notwithstanding his own multibillion-dollar success, Hoffman's language suggests an identity threat in which his sense of worth declined in response to others' successes. Albert Bandura (1988), one of the twentieth century's leading psychologists and an authority on self-esteem, writes, "In competitive, individualistic societies . . . where one person's success represents another person's failure, social comparison inevitably enters into self appraisal" (54). This aligns with Dartmouth scholar Erzo Luttmer's (2005) article, "Neighbors as Negatives," in which he found that regardless of objective well-being—whether one has enough to survive and even flourish, for instance—self-worth declines when salient others are more prosperous. Or as the Dalai Lama sums it up, "If you want to be poor find some rich friends, if you want to be rich find some poor friends" (Dalai Lama et al., 2016: 135).

Vertical individualists thus look with envy and resentment upon those bearing a fresh tulip lily or holding court in a corner office. This is known as **upward social comparison**, and these comparisons chip away at the vertical individualist's psychological well-being. By contrast, vertical individualists use **downward social comparisons** to reclaim self-esteem—and nourish a superiority complex—by gleeful reference to less-privileged others (White & Lehman, 2005).

High self-esteem is psychologically vital. It is key to setting and achieving goals and gaining the courage to take chances, and it is an important status predictor. It even enhances the likelihood of landing sexual partners—which, suffice it to say, is a strong evolutionary motive (Beach & Tesser, 2000). In fact, Stanford's Hazel Markus and coauthor Shinobu Kitayama (1991) write that maintaining a positive self-view is yet another universal human pursuit. In vertically individualistic America, however, this is accomplished by "separating oneself from others and seeing oneself as different from and *better than* others" (224, emphasis added).

In sharp contrast to American children, for instance, Japanese youth hold antagonistic views toward self-enhancement and self-promotion. Markus and Kitayama's study found that Japanese elementary schoolchildren viewed a modest classmate as morally superior and more skillful than an immodest classmate who publicly bragged about his own skills. This preference for modesty strengthened with age, showing the effects of cultural inoculation of the Japanese sense of self-restraint. Similar effects have been found in China and would likely be seen across many collectivistic cultures.

In the vertically individualistic West, by comparison, one does not rise with, or even independently of, others, but rather on others' backs. The natural effect is to inflame self-interested perceptions. In the same study, American children as young as four showed a self-favorability bias, and most children—like most adults—think themselves smarter, friendlier, and more skilled than average (Markus & Kitayama, 1991). Another study summarized in the Markus & Kitayama (1991) review article, for instance, showed that 70 percent of American students believed they possessed above-average leadership ability, and *zero percent* ranked their ability to get along with others below average.

With self-esteem contingent on others' perceived inferiority, vertical individualists actively seek social comparisons that allow them to maintain the fiction of their own superiority (Fujita, 2008). How to do this? By favoring downward social comparisons in self-relevant categories (Wheeler & Miyake, 1992; Wills, 1981). Most people consequently prefer being a "big fish in a small pond," or being successful in a relatively unsuccessful group, so that comparisons are mostly favorable (Gardner, Gabriel, & Hochschild, 2002).

As long as looking down upon others doesn't provoke a fear of joining them—as it might, for instance, if gazing upon demoted colleagues—then downward comparisons may boost self-confidence (Fujita, 2008). However, vertical individualists don't simply celebrate others' inferiority; as explored in earlier chapters, it may cause them to seek to maintain their elevated positions by preventing others from rising. As Leon Festinger wrote in 1954, a self-esteem that is contingent on one's comparative position generates "competitive behavior . . . to protect one's superiority" (126).

Whatever the immediate gains to self-confidence, therefore, they must be balanced against the societal costs of such destructive competition. Moreover, it is likely that any egoistic gains from downward comparisons are offset by the extrinsic orientation they entail. One of literature's most extrinsically oriented vertical individualists comes from hyper-individualistic author-philosopher Ayn Rand. In the classic novel *The Fountainhead*, anti-hero Peter Keating is a vertically individualistic foil to the sharply horizontal individualist Howard Roark (Rand, 2014).

Rand's story picks up with Keating's anxious, meandering thoughts during his much-ballyhooed college graduation: "They knew of his scholastic record and no one would beat his record today. . . . [Classmate] Shlinker had given him stiff competition, but he had beaten Shlinker this last year. He had worked like a dog, because he had wanted to beat Shlinker. He had no rivals today . . . he would always beat Shlinker and all the Shlinkers of the world, *he would let no one achieve what he could not achieve*" (45, emphasis added).

Years later, Keating has attained professional success: "He had everything he'd ever wanted. He had wanted superiority—and for the last year he had been the undisputed leader of his profession. He had wanted fame—and he had five thick albums of clippings. He had wanted wealth—and he had enough to insure luxury for the rest of his life. He had everything anyone ever wanted. What was his aim in life? *Greatness—in other people's eyes*. Fame, admiration, envy—all that which comes from others" (918, emphasis added).

Rand's Keating uses social comparisons in a narcissistic attempt to build his ego by and through others. He seeks professional achievements, in pursuit of which he is willing to smother others. To advance, he partners with a man he abhors and blackmails another partner. Keating's girlfriend—who later is jilted for lacking useful connections—explains his behaviors away, saying simply, "You're ambitious, Peter." (89).

Keating uses everyone, himself included, and in the end his accomplishments mean little. Keating says near the novel's apogee, "I hate it, all of it, my work and my profession, and what I'm doing and what I'm going to do!" The anti-hero Keating is a vertical individualist, extrinsically beholden to his place in comparison to others. Though he may have experienced the illusion of happiness while on the hedonic treadmill, in the end he is a wrecked and tragic soul, drinking too much, desperate for human connection, lacking a single friend in the world.

We know from decades of scholarly work that Keating's depicted end largely hues to reality. Key here is that the social comparisons of Keating and his vertically individualistic compatriots recall the extrinsic orientation, an orientation that is contingent on others, and thus tentative. Just as materialists' look to things for happiness, vertical individualists look to others for their self-worth. And just as using money toward extrinsic ends reduces well-being, the extrinsic motivations animating vertical individualists' social comparisons have the same negative effect.

Studies across a wide range of national cultures, for instance, find that merely *setting* extrinsically oriented goals—such as outperforming others—is associated with reduced life satisfaction (Kasser, 2002). The relationships of extrinsically oriented individuals are characterized by conflict as well as low levels of trust and love (Kasser & Ryan, 2001). Extrinsically oriented individuals are also more likely to engage in what psychologists blandly term "counterproductive behaviors," such as watching excessive hours of TV, smoking, drinking, using drugs (Williams, Hedberg, Cox, & Deci, 2000), and becoming a "shopaholic" (Dittmar, 2005). Extrinsically oriented individuals are even suspect ethically (Kasser, Vansteenkiste, & Deckop, 2006), with extrinsic motivation correlating with more ethnic prejudice (Duriez, Vansteenkiste, Soenens, & De Witte, 2007) and less environmentally friendly behaviors (Brown & Kasser, 2005). All of these undesirable traits are motivated by the belief—held far more commonly among the extrinsically motivated—that the world is zero-sum and dog-eat-dog (Duriez, et al., 2007).

Ghent University's Alain Van Hiel and Maarten Vansteenkiste (2009), furthermore, find that older Americans devoted to extrinsic pursuits saw precisely no boost to psychological well-being. To the contrary, the *successful* achievement of extrinsic goals, such as those seen during social comparisons, leads to higher levels of despair and regret and greater difficulty accepting one's own mortality—perhaps because such so-called victories leave people with time to consider the functional futility of efforts to surpass others.

By contrast, those who set intrinsic goals in pursuit of societal contributions, personal development, and meaningful interpersonal relationships experience greater life satisfaction and a stronger sense of connection with all humanity. As a result of these meaningful connections and accomplishments, both despair and regret decline while aging. Instead, less anxiety about and greater acceptance of mortality is experienced in comparison to the extrinsically motivated (Van Hiel & Vansteenkiste, 2009). Importantly, studies show that when self-esteem is not contingent on one's relative wealth, fewer social comparisons occur and little psychological trauma is experienced when observing materially successful others (Gardner et al., 2002).

All of this suggests that though downward comparisons may boost egos temporarily, overall well-being declines when self-esteem is extrinsically contingent on a perception of others' inferiority. What about when vertical individualists upwardly compare with their superiors? Lacking even the partial protection of an ego-boosting downward comparison, the consequences are yet more pernicious—and for all involved.

Malicious Envy and Schadenfreude

"Because I envy your normal life, it seems envy is my sin." So the 1995 Blockbuster film *Se7en* reaches its cinematic climax, with villain John Doe maliciously punishing seven sinners. In the scene, Doe has just revealed the murdered remains of Tracy Mills to her husband, lead character Detective David Mills. Doe implores Mills, played by Brad Pitt, to submit to his wrath and shoot him dead. In acquiescing, Mills implicates himself in a deadly sin while Doe suffers punishment for his sin of envy, thus completing the violent cycle.

In *Se7en* Doe grows envious while upwardly comparing himself to the happily married, professionally successful Detective Mills. As vertical individualists' need to maintain superiority leads them to kick those who are already down, those who compare upwards seek—if not quite with Doe's malice—superiors' downfall. In eliminating the cause of his discomfort, Doe experiences schadenfreude, or pleasure at another's suffering.

Though a dramatized, Hollywood version of envy, this is nonetheless a familiar narrative. A thousand years ago some medieval Parisian envied his neighbor's portlier pig. A thousand years before that, the Greek goddess Athena was busy turning Arachne into a spider for the unforgivable crime of besting Athena's weaving skills (Envy Canterbury, 2016). Half a millennium earlier still, envy took its place as one of the Seven Deadly Sins, with the story of Cane killing his brother, Abel, in a fit of jealousy.

Today verticalist individualists stand out by competing, and winning, in socially relevant arenas (Triandis & Gelfand, 1998). The result when the competition is lost? As Doe experienced, upward comparisons often leave stargazers envious of those above (Van de Ven, Zeelenberg, & Pieters, 2009). As psychiatrist Howard C. Cutler comments, "Our feelings of contentment are strongly influenced by our tendency to compare [and] constant comparison with those who are smarter, more beautiful, or more successful than we are also tends to breed envy, frustration, and unhappiness" (Dalai Lama & Cutler, 2010: 48).

Upward comparisons are indeed painful to the vertical individualist. For instance, research shows that as Westerners engage in more social comparisons, self-esteem declines and rates of depression increase (Wheeler & Miyake, 1992; Wood, 1996). In addition, the envy that results from upward comparisons is itself damaging. Envy reduces cooperation (Parks, Rumble, & Posey, 2002), for instance, and in turn group performance (Duffy & Shaw, 2000). Envy also increases irrational decision-making (Beckman, Formby, Smith, & Zheng, 2002; Hoelzl & Loewenstein, 2005), and may exacerbate depression and hostility (Smith, Parrott, Ozer, & Moniz, 1994).

Mark Twain, that astute chronicler of human nature, observed, "There's always something about your success that displeases even your best friends" (2014). Right he was. Socrates is said to have proposed this paradox: "The envious man finds something in the misfortunes of his neighbors at which he is pleased" (Smith, Powell, Combs, & Schurtz, 2009: 540). Socrates thus offered an early description of schadenfreude, when pleasure is taken at another's misfortune (Takahashi, Kato, Matsuura, Mobbs, Suhara, & Okubo, 2009).

As John Doe exemplifies, a superior's downfall is particularly rewarding for converting a painful upward comparison into a self-esteem-boosting downward comparison (Smith et al., 2009). Consider one study in which American students watched recorded interviews with either an average or a highly accomplished student. The study participants were then told that the interviewee was arrested for stealing drugs from a research lab and would consequently be forced to defer plans to attend medical school. "How do you feel about this student's setback?" the participants were asked. Some people in both groups experienced schadenfreude, though on average more pleasure was taken from the failure of the highly accomplished student (Smith et al., 1996).

These all highlight a cultural preference to see the fall of the high and mighty (rather than the ordinary and mediocre), something to recall the next time US society gleefully pounces upon yet another famous athlete, actor, politician, or philanthropist falling from grace. Indeed, researchers opine that a widespread tendency toward schadenfreude may help explain the preponderance of modern media highlighting others' suffering and misfortune—especially rich and famous others (Smith et al., 2009).

Closer to home, Americans' insecurities undermine what should be the strongest of relationships. Across multiple studies, psychology professor Abraham Tesser has shown that people are psychologically harmed more by the superior performance of family and friends than when bested by complete strangers (Tesser & Campbell, 1982; Tesser, Pilkington, & McIntosh, 1989). Similarly, the failure of close relations provides more *pleasure* than strangers' failures (Takahashi et al., 2009).

If given the choice, for instance, most Americans prefer that a sought-after promotion go to a stranger than to a close colleague (Gardner et al., 2002). Motivated by a similar desire to avoid seeing close others succeed, researchers find that business professionals are more open to ideas from outsiders than they are to ideas from their own teams or organizations, a phenomenon perhaps familiar to many family units as well (Menon, Thompson, & Choi, 2006). In sum, envy is felt when others succeed, pleasure is taken at others' setbacks, and both emotions are magnified when applied to emotionally close others.

As in John Doe's case, the passive pleasure at others' failures may give way to attempts to diminish superior performers. In the workplace, for instance, salary satisfaction is contingent on others' salaries (Gelfand, Erez, & Aycan, 2007). If other employees receive rewards perceived as unfairly high, resentment and demotivation increase, regardless of one's own compensation and benefits. Taking schadenfreude into their own hands, dissatisfied workers may retaliate by reducing contributions, stealing from the organization, or even seeking to harm or sabotage the aggravating employee (Colquitt et al., 2014).

Thus, verticalists feel temporarily satiated when looking down on others and would like them to stay right where they are, thank you very much. Conversely, they feel bad when looking up at superiors and would like to expeditiously bring them down to size. As the world grows ever more interconnected, moreover, people may find themselves looking not only at the nearby Joneses but also at the distant and far wealthier Smiths—or, such as it is with modern media, the Kardashians. The result of more and higher upward comparisons, as you can imagine, is not pretty.

Keeping Up with the Kardashians

Vertical individualists boost their esteem by competing, beating, and feeling superior to others. They suffer when others succeed and experience schadenfreude or pleasure at others' pain. The world of the vertical individualist is thus a contingent one, safe only so long as there are many more to look down upon rather than up toward. As seen with the fictional Peter Keating, it is a self-interested yet ultimately unfulfilling maneuver.

Yet many of us today have cognitively available far more upward comparisons than downward comparisons, a result that exacerbates the already harmful effects of upward comparisons. For instance, researchers find that most Americans overestimate the size of others' social circles and their number of friends, and they overestimate how often they dine out and attend parties (Deri, Davidai, & Gilovich, 2017). Similarly, Americans appear to overestimate others' wealth, which leads to the misperception that there are more wealthy people with which to upwardly compare than actually exist. When research by Michael Norton and Dan Ariely (2011) found that Americans underestimate inequality, researchers quickly came to question the validity of their results (Eriksson & Simpson, 2012). A subsequent study conducted in 2014 by St. Louis University's John Chambers further disputed the 2011 research. Chambers found that Americans in general—and especially political liberals—significantly *overestimated* the wealth of the top 1 percent. Americans also *underestimated* average income, leading to the perception that—bad as it is—US inequality is even worse than it truly is (Chambers, Swan, & Heesacker, 2014; Gimpelson & Treisman, 2018). This contrasts with global studies, which find that people tend to underestimate their society's wealth gap (Gimpelson & Treisman, 2018), a finding that reinforces Americans' distinctly harmful tendency toward upward comparisons.

In a term coined by sociologist Juliet Schor, moreover, the landscape of American media leads us not to keep up with the Joneses, but with the Kardashians (Annenberg Space for Photography, 2017). Perhaps contributing to this skewed perception of wealth, many Americans are bombarded daily with images of those not only materially "better," but so far ahead as to stifle any reasonable hope of catching up.

MTV housewives parading in high heels, Gucci purses by their side as they glide into well-polished Mercedes sedans. Supermodels on magazine covers perverting the measure of physical beauty. Daily, a new set of house hunters blithely shelling out for million-dollar oceanfront lots. And Twitter feeds tingling with exhortations from billionaire tech titans and overnight successes, as well as famous athletes, actors, and powerful politicians.

Never mind that—to reiterate—most Americans are better off than most humans living now or ever before. Incessantly confronting Americans are the most beautiful, wealthiest, extraverted, charismatic, and narcissistic. With so many rich and famous striding above, author Celeste Headlee (2020) writes, "People who are asked to compare their lives to the lives of others immediately think of celebrities, CEOs, and political leaders" (188). She also writes that people "used to yearn to break into the economic class just above their own. Now we strive to emulate the top 20 percent of income earners, because those are the families we're watching on TV. . . . At this point," Headlee continues, "Americans don't think someone is wealthy unless their income is about $2.5 million a year. That's thirty times the actual amount an individual needs in order to be classified as upper income in the United States, and thirty times the average net worth of American households" (187).

A profound discontent is experienced while examining the gap between where one is and where all the media suggest one deserves to be (Halliwell & Dittmar, 2006; Higgins, 1987). When upward comparisons are made to dissimilar others—magazine cover models, for instance—negative self-evaluations increase (Collins, 1996; Richins, 1994). Relatedly, fantasizing about unattainable lifestyles offers only a temporary boost to happiness, and eventually leaves its dreamers worse off than if they had never imagined life sailing a mega-yacht or as an elegant junior member of England's Royal Court (Oettingen, Mayer, & Portnow, 2016).

This may help explain why in 2015 Americans were rated thirteenth in global happiness, which may sound laudable until considering that America's average income ranked third (Pinker, 2018). As author and cognitive psychologist Stephen Pinker (2018) writes, "Americans consistently punch below their wealth in happiness" (271). This is no longer a problem only of the West, however, but is endemic worldwide.

Indeed, it is arguably *more* problematic in less developed parts of the world. Cut off from access to the wider world, ordinary people in impoverished nations once had little clue that others lived so well. This Kardashian Problem went global sometime in the twenty-first century. Satellite TV, DVDs, and the internet spread abroad the myth of widespread American affluence, and arguably the malevolent influence of exaggerated affluence has not yet peaked. As a result, members of the world's poorest nations are now also comparing themselves to the Kardashians and their ilk. The result is rising envy and frustration among the economically disadvantaged, as the poorest countries join the richest in craning their necks upward at the seemingly ubiquitous affluence of which surely they alone are missing out (Diener & Biswas-Diener, 2002).

The late Kenyan Nobel Prize winner and environmental activist Wangari Maathai (2009) reflects on this change. In her book she writes of her mother's generation, which "measured their happiness, their material and spiritual well-being, in ways far different from today. Their medium of exchange was goats. . . . Because most of their basic needs were met, they didn't consider themselves poor. . . . They didn't feel alienated, or adrift in a meaningless, highly materialistic world that assigns value in dollars and cents. . . . By the time my mother died . . . everything could be sacrificed for money: forests, land, goats, values, and even people" (162).

This artificial perception of glamour and affluence exacerbates the tendency to feel distant from others—who, after all, appear to be doing *just fine*—as individuals gain newfound justifications for materialism and self-interested ambitions. Upwardly comparing with more affluent others results in a double bind of self-interested motivations—as materialism and upward comparisons, each independently diminish generosity and enhance envy. As Headlee (2020) writes, "Comparing ourselves to the highest earners in the country has made us all feel poor and might be driving us to work harder and put in more hours in a futile attempt to create the lifestyle we think others have" (188).

The vertically individualistic pursuit of success, consequently, results in a series of harmful comparisons. And yet, social comparisons are evolutionary adaptations that once enhanced survival rates. What then is it that vertical individualists are missing, and how does acting with enlightened self-interest help?

11

Comparison, Inclusion, and *Mudita*

When Admiring Another Improves the Self

Envy is a pan-cultural phenomenon (Van de Ven et al., 2009). Dutch, German, Polish, and Thai languages all go so far as to distinguish between two sorts of envy: malicious and benign (Van de Ven, Zeelenberg, & Pieters, 2011). *Se7en's* John Doe illustrates malicious envy. This anticipates schadenfreude (Van de Ven et al., 2009), and is the experience most attributable to the vertical individualist who is threatened by others' successes.

Benign envy, by contrast, is *benign* precisely because it does not involve a desire to see others fail (Van de Ven et al., 2009). This is the envy most attributable to horizontal individualists, who are naturally self-seeking and may feel envious when others succeed at something they value. Because they are relatively uncompetitive horizontals, however, their own success does not require the failure of others. Those experiencing benign envy, similarly, are motivated not to diminish others, but to lift themselves. They tend to respond by enacting self-improvement regimens, and, research shows, their plans often succeed (Van de Ven et al., 2009, 2011). It is in this potential for self-interested improvement arising from upward comparisons that we see vertical individualists' first missed opportunity.

Yet another emotion that may arise during upward comparisons is admiration, which is characterized by scholar Niels van de Ven (2017) as "a feeling of delighted approval over the accomplishment of another person" (4). Americans most admire politicians, athletes, humanitarians, and others in the public eye, while envy is more commonly directed toward those with greater wealth and professional standing (Henniger & Harris, 2015). For instance, a recent Gallup poll of most admired people features politicians such as Donald Trump and Barrack Obama, former first lady Michelle Obama, as well as Pope Francis, the Dalai Lama, Bill Gates, and Lebron James (Jones, 2020). Most Americans are not themselves politicians, athletes, or humanitarians, and can therefore noncompetitively admire those who are without feeling threatened by their own relative sense of inferiority. However, a sense of inner worth is necessary to avoid envy and admire superiors on the same field of play.

In addition, even vertical individualists have little trouble admiring the successes of their children and a narrow set of others who are seen as inter-dependent with, or virtual extensions of, themselves. Horizontal collectiv-ists may see others, perhaps all others, as interdependent with the self. If, therefore, vertical individualists are subject to malicious envy, and horizontal individualists are candidates for benign envy, then it is horizontal collectivists who are most likely to revel in admiration.

Admiration is associated with a feeling of connectedness to the admired as well as a sense of openness which, far from crashing self-esteem, instead serves to enhance overall well-being (Van de Ven et al., 2011). As a result, collectivists can happily ponder others' successes—and in fact collectivists engage in more upward comparisons than do more ego-fragile individualists (White & Lehman, 2005).

Danish philosopher Søren Kierkegaard (2008 [1849]) reputedly said, "Admiration is happy self-surrender; envy is unhappy self-assertion" (139). While he is probably right about the underlying emotions of happiness and unhappiness, the idea of admiration as "self-surrender" overlooks its ani-mating potential. As Frank Fujita and Ed Diener (1997) discuss, those that inspire us to do or be better are almost inevitably seen through the lens of upward comparisons. In turn, research shows that admirers, inspired by their heroes, often seek to rise up and mimic them in word and deed (Schindler, Paech, & Löwenbrück, 2015; Schindler, Zink, Windrich, & Menninghaus, 2013). Collectivists are thus best positioned to leverage upward compari-sons in order to identify opportunities for personal and other focused growth (White & Lehman, 2005).

Here especially can be seen the benefits of upward comparisons that are lost on the competitive vertical individualist. In one study researchers found that Canadians of Asian descent were more likely to use social comparisons for self-improvement, whereas European Canadians compared in hopes of enhancing their egos. This resulted in more upward comparisons among the Asian Canadians, including more social comparisons after experiencing fail-ures. These collectivistic test subjects rightly understood that they could learn from those above them and, after experiencing failure, they were particularly motivated to do so. Indeed, studies suggest that exposure to superior others is "vital" to self-improvement (Collins, 1996).

These European Canadians might have understood this as well, but acknowledging their limitations proved too damaging to their extrinsically oriented self-esteems. As a result, they *reduced* social comparisons after failures and increased social comparisons only after achieving successes (White & Lehman, 2005).

Other studies similarly show that people engaging in social comparisons to build ego rather than to build upon successes are more likely to distort the truth in ego-enhancing ways (Gardner et. al., 2002). As Wendi Gardner and colleagues (2002) write, "Self-enhancement motives frequently overwhelm the desire for accurate self-knowledge and dominate the social comparison process" (239). Rather than attributing a peer's promotion to superior talent or hard work, for instance, vertical individualists would more likely claim managerial favoritism. But horizontal collectivists would celebrate that peer's promotion and may recognize, too, that superior talent was the reason (and then also reflect on ways to develop their own skills to gain the next open promotion).

Thus, both admiration and benign envy serve the utilitarian purpose of self-improvement, but the mechanisms differ. Admiration is an other-oriented and even transcendental experience—whereas envy, including benign envy, is individualistic and self-focused. ESIs, by combining self- and communal concerns, may consequently benefit from *both* benign envy and admiration. Upward comparisons are then opportunities for improvement and gratitude and help realize the evolutionary advantage that incentivized early humans to socially compare. By contrast, a zero-sum vertically individualistic competition converts that same ancient evolutionary advantage into a decided disadvantage.

Downward Comparisons: From Kicking Down to Helping Up

Let us return to former Greyston CEO Mike Brady, the Wharton-educated business leader. Brady explains that the New York–based Greyston Foundation and its industrial bakery both operate according to the Buddhist ideology of "nonjudgment" toward all living things. This is not as surprising as it might appear—Greyston, after all, was founded in 1982 by Bernie Glassman, a rather eccentric and mystical figure characterized in a *New York Times* obituary as a Buddhist Zen master and social activist" (Seeylve, 2018).

Glassman popularized so-called street retreats in an effort to build empathy toward New York's underserved communities. Author James Ishmael Ford (2006) writes that during street retreats, "participants eat in soup kitchens and, if they know they're not displacing homeless people, sleep in homeless shelters or, otherwise, sleep in public places" (168). Glassman gained notoriety as a spiritual guru to, and eventual coauthor with, actor Jeff Bridges. This resulted in the delightfully titled book *The Dude and the Zen Master* (Seeyle, 2018).

Mike Brady speaks about Glassman's ongoing legacy. Business, he explained, is too often characterized by moralizing judgments and conscious or unconscious bias. Yet by managing with an open mind, Brady argues, businesses may select from the full pool of workers and help the best workers rise.

Indeed, workplace bias is well-documented, adversely impacting people based on characteristics ranging from gender, nationality, and religion to weight, height, and more. As mentioned earlier, Greyston's principle of non-judgment offers opportunities to workers from all backgrounds—and thereby seeks to overcome the implicit discrimination experienced by traditionally marginalized peoples and communities. Brady took this policy mainstream in 2018 by launching the Center for Open Hiring, through which best practices are disseminated to employers (Frederick, 2019).

Dion Drew, whose criminal history made it nearly impossible for him to gain employment, exemplifies Brady's judgment-free hiring policy. In an emotional Ted Talk co-presented with Brady, Drew tells the crowd, "I would like to tell you a little bit about myself. I grew up in the projects. At a very young age I see a lot of drug selling and a lot of drug use. I started selling drugs at the age of fifteen. I've been in and out of jail from the age of seventeen. In 2004, I had to do four years. That's when I decided to change my life. When I was incarcerated, I set some goals for when I came home. First, get a job, secondly save some money, third start my own family, and the most important goal," Drew says, pausing to choke back tears, "it was to make my mom proud of me again" (Brady & Drew, 2022).

"When I came home, I looked for work, like, every day. But," he continues, "nobody would hire me." This is the judgment about which Brady spoke, a belief that Drew did not fit the prototype of a good worker—even for entry-level jobs requiring no special skills. Drew had applied under Greyston's open hire system, however, which offers work to anyone and everyone in the order an application is received. "I was riding around with a friend, and I got a call from Greyston asking if I wanted to work for Greyston," Drew explains. "That was 2015, and I've been there since then."

"They empower me every day," Drew says on stage. "When I came to Greyston I started as an apprentice. [Since then] I got three promotions. I have three bank accounts, I have life insurance, dental insurance, health insurance—Aflac," Drew laughs. "I have a beautiful three-year-old daughter. And my mom calls me a least twice a week to let me know how proud she is."

It is this nonjudgment that brought Drew to Greyston when no one else would hire him. It is nonjudgment that has kept him there, in a place that sees him not just as a token hire but someone worthy of development and promotion. And it is Greyston that benefits from deeply loyal employees like Drew, and a reputation that makes it easy for other socially responsible organizations like Ben & Jerry's to do big business with the foundation.

All of this was made possible by the framework of enlightened self-interest. Just as an individual acting with enlightened self-interest can engage in upward comparisons without feeling envy, that individual can engage in downward comparisons without feeling superior or wishing to hold others down. Brady, for instance, expresses his unreserved admiration for Drew. "He's a tremendous story," Brady (2021) explains. "I draw inspiration from him and many others, to know that they were given an opportunity to change their lives and they did. And if you can do that a million times over, the world's going to be a heck of a lot better place."

Brady understands that in a world of abundance, he need not diminish others to maintain his position or his self-esteem. He understands all can rise together. He acts unhindered by judgment about what is or is not possible, and in return he experiences joy. The joy, that is, of *mudita*.

In *Mudita*, East Meets West

While Western thinkers such as Mark Twain and Socrates were busy contemplating schadenfreude and envy, Buddhist philosophers were meditating on the opposite: *mudita*. Mudita, an ancient Sanskrit word, views joy as limitless. In the context of mudita, and consistent with Brady's reaction to Drew, the joy of others not only fails to diminish one's own joy but is a *source* of joy.

As noted previously, individuals with more communal orientations—those not subjected to malicious envy at others' successes—engage in healthier upward comparisons (Kemmelmeier & Oyserman, 2001). While gazing at the glittering successes of any one of eight billion-odd people, practitioners of mudita can socially compare upward and take uncomplicated joy in their well-being. A welcome difference from the self-conscious individualist who would root for strangers before friends and family, mudita practitioners celebrate the successes—even the surpassing excellence—of close friends and acquaintances (Gardner et al., 2002).

The benefits of mudita—better known in the social sciences as "empathic joy"—are significant. Celebrating the successes of others strengthens one's relationships with them, creating a mutual sense of intimacy, commitment, and trust (Pittinsky & Montoya, 2016). In one study, couples who were joyous about one another's successes experienced higher relationship satisfaction and a greater chance of remaining together two months after the study (Gable, Gonzaga, & Strachman, 2006). This result is not so much a surprise as it is a reminder of the costs of schadenfreude when leveled against loved ones.

Empathic joy researchers Todd Pittinsky and R. Matthew Montoya (2016) highlight mudita's hodgepodge of desirable outcomes. Mudita, they write, "generates positive emotions, positive thoughts, enhanced memory (including better recall of pleasant events), more exploratory and more flexible thinking, and the psychological states that prepare a person to build friendships and social networks" (514).

Pittinsky and Montoya also describe the refreshing consequences of mudita on diversity attitudes. Their study (2016) measured mudita among white American teachers arising from the successes of their predominantly minority students. The teachers' indicated their level of agreement with questions such as: "When my students celebrate things, I am happy for them," and "When my students feel happy, I feel happy." They found that as mudita increases, discrimination declines, while deepening teachers' positive and beneficial relationships with students.

Aristotle advised, "The good person is related to his friend as he is related to himself (because his friend is another)" (Crisp, 2000: 179). Worthy advice though this may be, we can go further. The Pittinsky and Montoya study suggests that mudita is a tool to overcoming limiting tendencies, going beyond rooting for spouses and friends—a step away from schadenfreude though that is—and see ourselves as interconnected with and rooting for a diverse array of "others." The scholars suggest that mudita may be experienced in relation to "not only close relationships such as family, friends, romantic partners, and roommates, but also strangers, coworkers, and acquaintances" (153).

The Pittinsky and Montoya study, conducted on American teachers, reaffirms that while concepts like mudita and power-as-responsibility are philosophically rooted in the East, these values are open to cultivation by anyone, anywhere. Americans may even have some advantages incorporating these inclusive practices. Far Easterners are in general able to engage in more productive upward comparisons. Yet vertically collectivist cultures, which promote in-group / out-group competition, may inhibit constructive social comparisons with out-group members. In addition, the strict social hierarchies of the East mean that though willing to compare with better-performing peers, East Asians are resistant to making self-comparisons to more powerful others such as employers or those advanced in age. Together these taboos imply that the vertical collectivist may look to a successful colleague or countryman to learn, but miss learning opportunities that come from foreign nationals or social superiors (Guimond et al., 2007).

By contrast, the power of mudita to experience joy at *all* others' successes may be compatible with the somewhat more egalitarian West. With a genuine view of humanity as interconnected, healthy and affirming social comparisons may occur nondiscriminately, both upward and downward, and irrespective of in-group / out-group dynamics and power dynamics (Guimond et al., 2007). A real leap forward, then, would combine disparate cultural strengths: the benign envy or admiration in the East, which sees upward comparisons as opportunities for growth, with the West's more inclusive social comparisons. Beyond the broad parameters of a lifestyle motivated by enlightened self-interest, what more can be done to kindle our latent mudita?

Cultivating *Mudita*

Ayn Rand's character Peter Keating claimed superiority while utterly lacking self-confidence. Keating is the quintessential vertical individualist: hyper-competitive because his self-worth is derived from winning out over others. Individuals like Keating with low self-esteem tend to fall prey to unhealthy competitive instincts and, when competing, to see others' failures as the only salve to their wounded pride (Eastern Oregon University, 2020; Fujita, 2008). By contrast, as scholar Alfie Kohn (1992) writes, "An adult with a reasonably healthy self-concept... does not need to continue asking ritualistically, "How'm I doin'?" or even to compare herself or himself with others" (42).

The researchers Tanya Menon of Ohio State University and Leigh Thompson (2010) of Northwestern University are among the few American researchers studying mudita. They acknowledge, "It is the rare person whose automatic impulse is to feel glad when meeting someone smarter, prettier, or richer. Nevertheless, it is possible to cultivate more generosity of spirit and quiet the cruel voice of envy."

Research suggests that infants may possess a certain amount of generosity, which is lost as cultural values take hold. In one study, infant children—unprompted by researchers—sacrificed playtime in order to offer help to another child in the study (Warneken & Tomasello, 2009). As children grew older, however, they increasingly preferred to maximize their own well-being, even at another's cost. In fact, older children chose to accept less for themselves because it would have meant giving more to another—a clear illustration of a vertically individualistic mindset (Warneken & Tomasello, 2009).

Yale psychologist Paul Bloom explains that many people learn to hide—but not actually overcome—these self-interested actions (Stahl, 2012). Yet the key to genuinely acting with nonjudgment is not to cease judging, because social comparisons are often automatic and unconscious. Rather, Menon and Thompson (2010) encourage mindfully acknowledging and releasing judgments as they form, with particular attention to situations that evoke jealousy or envy. Just as boxing legend Muhammad Ali (2003) once said, "We can't be brave without fear," it may be that mudita bubbles to the surface when acknowledging the presence of its opposite—envy (28). We should recognize envy—feeling that unconscious stiffening and flutter of anxiety—but then replace it with more virtuous thoughts. By repeating this process, the neural connections that process envious emotions begin to atrophy like an unused muscle, while compassion muscles grow well-toned.

Similarly, by taking steps to strengthen self-esteem, envy is felt less for the simple reason that well-being is not challenged by others' successes. Menon and Thompson (2010) offer a surprisingly simple solution for strengthening self-esteem. Like a mantra, they advise, remind yourself of your many strengths and successes. That's it: the power of positive thinking and positive affirmations.

If it sounds just a bit too easy or new-worldly, then consider the surprisingly robust results of their study. "In one experiment we asked people to think about a rival and prepare for a task in which they would evaluate that person's latest idea. Before the task, half the participants listed some of their own accomplishments ("I'm a good tennis player") or cherished values ("I put my family first"). The other half did not. This simple exercise yielded profound results," Menon and Thompson write. "When we asked the participants what percentage of their working hours they'd be willing to devote to learning about their rival's plan, we found that managers who had affirmed themselves were willing to allocate about 60% more time than those who had not affirmed themselves."

These affirmations—used to protect participants' egos—allowed them to use social comparisons more constructively. Similarly, other research suggests that confident people are more likely to cheer on others' successes (Wheeler & Miyake, 1992). Interestingly, however, it would not be accurate to say that the participants in Menon and Thompson's study engaged in healthier *upward* comparisons. Rather, they elevated their view of themselves, which allowed them to see themselves as somewhat better than others. This act of "elevation" replaced threatening upward comparisons with more palatable downward comparisons.

Yet do we not wish to hold *accurate* self-portrayals, rather than needing to inflate our self-views to get by? Do we not wish to be able to serenely look upon not just others who we judge below us, but also those who will— inevitably—continue to stand above, no matter how many positive mantras we chant? After all, no matter how effective your piano playing, scientific skills, or leadership lessons, there will always be a Mozart, a Mendel, or a Mandela.

Presumably the participants in Menon and Thompson's study would have struggled to compare themselves to Mozart, Mendel, or Mandela, for these would represent unambiguously upward comparisons that no amount of mental finagling could deny. Indeed, studies involving American college students have found that those with the highest self-esteem engaged in the *most* downward comparisons. They did so because they found their self-esteem at its strongest when averting their gaze from Messianic superiors while spending more time contemplating hum-drum inferiors (Wheeler & Miyake, 1992). This suggests that their self-esteem was, much like Peter Keating's, extrinsically oriented. Able though they were at shielding their eyes from painful upward comparisons, their self-esteem was nonetheless contingent on the standing of others (Deci & Ryan, 1995; Kernis, 2003). When they did ponder the successes of superiors, these students were no less likely to experience schadenfreude than any other extrinsically oriented verticalist. They had, in essence, gained self-esteem but lost the virtues of healthy social comparisons.

What is missing, then, is the chance to have our cake and eat it too. Or, such as it is, to enjoy healthy social comparisons *and* a healthy ego. One must, therefore, draw self-worth from within. And this, paradoxically, comes also from without.

12

Altruistic to All

Tapping into the Horizontal Collectivist Global Identity

As the Dalai Lama once observed, "In Judaism, it is called *tzedakah* . . . In Hinduism and Buddhism, it is called *dana*. And in Christianity, it is called charity" (Dalai Lama et al., 2016: 250). Yet for all our species' altruism, the age-old question remains: Are humans inherently good? Or basically selfish? If claiming that Americans can adopt a more inclusive, cooperative lens, the answer to this question is essential. If people are ultimately selfish, then it does little good to ask more of anyone. Instead, we ought to restrain humanities' worst excesses and align incentives and rewards with self-interested motives.

Indeed, this represents the current working mechanisms of American government and business, which assume the worst and organize accordingly. American corporations, for instance, assume that workers are better incentivized by individual rewards than by distributing corporate gains across the team or organization (much less sharing those gains with either the local or global community). American government, similarly, is organized around a system of checks and balances that reflexively mistrusts and restrains powerholders.

But if it is culture and environmental circumstance rather than human nature that drives selfish behaviors, then it is reasonable to expect more of everyone—and devise systems premised on somewhat more altruistic assumptions. Undoubtedly, membership in a social group is beneficial, and inclusion offered early humans a distinct survival advantage. But whether we humans can consciously join and support others to ultimately benefit ourselves is a hotly debated question. One prominent advocate of the cynical school of thought is British evolutionary biologist Richard Dawkins, who wrote, in the aptly titled book *The Selfish Gene*, that human societies ought to "try to teach generosity and altruism, because we are born selfish" (Dawkins & Davis, 2017: 4).

Some research supports the cynical view that we are, basically, all about ourselves. For instance, individuals working in groups often seek to *appear* helpful, but in fact minimize their contributions at every opportunity. In a classic study from 1913, Max Ringelmann found that people worked harder in a tug-of-war game when facing off individually than when they were on a team. Similarly, students and professionals alike may prefer to let colleagues do most of the work. This phenomenon suggests that free riders reap the benefits of group membership without equitably contributing (Earley, 1989).

The University of Zurich's Ernst Fehr and coauthor Urs Fischbacher (2003), however, note that cultural norms are among the most important predictors of self-interested behaviors. Similar to research findings on power, society tends to get just about as much selfishness as it expects. Vertical collectivists, for instance, exert *more* effort when working with others, so long as they see those others as in-group members (Earley, 1993). And, though we don't have the data to say with certainty, it is reasonable to expect that horizontal collectivists—with weaker in-group / out-group dynamics—will exert more effort in group work, regardless of group composition.

Yet individualists are basically expected to act selfishly and free ride. In the absence of social pressure and sanctions, rates of free riding do indeed increase relative to groups that sanction free riders (Fehr & Fischbacher, 2003). As University of Oxford scholar Dominic Johnson writes, "The punishment of free-riders is widely regarded as central to the evolution of human cooperation" (Johnson, 2009: 169). In highly religious and thus communal societies, these sanctions may come in the form of a supernatural power— that is, free riders are punished, if not in this life, then in the next. For instance, many religions teach that upon death one must "atone for one's sins." Johnson, in an article titled "Hand of God, Mind of Man," comments that examples of divine retribution are to be found in all the world's major religions. He and coauthor Jesse Bering argue that most religions across history have likewise favored the threat of spiritual punishment. Christians stress the day of judgment (Johnson & Bering, 2006), for instance, while Hindu karma suggests that one's behavior in this life influences reincarnation as a more or less desirable being (Wilkerson, 2020).

As Johnson explains in a series of well-cited articles, such supernatural sanctions are rather low cost: no investigation or even close monitoring is needed because God(s) sees and hears all; no tribunal is needed, because a higher power does the judging. These societies, as a result, are thought to experience lower rates of free riding and consequently have a significant evolutionary advantage relative to other societies (Johnson, 2009; Johnson & Bering, 2006; Johnson & Krüger, 2004).

This research emphasizes the essentiality of social norms that demand more altruistic and communal behaviors. It also hints that cooperation is, at least in part, a function of societal taboos and sanctions. People may engage in more altruistic behaviors when it is personally advantageous. Men, for instance, are more altruistic and charitable when in the presence of women, and even more so if on a first date; men and women both act more altruistically toward those they find attractive (Van Vugt & Tybur, 2015).

Yet there is more to the story than Richard Dawkins's selfish gene. Our closest cousins and evolutionary predecessors, the primates, shed light on the workings of contemporary human minds. And, among primates, selfless altruism is repeatedly documented. Primates act altruistically not only when the personal cost is low, but even when the altruistic behavior risks harm or death.

As primatologist Frans De Waal (2008) writes, "Altruism in response to another's pain, need, or distress . . . is phylogenetically ancient, probably as old as mammals and birds" (279). There exist "literally hundreds" of stories of apes engaging in helping behaviors, including sacrificing their lives in efforts to save unrelated others from drowning in lakes or pools; of dolphins holding their sick to the surface to prevent drowning; of whales heart-wrenchingly positioning themselves between a harpooner and an already injured mate (De Waal, 2008). These actions occur in an animal world in which power is claimed via force rather than prestige; and yet, still, altruism arises.

Apes, for instance, not only may avoid taking advantage of weak group members, but may actively help them. Author Yuval Noah Harari (2018) details the story of an ape, Kidogo, whose weakened heart caused it anxiety and confusion. Harari writes: "If he became distressed, he would send out signals and others would rush to help." Harari continues: "In another story, in the jungles of Ivory Coast, a young chimp lost his mother and none of the other females would adopt and care for him because they had their own young. Oscar lost weight, health and vitality. But then the alpha male, Freddie, adopted him. He made sure he ate well and even carried him on his back. Tests confirmed they were not related." "Apparently," Harari concludes triumphantly, "ape leaders developed the tendency to help the poor, the needy and the fatherless" (254).

As for humans, the stories of selfless altruism are endless, even if the dark and dangerous tend to dominate headlines. As scholars Ernst Fehr and Simon Gächter (2002) write, "People frequently cooperate with genetically unrelated strangers, often in large groups, with people they will never meet again, and when reputation gains are small or absent" (137).

Along with the many real-world examples of this cooperation, researchers repeatedly demonstrate these altruistic behaviors in laboratory experiments. As just one example, when scholars give participants money and ask them to distribute the money as they see fit, a Dawkins-like cynic might assume most would choose to keep the money for themselves (as they were allowed to do). While just a few choose to do so, the vast majority seem to have an innate sense of fairness. In study after study, most participants voluntarily distribute the money to their anonymous, sometimes unseen, research partners (Fehr & Fischbacher, 2003).

When engaging in altruistic behaviors, altruists are rewarded with the release of pleasure-chemical endorphins (Headlee, 2020). Generosity is associated with better health and longer life, too. According to David McClelland and Carol Kirshnit (1988), just thinking about acting with generosity increases a protein used to support the immune system. Furthermore, individuals with a reputation for helping are far more likely to *receive* help, to have stronger relationships, and in turn lead happier lives (Fehr & Fischbacher, 2003). While it may be argued that this represents yet another example of behaving selfishly (to gain pleasure, reputation, or health), it is clear evidence that altruism is, as with selfishness, internally programmed.

Consequently, we humans may act altruistically due to a fear of punishment (divine or worldly). We may also see reputational benefits from generous acts, such as those peacocking men who act better in the presence of an adored woman. However, the preponderance of evidence suggests that most humans are some combination of selfish and selfless, with the precise ratio varying from person to person and culture to culture. Indeed, in Harari's story of the weak-hearted ape asking for and receiving help from his tribe, the author also mentions a bully that the tribe leader regularly needed to run off (Harari, 2018).

Jonathan Haidt (2012) ably presents this selfish-selfless argument in *The Righteous Mind*, where he notes that among early humans, the entirely selfless person might have literally given away his last meal, and by starving to death failed to pass on his genes. Consequently, evolution put some limits on altruistic impulses, ensuring that each of us looks out for the proverbial number one. At the same time, the entirely selfish person lacked the trust and respect of tribal mates, and so faced a bleak future. Those who struck this Goldilocks balance between selfish and selfless lived to pass along their genes to future generations, and in so doing, finely tuned human nature's in-group / out-group orientation (Haidt, 2012).

These findings suggest that altruism can arise from genuine concern for others rather than mere conformance to social norms or fear of social sanction. The next question that arises is how to extend communality beyond a small, local in-group? And, once extended, just how large can an in-group grow? In answering these questions, we begin to see a pathway to healthier social comparisons as well as to a natural inclination to use money and power on others' behalf. We will see how a wider communal concern is, perhaps surprisingly, yet another vehicle to attain improved self-esteem.

A Global Identity at the Tip of the Spear

Some might reckon Jerónimo Calderón a wunderkind. Beginning his career as an instructor at Switzerland's University of Geneva, Calderón received a half million-dollar grant to "spread health, wealth, and happiness" from the Swiss Business Council for Sustainable Development. He holds a laundry list of prestige positions: a World Wildlife Federation–Switzerland board member, an Ashoka Fellow in the company of Nobel Prize winners and revolutionary thinkers, a World Economic Forum Global Shaper, a fellow of the Royal Society for the Encouragement of Arts, Manufactures and Commerce, and a Compassionate Leader of the Healthy Minds Institute.

But this is not his story. His is a story of a homecoming that was generations in the making. Of a man that went from working ninety to one hundred hours every week in Switzerland to spending his days in communion with Aymaran Ancestors atop Bolivia's Andes Mountains. From an endless achievement loop to a view of the cosmos as circular and ever-connected. From generational pain, suffering, and doubt to an identity restored and a heritage reclaimed for himself and his lineage.

The first hint that his demeanor was not the carefully curated, hard-charging overachiever one might expect, came from an auto-email response. Calderón's auto-responder to a request for an interview shot back with this:

> Mighty clouds are hanging over the majestic peaks of the Andes as I'm returning "home" to our neighbourhood "Nuevos Horizontes" in El Alto, towering above La Paz. Everything seems closer here at 4'000 m. above the sea, the stars, the thunder and the family. Learning Aymara and connecting more deeply with the wisdom tradition of my ancestors have taken over the command of my agenda for the unforeseeable future.
>
> I'm mostly offline, celebrating life and honouring death. Depending on your hemisphere, I wish you a fab beginning of spring/ending of the rainy season. May you surf and duck any waves life throws at you with ease, pleasure and grace in the new season. Thank you for your intention to connect, I'll see you on the other side!
>
> ¡Sarantaskakiñani! > May we continue walking together!

Calderón did eventually accept my invitation to speak. I sought to understand Calderón's motivations to use his considerable talent for the benefit of others—working with the World Wildlife Federation, for instance, and toward more sustainable development.

We met on a virtual video call: Calderón sporting shoulder-length hair, horn-rimmed glasses, and a blue denim shirt, his profile framed by the sunsoaked skyline of the world's highest major city, El Alto, Bolivia. Calderón appeared to have shed the wunderkind label, expressing surprise when I commented on his many career achievements. "It's a curious observation," he explained, "because I've been on something of a sabbatical for the past four to five years" (Calderón, 2021).

Calderón was living among his lineal descendants in Bolivia, in a graduate school of sorts. But this grad school, he explained, "isn't one that has been at the center of power, which is all these other places I've been studying. I'm here at the university of our people."

Just five minutes into our discussion and the interview questions were scrapped as nothing more than a distraction. We returned to the basics: Who is Jerónimo Calderón? He offered these enigmatic words: "I'm an accident. I'm a mistake in the matrix. I shouldn't be here, and yet I am. I come from an imaginary place, where the Bolivian Andes meet the Swiss Alps. Where the condor flies with the eagle."

Calderón, you see, is Swiss-Bolivian. I revealed my own bias—to myself, if not to Calderón—by assuming that a Swiss Bolivian educated at elite schools would himself be a jet-setting elite, rubbing shoulders with the European-descended oligarchs of Bolivia when not relaxing by the fire of a Swiss ski chalet. Instead, Calderón was living in the slums outside Bolivia's capital city, La Paz, embracing if not glamorizing the impoverishment of his community and family.

Calderón appeared constitutionally unable to characterize himself without reference to his forebears, a tale that incorporates the rich details of his maternal and paternal grandparents, his mother, and his father. To do less would for Calderón be like coming on stage to play nothing more than the crashing crescendo of a musical piece—an ending, perhaps, but one stripped of significance and context without all that comes before it. Who are *you*, I pressed after a lengthy introduction to everyone but Calderón himself. "I am the spear tip of this lineage," he explained.

The spear analogy was apt, I soon learned; a weapon against discrimination and injustice that seeps deep into Calderón's history. His Swiss mother "was considered lower class, a farmer peasant descended from a long lineage of subsistence farmers at the foothills of the Swiss alps." She dreamed of a university degree and had the grades for it, too, but was told that peasant girls like her dare not dream.

"On my father's side," Calderón continued, "I descend from a lineage of Aymara, Indigenous people from the Altiplano in Bolivia here at four thousand meters [about 13,000 feet in elevation]. It's where my father grew up in extreme poverty. With everything that comes from that poverty," Calderón explained simply.

Though Calderón's story is not of a wunderkind but of a homecoming, the pain of his ancestors is the fiery crucible in which Calderón's iron spear took shape. Calderón described his mother as an "independent, strong, very smart woman that really fought hard." Far from bowing to discrimination, she expressed a "very strong feminist stance, with this drive and determination to make our place, and make our voice heard."

A profound and deep love for spirit and nature inherited from her father animated this resilience. Calderón continues, "My grandfather would have me just sit down and admire the sky and a particular tone of blue that he hadn't seen in twenty years. What we really celebrated is to see God's creation and wonder in nature." This sense of connection with something infinite and inexhaustible, Calderón explains, "imbued [my mother] with the strength of faith to overcome real hardship." Eventually Calderón's mother quit her job and graduated from university, naysayers be damned.

Calderón's father, for his part, would make his way to Switzerland and find that the unremitting discrimination of his Bolivian homeland continued in his adopted land. "To give a very simple example," Calderón tells me, "when he tried to enter the border of Switzerland, because he didn't speak German he was slapped in the face by the guards. He struggled with that kind of discrimination throughout his lifetime." But the embers igniting his father's passions burned long and bright too. "He has become a very successful lawyer, speaking French, German, English, learning all these languages. And now he is a writer, too," Calderón says.

When Calderón's father left Bolivia for Switzerland, following his paternal grandmother's religious conversion in the face of colonialism, it seemed that much of this ancestral tradition had been lost. The beliefs of centuries, if not millennia, were wiped away in a matter of a few generations. He comments: "I somehow still feel the pain of how that heritage was lost."

Calderón's youngest years were characterized by relative impoverishment by Swiss terms. Yet Calderón became a child of reluctant privilege as his parents attained professional success. Reluctant, because his parents' history of resistance had seared deep into his bones. "I was given the name Jerónimo in honor of an Apache chief who fought with the resistance against the Mexican Army. There is a very strong spirit of resistance that I hold dear."

Calderón learned to see his relatively scarce living standards as a source of pride, and indeed he remains prideful of his perch in the slums of El Alto today. But, as he attended leading academic institutions such as INSEAD on the edges of Paris, and as he did indeed enter the ranks of the elite jet-setting crowd, he nonetheless felt ill at ease in this elevated company. At the same time, he feared that by getting too close to the clubby elite, he would somehow betray the memory of his long-suffering ancestors. A Swiss-Bolivian, "an accident of the Matrix," Calderón was ideologically unmoored.

These insecurities pushed Calderón to achieve what to an outsider may look like the epitome of mainstream success. "Throughout my childhood it just was me against the world," Calderón explains, in vertically individualistic terms. "I was showing my worth and value through certain achievements and success. I was always top of my class. I went to university with excellent scholarships. I played soccer at the national level from thirteen until I was eighteen, and only decided against a professional soccer career in favor of an academic career. These were the drugs that I used to stimulate my self-esteem. I needed success to know that I deserved all of the privilege that I had."

Slowly, painfully, Calderón exchanged extrinsic rewards for intrinsic self-worth. "What shifted is I'm in a place of such profound, deep inner peace with who I am, with my lineages. I'm at the moment in life where I don't need to do anything or be anywhere other than where I am."

He relocated from Switzerland to El Alto. He put aside the ninety-hour work weeks. Today Calderón spends a few hours each day working on what he calls high-impact projects, including an ambitious multinational effort to protect the Amazonian rainforest. But his growth springs not just from slowing down and resting more but from connection and learning from those before him.

Calderón credits his ideological development to a series of teachers— one, an "Aymaran wisdom keeper" (and, incidentally, Bolivia's former foreign minister), and the other an Amazonian spiritual leader and esteemed environmentalist working on behalf of the beleaguered Sapara People. "Growing up in Switzerland, I inherited one of the finest forms of European education— rational, linear, logical thinking, combined with the European ideals of individual human rights, free speech, and all of these things," Calderón explains. "But what I inherited from my father's side [in Bolivia] is one of the most marvelous traditions there is. I received here the circular logic; the holistic, complimentary, integrative, collective view. There is a community here, where all is one. There is no separation between Earth, [between] the visible and the invisible."

This interconnectivity is the root upon which Calderón's ideology blooms. In the West, he explains, all is binary. To see the self and others as separate, Calderón argues, "might be one of the greatest shortcomings of our current monomyth. Everything is completely interconnected. And the key is, How do we bend that binary line so that we see we are all part of that same circle?"

We in the West arbitrarily separate ourselves from others in this life and, Calderón notes, we separate ourselves from all those who have come before and all those who will come after. "We in the Western world, we're raised with this belief that life is linear. It starts with birth, there's nothing before, and it ends with death, there's nothing afterwards."

But that's not right, Calderón insists. Evoking Ovid's *Metamorphoses*, he said, "I look at nature, nothing is linear. Everything is cyclical. Death is actually a creation of our human mind. It doesn't exist in nature. We can look at something and say, 'Yeah, this is dying, but it actually is just transforming.' I'm eating a carrot and the carrot is dying, but it's physically—*physically*," Calderón emphasizes, "turning into me. This whole idea of separation doesn't exist."

By this same logic, Calderón declares, we are connected to everything: the mountains and the rivers are our very ancestors—the rocks our bones, the water our blood. "If you look at the forest, you're looking at the past. The forest is the result of millions of years of creations. They're our ancestors."

Calderón discusses the heady implications of such unity. "In this human form in which I am right now, the programming of my ancestors is in my DNA" and roughly akin to what Western scholars today know as evolutionary psychology and inherited personality traits. "But it's only their experiences that they had during their lifetime. So, it comes still from a place of separation," a human experience full of "fear, of self-preservation, of answering why I'm here."

This is the ancestral inheritance with which most in the West are familiar. But it is not all, Calderón insists. In the Amhara Cosmovision from which Calderón descends, the physical body is but a single thread in an endless tapestry.

The mythology of my ancestors is we come from a place of eternity, and we come into this lifetime through an eternal gate at which point we experience separation from time, from space, from matter, from life, from death, from all of it. And once we die, we go back through that gate into eternity and are again at one with everything.

As soon as an ancestor passes into the gate of eternity, the ancestor realizes all of his or her mistakes, and learns all of the lessons. It happens right before you go through the gate, so you're in your last breath in your last day of life, and you're like, "Shoot, I really messed this one up. I should have done more of this, less of this." There's this wisdom that comes through the notion of finality, or the impression of finality.

And this doesn't get lost, it actually deepens once you go through the gate. So afterwards, these ancestors *know*.... Once we're able to listen, all of that knowledge informs and guides us.

This connection only grows stronger, Calderón explains, "the deeper you go into this place of humility and silence, of trust that your consciousness doesn't stop inside of you at your brain."

Today, Calderón says openly, he is in near-constant communion with the spirits of his ancestors. "Ancestors actively speak, whisper, and sing to me," he reveals. "Psychologists would tell me I'm completely nuts, with all of these beings that interact with me. I've just come to a place where I'm accepting that this is a possibility either of my imagination, or of an external reality that exists independently of me. I'm not judging, I'm not pretending I know, I'm just witnessing that I've let go of my fear and I'm integrating and evolving it into my practice."

Calderón has not only released his fear. He has healed, for himself and for his ancestors. He has restored his identity, anchored his ideology, and rooted himself with family, taking his rightful spot at the tip of the iron spear. He is, after generations lost, home again.

13

Loving Billions to Love Oneself

Generating Inner Self-Esteem from Without

Perhaps the cosmology of Bolivian highlanders is a novel taste for the Western palate, but its interconnected ideology is deeply ingrained within most of the world's major religions. In Galatians 3:28, Paul writes to the people of Central Anatolia in the Turkish highlands. The letter reads, in part, "There is neither Jew nor Gentile, neither slave nor free, nor is their male nor female. For you are all one in Christ Jesus" (Scott, 2009).

Similar ideas of interconnectivity were espoused in the East by Confucius (Confucianism), Lao Tzu (Taoism), Buddha (Buddhism), and Mahavira (Jainism), all of whom established universal ethical codes that predate Christianity. Confucius taught that every person must love others before loving themselves. Buddha and Mahavira instructed followers to avoid harming not only other human beings but any sentient being whatsoever—including even insects (Harari, 2018). Members of the Jain community may take nonviolence to its extreme, with those who voluntarily take the mercifully rare vow of Sallekhana fasting to the point of death rather than consuming organic matter.

Among contemporary societies, it is the Israeli kibbutz and the monastic orders of various religions that continue to exemplify what is a horizontal collectivistic ideology in which others are held as inseparable from self (Singelis et al., 1995). Horizontal collectivism is not, however, limited to the religious domain, and therein lies the power of this inclusive ideology among educated and broad-minded but sometimes secular twenty-first-century sensibilities.

Consider the popularity of the nonsectarian Eckart Tolle, who advocates a form of universalism, or unity, to his millions of followers. Tolle (2006) writes in tones reminiscent of his sectarian forebears, "You are neither inferior nor superior to anyone. True self-esteem and true humility rise out of that recognition" (109).

In decidedly contemporary terms, Johns Hopkins University's awe researcher David Yaden has identified space travel as one path to "that recognition" (Yaden et al., 2016). In 2021 actor William Shatner became the oldest person to reach space when he departed on one of Jeff Bezos's Blue Origin flights. On his return, a visibly emotional Shatner explained, "It's so much larger than me. It hasn't got anything to do with the little green men and the blue orb. It has to do with the enormity and the quickness and the suddenness of life and death" (Wattles et al., 2021). Describing a completely different view of life, he said, "It would be so important for everybody to have that experience through one means or another."

Jerónimo Calderón, Saint Paul, the Eastern philosophers, even William Shatner: all express a global identity, or what is sometimes known as "self-transcendence." Self-transcendence is to move to a view of the self as part of a connected and unified whole (Gutierrez-Zotes et al., 2015; Le & Levenson, 2005). Self-transcendence is opposite of self-enhancement. Self-enhancers, akin to vertical individualists, are interested in power, hedonism, and personal achievement. Studies show that self-enhancing individuals see others as a means to their own self-interested ends (Roccas, 2003).

By using self-transcendence and related global identity measures, research shows that a global identity is associated with a prosocial motivation and increased empathy for outside social groups, for social justice and human rights, and for environmental sustainability, as well as "a felt responsibility to act for the betterment of the world" (McFarland, Webb, & Brown, 2012; Reysen & Katzarska-Miller, 2013). Furthermore, participants possessing global identifications yet coming from such diverse countries as the United States, Iran, South Africa, Argentina, and Russia show a greater willingness to engage in global cooperation for the benefit of all—even at the expense of self-interests (Buchan et al., 2011).

This global concern may reduce social comparison biases and facilitate mudita, or joy at others' well-being. Relatedly, studies show that those high in self-transcendence also hold higher levels of optimal self-esteem and are more likely to answer, for instance, that "my sense of self is less dependent on other people and things" (Le & Levenson, 2005).

Individuals with a global identity may thus learn from their betters and improve themselves along the way. Through downward comparisons they can also look at suffering others and not feel superiority, but instead feel obliged to help them rise. They also can leverage this sense of connectedness to avoid competing for material gains and use their prosperity in pursuit of intrinsic pursuits including self- and other development. Finally, with a sense of connectedness to others, power is seen less as freeing *from* others and more as responsibility and obligation *to* others. A global identity is consequently an essential component of a lifestyle motivated by enlightened self-interest, one in which money, power, and fame are repurposed to the greater good of self and others.

Unsurprisingly, a global identity is incompatible with the psychology of verticalist individualism. In one telling study, participants from the United States, Russia, across Southeast Asia, and in Tibet completed a survey that measured self-transcendence and self-enhancement. Results showed that as vertical individualism increases, self-transcendence decreases. Participants high in vertical individualism exhibit less mature forms of love, for instance, seeing loved ones as means to self-aggrandizement. The authors conclude: "An exclusive focus on self and egoistic concerns may hinder the ability to see others and experiences objectively" (Le & Levenson, 2005: 444).

In moving away from vertical orientations toward a more connected, global identity, however, we all must reckon with our ancient, and slowly evolving, minds. As the scholar Henri Tajfel and colleagues (1971) showed in a series of experiments, humanity is astoundingly talented at creating in-groups and distressingly capable of delineating out-groups. Esteemed scholar though he was, Tajfel was not just another academic figure. He was also a survivor of humanity's worst excesses. Being Jewish, he emigrated to France in the 1930s to escape rising discrimination in Poland. Alas, none of Europe was safe at this dark juncture, and while fighting with French forces in World War II he was captured by the Nazi war machine.

Had he been recognized by his captors as Jewish he would have been tossed into a concentration camp and, very likely, perished. Tragically, this is the fate that befell Tajfel's immediate family. The Nazis instead labeled Tajfel as an enemy combatant. He was able to survive the war in a somewhat less horrific prisoner-of-war camp. This social categorization—being identified as a soldier and not a Jew—saved Tajfel's life. After the war he joined Stanley Milgram and other scholars in seeking to understand how humanity could so utterly descend. Specifically, he sought to understand the capacity and need to categorize humans into one group or another.

Tajfel published the results of his classic study in 1971. In it, he asked study participants (all of whom knew each other, attending the same school) to estimate the number of dots projected onto a screen. Next, he divided participants into two groups. The first group, he explained, consists of those who underestimated the number of dots on screen; the second group were those who overestimated the number. He further told the participants that they would work with their new groups as they participated in a money-allocation game, entirely unrelated to the first activity. Participants would distribute the money that researchers provided to them. It didn't matter how they distributed it, for there were no points or winners. The researchers then observed whether the participants would favor their own groups—groups chosen, remember, based on nothing more than dot-count similarities.

Tajfel's prediction? That of course the participants would not favor their own teams. Because all participants across both groups knew each other, Tajfel reasoned, that connection was a far stronger one than simple dot-counting similarities. What, after all, did it matter whether someone over- or underestimated the *number of dots on a screen*? Anyway, the expressed division was arbitrary—the researchers had in reality divided the participants randomly, rather than according to their actual dot estimates.

Yet time and again the participants favored their own groups with extra money. Tajfel called this the Minimal Group Paradigm Study (Tajfel, Billig, Bundy, & Flament, 1971). He had intended to demonstrate a baseline level at which individuals would *not* engage in out-group bias or in-group favoritism. In this he failed. Instead, his research birthed what is known as social categorization theory. Thanks to Tajfel, we now understand humans can use even the most arbitrary of distinctions to separate and divide.

Consider, in turn, a study conducted by researchers Wendi Gardner, Shira Gabriel, and Laura Hochschild (2002). These social scientists were intrigued by studies in the 1990s showing that some people were *less* harmed by the successes of their romantic partners (though still not exactly jumping for joy) than the successes of complete strangers. This seemed to contradict the expectation of schadenfreude, especially salient in close relationships, that researchers had come to expect in vertically individualistic Westerners.

Gardner and company parsed the results and found that when the romantic partners reported low relationship satisfaction, schadenfreude returned to expectedly high levels. The researchers speculated that in particularly close relationships, one's partner is seen almost as an extension of the self and thus exempt from otherwise-applicable competitive tendencies. The team labeled this the "expanded self."

To test their hypothesis, the trio invited undergraduate students to participate in a study and asked each to bring a close friend. They then primed half of the participants to see themselves as more interdependent with close others, including especially the attending friend. Finally, they asked everyone to participate in a test styled on the Graduate Record Exam, which is used to determine postgraduate admissions. The research team speculated that these undergraduate students, perhaps eyeing graduate school, would typically compete with one another for the highest scores.

They found that those primed to see close others as interdependent with themselves were better able to root for the success of their friends; those not so primed preferred strangers' success to their friends' success. Thus, the "expanded self" allowed the study participants to see others' successes as something like their own.

The researchers speculated further that this sense of interconnectedness likely comes easier for members of collectivistic cultures. However, by successfully "priming" the expanded self in some participants, their research shows that even individualists can expand their semi-hibernating other orientation.

Exactly how to "prime" this view of others as expanded selves, it turns out, was hiding in plain sight in Tajfel's study. For while it is unfortunate just how easily out-group distinctions form, Tajfel also showed just how easy it is to form in-groups, even upon a bedrock of rather flimsy foundations. As Jonathan Haidt (2012) memorably writes, we can "drown [differences] in a sea of similarities" (277). Adam Grant (2013) goes further, writing that while commonalities are useful, "uncommon commonalities" are better still. Grant cites a study in which participants were asked to review an eight-page essay of their randomly assigned research partner, offering one page of feedback within twenty-four hours. Somewhat surprisingly, 48 percent in the control group agreed to the thankless task.

Other study participants were told that they and their partner shared an e-type fingerprint. Half of these participants were told that 80 percent of the population also had e-type fingerprints. Of these, 55 percent agreed to review the essay—a slight uptick based on a rather common similarity. When the remaining participants were told that only 2 percent of the world's population shared that same fingerprint type, an astounding 82 percent agreed to review the essay for their previously unknown research partner (Burger, Messian, Patel, Del Prado, & Anderson, 2004). E-type fingerprints, it's worth noting, are fictitious.

In addition, even when forming in-groups readily, as Tajfel showed, people tend to favor in-groups more than they seek to harm out-groups. As Stanford University's Nathanael Fast and colleagues (2012) showed in a series of studies, people tend to bias out-groups primarily when the out-group is seen as threatening their in-group. But if the out-group is seen as relatively harmless, the out-group is given little thought (Fast et al., 2012; Halevy, Bornstein, & Savig, 2008). This helps explain why national citizens may hold rather adverse feelings toward immediate neighbors with whom resources are in dispute, but not toward distant, and thus relatively harmless, nation-states.

By contrast, most people take every opportunity to favor in-groups. Collectivism is the process by which in-group members are seen as mere extensions of oneself. Recall Aristotle, noting that a friend is "another self" (Crisp, 2000). In fact, so blinded by in-group love are we that we think favorably of in-group members even if we don't particularly like them (Turner &

Reynolds, 2011). In this way, football fans of diverse backgrounds bond over their teams just as multigenerational and geographically dispersed families argue without hating.

Combining the logic of these studies, it seems that by identifying ever-more similarities with others, it becomes possible to convert out-groups into in-groups. Importantly, we can do this without thinking any worse of those who, for one reason or another, remain outside our extended-self view.

While aspiring toward global identities, the challenge is to put aside nationality. Put aside religion, ethnicity, and other limiting categories. Instead, think bigger. Consider, if you dare, as Jerónimo Calderón now does, that we are all the dust of stars and dinosaurs. Jerry White (2020), the land mine eradication activist, encourages others similarly to "hold everyone in equal dignity." To recognize that "you are no better and no worse. We're all [in the] dirt together."

A genuinely global identity is admittedly a radical concept, and few—perhaps none—can fully embody it. Rather, this is the idea upon which to measure, benchmark, and aspire to reach, even while admitting that we remain biased in favor of our families, especially our children, and perhaps many others as well.

Imagining a Global Identity

An inclusive mindset does not necessarily demand the expression of tender love for all eight or so billion people on earth. Nor is that needed. In fact, the challenge comes not in contemplating millions or billions of others, but more like hundreds or thousands of others. That is, beyond those modest numbers and the human capacity for empathy flags. Our minds evolved in the context of hunter-gatherer bands that typically consisted of dozens or hundreds of people. Today, more people fly abroad on a typical commercial flight. We are thus not well-adapted—empathetically speaking—to consider the plight of large numbers of people.

Dan Ariely (2011), in his book *The Upside of Irrationality*, documents this psychological blind spot. He cites one study in which participants were given money and asked to make a donation. When participants were cited the sobering statistics about the rate of famine and then asked to donate money to fight hunger, the average individual donated 23 percent of their available money. But donations nearly doubled when, instead of global statistics, participants were introduced simply to Rokia, a young starving girl.

This may seem counterintuitive. Participants appeared more prepared to help one individual than millions. Ariely describes "what social scientists call 'the identifiable victim effect': once we have a face, a picture, and details about a person," Ariely writes, "we feel for them, and our actions—and money—follow. However, when the information is not individualized, we simply don't feel as much empathy and, as a consequence, fail to act" (159).

The identifiable victim effect has three key elements. The first is that we fail to empathize with others when there is the feeling that there are simply too many victims for our actions to make any difference—what Ariely calls the drop-in-the-bucket effect. The second is when others' suffering is perceived as vague rather than vivid. Third, we often fail to act or even be aroused to act when we do not feel a sense of kinship with the victim.

Developing a global identity helps us overcome this third limitation by ensuring that we see all in need as equally deserving of aid. The identifiable victim effect nonetheless suggests that we are more likely to help those whose problems are salient to our own lives. The sense of suffering as something vague and distant is heightened by geography—from the reality that suburban enclaves are buffered from both inner-city strife and rural hardship to the fact that much of the world's most egregious poverty is centered in a handful of countries.

In addition, the well-to-do—meaning those with solid homes and little question of meeting basic needs—struggle to understand the real effects of poverty for the average Bangladeshi or continental African. When a neighbor loses her job, we send cake; when nations are ravaged by famine, we send sympathy but otherwise move on. This failure to act on behalf of a "nation" of people is exacerbated by the drop-in-the-bucket effect—the belief that we can't really make a difference.

Yet even while supporting our struggling neighbor but not a starving nation, there is a middle way forward, and it can come from the strength of one's in-group orientation. Many people are willing to support their fellow countrymen in suffering, or their co-religionists, or their ethnic counterparts, even if they do not know their names or faces. They imagine they know these people; that they have some idea of the lives they live and the values they hold. For strong in-groups, therefore, seeing little Rokia's suffering is less important; to act with greater altruism, we need know only that she is one of "us" (Morishima, Schunk, Bruhin, Ruff, & Fehr, 2012).

An American identity (or a Finnish or an Indian identity), however, is an imagined community. It is imagined in the sense that an American identity is an intersubjective belief that there is such a thing as "America" residing within people located at a few corners of the Earth (De Rivera & Carson, 2015). Imagined, but accepted and acted upon as though real.

As a result of this seeming reality, its capacity to arouse empathy and enhance in-group love is real. Many Americans, for instance, may already feel real affection for American citizens numbering 330 million (or at least the roughly half in their political camp). Entirely unknown though they may be, they are "extended selves" by virtue of their inclusion in one's in-group.

With national and religious groups in the hundreds of millions, these in-groups are proof of concept for a global identity which would encompass billions of people. Indeed, this global identity is psychologically robust no matter how many humans are included, or even if opting to incorporate, like Jerónimo Calderón, *all beings* into the equation. As thought-leader Yuval Noah Harari (2018) writes, "We know of no upper limit to the size of a group with which people can identify," then continuing, "most present-day nations include more people than the entire world population ten thousand years ago" (155).

Nor does a universal identity require sacrificing on behalf of everyone, all the time. Rather, as Scottish philosopher John Macmurray (1977) summed it up, the implications of a universal identity implies a preference and intention to care for any others with whom one comes into contact. Geography, therefore, remains important, but only insofar as it brings us into greater contact with some and not others. As Stephen Covey (2014) recommended in *The 7 Habits of Highly Effective People*, we each ought to act within our "circle of influence."

You may feel you can more effectively rail against the strife and inequities of your own community than against those of Calcutta or Nairobi. You may be forgiven for neglecting the concerns of universal health care if you are a teacher working toward greater access to education—and even then only one student at a time. But know also that the world today is the most interconnected it has ever been. Consequently, our own circles of influence may have a circumference large indeed.

By leveraging the strength of in-group orientations, by identifying "uncommon commonalities" with diverse others, we make the way toward a global identity possible. Yet amid the insecurities of a vertical individualistic culture, more is needed to avoid seeing others as better or worse and instead seeing them simply as extended selves. To accomplish this we must burnish our optimal self-esteem.

Optimal Self-Esteem

The Japanese culture values self-esteem far less than Western ones, "if in fact it is important at all," writes scholar Chen-Bo Zhong (Zhong et al., 2006: 57). It is self-defeating to see oneself as superior to those with whom one is deeply connected. Indeed, even if one were to gain some semblance of objectively measurable superiority, people with interdependent identities report caring little for, or psychologically benefiting from, that superiority. They are uninterested in self-promotion and far more interested in advancing others. Those others are valued for who they are, not what they may offer—a viewpoint anathema to the competitive world of the vertical individualist who sees others as a means to self-interested ends (Markus & Kitayama, 1991). Consequently, self-esteem is paradoxically steadied by positively reflecting on others (Markus & Kitayama, 1991).

For the individual acting from enlightened self-interest, this communal orientation is harmonized with intrinsically meaningful—individualistic—self-interested pursuits. Those acting with enlightened self-interest, therefore, hold others *and themselves* in high regard, unlike in the Far East, where self-esteem is perhaps not "important at all." Researchers label this state of affairs as "optimal self-esteem" (Kernis, 2003), a case of researchers unambiguously telegraphing a preferred cognitive state. With optimal self-esteem, one no longer need compete for superiority nor conform for acceptance. One need not engage in downward comparisons to feel superior, nor shrink from upward comparisons. Those with optimal self-esteem are, in the words of the late psychology professor Michael Kernis (2003), "content to be on an equal plane with others" (4).

From this place, mudita, as well as the full benefits of social comparisons, money, and power, all follow readily. So how do we get here? Consider again psychologist Howard Cutler, who explains: "We can increase our feeling of life satisfaction by comparing ourselves with those who are less fortunate than we are and by reflecting on all the things we have" (Dalai Lama & Cutler, 2010: 48). Breast cancer patients, in one study, were better able to cope with their challenges by using strategic downward comparisons. As one patient remarked, "I only had a lumpectomy, but those other women lost a breast" (Suls, Martin, & Wheeler, 2002). In Cutler's reckoning, therefore, gratitude is posed as envy's counter.

This is consistent with the approach we advocate here, as well: to focus not on being worse off than a few million prosperous Americans, but on the likelihood that you are *more fortunate* than billions around the world. The late Archbishop Tutu says similarly to count your blessings: "That might sound very old, old, old, old, old, grandfatherly style, but yes, it does help. You know you might not have as big a house as that [person. But] you know what? You're not living in a shack. So being thankful for the things that you do in fact have can help.... Certainly with envy, it can also be a spur" (Dalai Lama et al., 2016: 137).

Yet Cutler's approach remains steeped in individualism—savoring our fortunes because we are lucky to not be among the suffering masses. This individualism is not a fatal flaw. Cutler is not espousing a vertical individualism, for instance, in which self-esteem increases because "I am better." Instead, a more horizontally individualistic mentality seems an appropriate label for Cutler's and, for that matter, Tutu's description. Horizontal individualists are, as we know, self-reliant, disinterested in status, and low in hedonistic motives (Triandis & Gelfand, 1998). Cutler's subjects, for instance, didn't take joy in the suffering of those "less fortunate," but in typically horizontally individualistic fashion they used that recognition to establish that they are not better, just better off.

Perhaps it is possible to go a step further and incorporate the life-affirming oxygen of the collectivistic approach, too. Not just gratitude to float above those suffering worse miseries, but to genuinely *connect* with those down the hierarchy. The Dalai Lama—a horizontal collectivist par excellence—explains that he uses just this sort of downward comparison when pondering his exile decades earlier from his Tibetan homeland, not to mention his thousand-room palace in the capital of Lhasa.

In considering his predicament, the Dalai Lama notes the millions globally that suffered similar, or worse, fates. Pondering these suffering others does not diminish nor deny his own suffering; rather, it is a reminder that he is not alone—that all humans are connected by both pain and joy (Dalai Lama et al., 2016). He thus uses downward comparisons, but goes one step beyond Cutler in using these comparisons not to separate, but to connect.

Land mine survivor Jerry White wrote in similar terms that disaster is "one of the things connecting us all, regardless of faith, culture, and geography. But it's more than just pain that unites. The strength and resilience it takes to get through the pain also binds us" (White, 2008: 10).

Cutler's approach may increase self-esteem by revealing the many inferior others out there, and this may in turn facilitate more useful social comparisons. But if we wish to look unyieldingly at those who are above, and with more gratitude toward those below, then look to the Dalai Lama. The Dalai Lama identifies with all those who share in misfortune, and views that connectedness as a salve to his own wounds. Because everyone suffers at some time or another, we are then *all* connected. Here, then, we see truly "optimal self-esteem."

The Dalai Lama engages in downward social comparisons without feeling superior; that same equanimity, or sense of connectedness, allows for upward comparisons as well. This is because, in fact, the horizontal collectivist doesn't see others as worse or better, and thus *does not engage in downward or upward social comparisons*. He or she engages only in comparisons with equals, and uses these comparisons to enhance gratitude for self, compassion for others, and opportunities for growth.

In a benevolent twist on the old expression, the Dalai Lama gained company in his misery. It is easy to see how "upward" and "downward" social comparisons give way to fully horizontal comparisons, when others are seen as part of this "expanded self." From this position, self-esteem can no longer be threatened by others, because they are not (psychologically) fully other. Gratitude and mudita follow easily.

Scholars studied another Buddhist monk to gain greater clarity on the psychology of social comparisons. Psychologist Tania Singer, head of the Max Planck Institute in Berlin, invited the monk Matthieu Ricard to watch a disheartening documentary about Romanian orphans. Singer then asked Ricard to enter a brain-scanning MRI machine and to recall the pain and suffering of those languishing children.

Ricard, the son of French philosopher Jean-François Revel and artist Yahne Le Toumelin, has lived most of his adult life in the Himalaya Mountains. There he devotes himself to contemplation, meditating, by his own estimate, around eighty thousand hours (for context, that's equivalent to working full-time for forty years). When researchers in an earlier study hooked Ricard up to a brain scanner, their results left them astounded. Those interminable hours of meditation left him with "an abnormally large capacity for happiness and a reduced propensity towards negativity," as summarized by *Smithsonian Magazine* journalist Rachel Nuwer (2012). Ricard is, as a result, sometimes considered the world's happiest person.

And yet, when Ricard contemplated those children's misery in Singer's study, this man of profound compassion was deeply pained—in fact, his capacity for empathy led him to a deep ravine of suffering. Singer asked Ricard to return the next day (and, surprisingly, he agreed). This time she asked him to do something different: not to imagine their pain, but instead try to feel warmth, concern, and compassion for those children. Once engaged in the task, Singer observed entirely different parts of Ricard's brain light up on her screen. He had activated gamma waves at levels that were virtually unprecedented in humans. His compassion was off the charts. Far from feeling exhaustion as he had the previous day, Ricard now reported positive emotions.

The takeaway? Empathy, putting ourselves in another's shoes, can lead to burnout and negative affect, such as sadness, anger, or depression. Compassion, when contemplating others with love, patience, and concern, is positively energizing (Bregman, 2020). In seeking to emulate the Dalai Lama, then, we do need not to contemplate the misery of others; rather, we need simply to extend to them feelings of compassion as we would to our own children. In so doing, we defend our psychological well-being while gaining the evolutionary advantages of social comparison.

Part 2 Conclusion

There are at least two keys to cultivating mudita: through optimal self-esteem, such that social comparisons are not so heavily relied upon to develop self-worth; and through a global identity, to facilitate positive emotions toward diverse others. These concepts are very much intertwined, with a global identity fueling a stronger, more resilient self-worth. Combining self-esteem with a global and interconnected identity makes possible the far-reaching, non-discriminatory social comparisons upon which benign envy or admiration is experienced when looking up, and Brady-like gratitude when looking down.

Both self-esteem and interconnectedness are, furthermore, crucial to support a lifestyle characterized by enlightened self-interest. We have seen how money and power harm the vertical individualist, who sees each as a medium for higher status. To this end, money is conspicuously consumed in a materialistic lifestyle, while power is more likely to be seen as an opportunity to advance oneself rather than triggering a sense of responsibility to advance others. With optimal self-esteem, however, one need not engage in conspicuous consumption to impress others or use power to establish superiority. Instead, seeing that others are extensions of oneself makes it natural to use both money and power for those others, which as we have seen is to one's personal advantage as well.

In the next chapters, prospects for the rise of those driven by enlightened self-interest are explored, with a particular focus on the potential rise of ESI within American society. In closing, a series of methods for jump-starting a transition to acting with ESI are identified.

Part 3

Society and Self

Prospects and Pathways to Enlightened Self-Interest

14

Enlightened Self-Interest in Theory and Practice

Ubuntu and Ambition as Pathways

For thousands of years ancient Egyptians living along the Nile River were at the mercy of annual—and often destructive—flood waters. As Yuval Noah Harari (2018) writes, "No tribe could solve this problem by itself because each tribe . . . could mobilize no more than a few hundred labourers. Only a common effort to build huge dams and dig hundreds of miles of canals could hope to harness the mighty river. This was one of the reasons why the tribes gradually coalesced into a single nation that had the power to build dams and canals, regulate the flow of the river, build grain reserves for lean years, and establish a countrywide system of transport and communication" (111). Thus the Egyptian state formed, anticipating a great administrative state overseen by pyramid-building pharaohs. This coalescence is part of a historic trend in which societies expanded from tribal clans to city-states to national and finally supranational entities like the European Union.

The time for a global identity is and long has been here. In the same way that the people along the Nile required unification to manage regional challenges, so too does the world today require the combined capacity of its many billions to solve intractable, global challenges. As Joseph De Rivera and Harry A. Carson (2015) argue, globe-spanning conflicts "can only be constructively managed if individuals and groups realize they now belong to a single people" (310).

We all will sink together without global cooperation to combat climate change, for instance. The recent Covid-19 pandemic represents another example of needed (but often insufficient) global cooperation. As the World Health Organization reported, the initial hoarding of vaccines by rich countries was a self-interested yet self-defeating action. The failure to expeditiously vaccinate much of the developed world—a painfully slow process I observed from my perch in Rwanda—allowed new viral variants to take hold and quickly infiltrate the porous fortresses of the world's richest countries (WHO, 2021).

The challenges of today require a coordinated response, but silent is the self-interested vertical individualism that got us here. Indeed, the competitive, go-it-alone ideology of America's vertical individualism is arguably driving its evermore polarized populace. American culture, having reached an apparent apogee, is now in decay. The rot spreads as Americans bicker rather than unite, with many still celebrating national greatness while rarely questioning how to confront its challenges, focusing more on maintaining prerogatives of wealth and power than on the fundamentals that make human progress possible.

Across the world, popular cultures and value systems in many ways reflect those of the United States, yet while departing from its worst excesses. Most societies, for instance, have accepted the value (or inevitability) of a globalized economic system but also have aggressively sought to restrain some of capitalism's most deleterious externalities. Similarly, some societies have embraced individualism amid the perquisites of rising personal wealth without accepting workaholic notions or hypercompetitive and aggressive tendencies.

The challenge is for the United States to reverse engineer this process of cultural adaptation by learning from others. As Fareed Zakaria (2020) writes of the economic and moral inequities hampering American society, "For many decades, the world needed to learn from America. But now, America needs to learn from the world" (55).

Consider the lessons coming out of Africa, a part of the world long relegated to second fiddle and third world. There the philosophy of *ubuntu* counts among its prominent supporters the late Desmond Tutu, a beacon of morality and a lion of a man who once proclaimed that the Dalai Lama would go to heaven despite his decidedly un-Christian credentials (Dalai Lama et al., 2016).

As Tutu explains, ubuntu means that one "does not feel threatened that others are able and good" (Tutu, 2009: 31). Ubuntu further holds that "self-identity is not optimally formed through competition" and "perpetual competition is dangerous for our relationships with other people as well as the planet." Instead, "we need to be part of something larger than ourselves" (Battle, 2009: 8). Ubuntu thus militates against the winner-take-all, hypercompetitive orientation of vertical individualism (Lutz, 2009). It instead represents an extension of the globally minded horizontal collectivist identity.

Ubuntu also incorporates elements of horizontal individualism, thus mirroring the ideals of the enlightened self-interests presented here (Shutte, 2009). A proverb from the Akan people in West Africa says, "The clan is like a cluster of trees which, when seen from afar, appear huddled together, but which would be seen to stand individually when closely approached" (Gyekye, 1996: 31). As the philosopher Kwame Gyekye (1996) explains, "The proverb stresses . . . that the individual has a *separate identity* and that, like the tree, some of whose branches may touch other trees, the individual is separately rooted and is not completely absorbed by the cluster. That is, *communality does not obliterate or squeeze out individuality*" (31, emphasis added).

As the scholar David Lutz (2009) explains, "The individual does not pursue the common good instead of his or her own good, but rather pursues his or her own good through pursuing the common good" (1). Therefore, individuals are not asked to "sacrifice their own good in order to promote the good of others," but instead to "attain their own true good . . . by promoting the good of others" (1). In this way, a relentlessly ambitious and achievement-oriented American culture is given an outlet, but ambition and achievement are reframed such that personal growth is harmoniously intertwined with the growth of others.

We have by now seen numerous ESIs, many American, and many male—both demographics in which vertical individualism remains deeply embedded. Few if any began their lives acting with enlightened self-interest, but rather experienced a transformation toward the ESI ideal. While they help to illustrate the viability of the ESI pathway, it bears examining how ESIs attain true good by promoting the good of others. To this end, we introduce not a social climber but a socially beneficial climber.

Ambition with Enlightened Self-Interest

We are the first humans with regular access to clean water and abundant and healthy food, not to mention a never-ending buffet of education, entertainment, and the arts. Yet Americans are among the most ambitious on Earth. These ambitions too often mean conforming to the societally sanctioned quest for money, power, and fame. Ohio State University's Timothy Judge, one of this generation's leading scholars on organizational behavior, writes that for most people ambition has little to do with hopes of achieving higher levels of life satisfaction (Judge & Kammeyer-Mueller, 2012). Instead, he and colleague John Kammeyer-Mueller (2012) define ambition as "the desire to achieve ends, especially ends like success, power and wealth" (759).

We see this view of ambition as the pursuit of money, power, and fame from a variety of Western intellectuals. As for money, the nineteenth-century poet Walter Savage Landor (1829) wrote, "Ambition is but avarice on stilts, in a mask." Scottish Enlightenment philosopher David Hume was one of a long line to characterize ambition as a desire for power (Pettigrove, 2007).

It seems, however, that ambition is most commonly thought to pertain to fame or social distinction. The ancient Greek poet Homer assumed that his contemporaries aspired most for honor. He—and later Aristotle, Thomas Aquinas, and others—viewed ambition as something externally oriented and contingent on another's recognition of one's own success. A twenty-first-century definition of ambition in *Wiktionary* (2022) is no less extrinsically oriented: "An eager or inordinate desire for some object that confers distinction, as preferment, honor, superiority, political power, or literary fame." Emphasizing the socially comparative element of extrinsic ambition, the definition continues in saying that ambition is the "*desire to distinguish one's self from other people*" (emphasis added).

Moreover, many writers conceptualize ambition as motivated not only by the desire to appear better than others, but in some cases by the *fear* of appearing worse. This insecurity, as philosopher-psychologist William James (2019) wrote, leads us to "imitate what you see another doing, in order not to appear inferior" (39). In the West, therefore, many imitate others in their ambitious pursuits for money, power, and fame. The general public, meanwhile, not to mention some of these aforementioned thinkers, publicly decry naked ambition and claim not to possess any quite so ugly tendencies.

It is true that the dangers of ambition are varied and significant. For instance, research suggests that children of lower socioeconomic backgrounds tend to be highly ambitious. The adverse consequences of hypercompetition may be to blame. Scholars theorize that these children's parents encourage them to ambitiously seek to better themselves—they, after all, are not beneficiaries of the world of abundance available to others.

Unfortunately, this well-intended ambition backfires. These children act more aggressively and competitively on their parents' orders than do socioeconomically advantaged children. Not yet fully mature or aware of their limitations, however, these children engage in competitions they have little chance of winning. As the losses accumulate, they come to associate competition with stress and anxiety—which likely *lower* their ambitions over time.

Vrije University of Amsterdam's Menusch Khadjavi and Andreas Nicklisch (2018) write: "The long-term effect of too much competition in early years could be the avoidance of competition later on, laying the foundations for less success in their future life. . . . Therefore, extreme ambitions on the parents' side do not reduce but rather strengthen the existing status and income structure within societies" (97). While Khadjavi and Nicklisch show that children of lower-status parents are more ambitious, Judge and

Kammeyer-Mueller (2012) found that as adults, children from *higher* status backgrounds are the more ambitious. Their finding thus serves to support Khadjavi and Nicklisch's claim that unfulfilled ambitions may dim the future ambitions of socioeconomically disadvantaged children.

More generally, setting overly audacious goals may also backfire. For instance, one study found that individuals daydreaming about achieving their ambitions experienced short-term boosts to their happiness. If they were not able to achieve those ambitions, however, they were even more unhappy than if they had never set the goal (Oettingen et al., 2016).

Despite these dangers, it would seem that if ambitions are achieved, all is well. Except, not quite. In a groundbreaking study later replicated by other researchers (Otto, Roe, Sobiraj, Baluku, & Vásquez, 2017), Judge and colleagues explored the relationship between ambition and career success (Judge, Cable, Boudreau, & Bretz, 1995). They found that ambitious people—which the researchers defined for purposes of the study as those desiring to work more hours each week, with a strong desire for advancement, and for whom work played a central part in their lives—were objectively more successful. They made more money than the less ambitious and rose to higher ranks (Judge et al., 1995).

This finding was consistent with other studies, including an influential study exploring the variables that led to the advancement of AT&T managers (Howard & Bray, 1988). Studies have similarly shown that more ambitious people achieve more academic success (Judge & Kammeyer-Mueller, 2012). But subjectively, Judge and Kammeyer-Mueller found that these ambitious types were *less* successful. They showed less satisfaction with their current jobs and with their careers than did their less-ambitious peers, a finding that undoubtedly weighed on overall life satisfaction (Tait, Padgett, & Baldwin, 1989). How do we make sense of this?

William James once wrote of the "ambitious impulse" as the driving force of human progress itself (Pettigrove, 2007). Ambition, at its best, encompasses resilience in the face of setbacks, a long-term commitment, and strategic problem-solving to achieve goals (Pettigrove, 2007). Warren Buffett famously recommended that his private pilot list his top twenty-five goals, then cross out all but five of them. Follow those five only, Buffett said, and avoid the rest as harmful distractions, for you don't have enough time in life for much more than those few goals (Duckworth, 2016). The ambitious may, like Buffett, gain clarity from their objectives and respond by narrowing their objectives in single-minded pursuit of an ambitious set of goals—and thereby increase the likelihood of success (Mahan, 2002). For instance, ambition facilitates "take-charge" behaviors such as making recommendations to a supervisor or team about ways to better attain goals, and this proactivity in turn facilitates career success (El Baroudi, Fleisher, Khapova, Jansen, & Richardson, 2017). Similarly, the ambitious may respond with greater conscientiousness, which is associated with careful and diligent work performance and is one of the primary drivers of highly rated job performance (Judge & Kammeyer-Mueller, 2012).

The objective successes, therefore, should not surprise. But what of the *subjective* failures reported by Judge? Judge and colleagues (1995) explain that many objectively successful people "do not feel successful or satisfied with their achievements" (487). They write, "The variables that lead to objective career success often are quite different from those that lead to subjectively defined success" (485).

As the University of Glasgow's Glen Pettigrove (2007) explains, part of the problem may be that extrinsically oriented ambitions may never be fully realized. Pettigrove writes: "Ordinarily the objects of ambition are such as allow of continual, unending increase. However much wealth, power, esteem, knowledge or perfection one has, there is always more that one could desire.... In such cases ambition's desire may *never* be fully discharged" (57, emphasis added).

Similarly, Judge and Edwin Locke (1993) speculate that individuals tend to use their goals as proxies of well-being and success. It follows, they write, that the more ambitious one's goals, the harder the person will be to satisfy. "This suggests that high ambition, because it represents a high standard of aspiration, should be associated with low satisfaction" (479).

Recall that "power itself is morally neutral" (Donaldson, 1989: 32). Its consequences are dependent on the intentions of its user. So, too, with ambition. When ambition is used in a self-interested pursuit of money, power, and fame, the consequences are typically adverse for all of the reasons we have already explored. Yet ambition need not only be used in pursuit of vertically individualistic ends. When self-interested values give way to enlightened self-interest, the benefits of ambition begin to bloom.

To Be Ethically Ambitious: Life Lessons from a Lifelong Climber

It is 2014 and Shaun McElhatton is standing atop a mountain in Naryn Province, Kyrgyzstan, an isolated country best known—if known at all—for its location along the historic Silk Road. It is bitterly cold, but this is nothing new for McElhatton. During his twenty-seven months in-country, McElhatton experienced frostbite repeatedly. "Winters in Naryn are tough," McElhatton (2021) explains during our interview. "My first year it never got above about forty-something degrees *inside* the whole winter. So that was kind of miserable."

McElhatton is seven thousand feet above sea level and six thousand miles away from his Minnesota home. It is just another day in the Peace Corps for McElhatton. Along with fifty or so other Kyrgyzstan-based volunteers, McElhatton earns about $10 a day serving in one of the remotest and coldest parts of a remote and cold country. While most of his Peace Corps colleagues are early twenty-somethings, many fresh out of college, McElhatton is a professionally accomplished fifty-six years of age.

The mountains of a remote Central Asian republic might sound like rock bottom. But McElhatton isn't a recovering alcoholic and he isn't running from some messy divorce or financial setback. To the contrary, McElhatton left the comforts of home at the height of success: a Harvard-trained lawyer, a partner in a prestigious law firm, and once named the "go-to" lawyer for developers and investors (Hellman, 2011).

McElhatton surveys the snow-covered horizon, then notes the small town he now calls home far below. His mind flashes to the wood-paneled boardrooms and sun-lapped law firms in which he made a career, as well as to his wife and children and the calling that brought him here. Shaun McElhatton's story is one of ethical ambition, of one man's relentless "climb" to advance the causes of others. It is a story in which opportunity is, unusually, seen as evoking responsibility. It is a story of communality expressed globally. It is the story of a man who made good on a decades-old promise to himself.

A Rising Star: Community and Ethical Ambition

McElhatton grew up poor. His father "left and never came back" when McElhatton was just five years old, and his "super-hard-working" mother kept her family of eight afloat with the aid of food stamps and the support of a tight-knit Roman Catholic community.

This upbringing imbued McElhatton with resilience and a sense that he would have to work hard for everything he wanted. "I learned at a pretty young age, you've got to make your own way in life," McElhatton said. But far from separating from or competing with others, McElhatton gained an appreciation for the value of community. "Growing up, community was important, and service, giving back to community, was a big thing."

This ethically oriented ambition led McElhatton to see opportunity as responsibility, to ask how he could bring others through the same gilded doors that a Harvard law degree had opened for him. "You know, I've been very fortunate in life," McElhatton said, explaining that he saw law as an opportunity to give back to the communities that were instrumental in his upbringing. "I actually went to law school intending to be a legal aid lawyer, and I clerked for legal aid my first summer and just decided that that wasn't what I wanted to do." After taking time off to support his wife's graduate school studies, "I worked for a labor law firm. That was my next idea, that I'd be a union labor lawyer, and that didn't really pan out either," McElhatton laughs. "I consider myself a working person, and what I found out is that the unions are f*ing over the workers as much as the management is."

This could have been a turning point for McElhatton, the moment when he told himself that the world is corrupt and beyond help—yes, zero-sum after all—and would have excused himself to pursue his own interests without fetter. But McElhatton is a climber. He climbed out of a childhood of scarcity, he scaled the heights of law school, and he was not about to stop rising now. So he quit. Again. "My third idea was kind of a community development attorney, doing affordable housing. And that stuck and provided me a really rewarding career. The more I did it, the more I liked it." He would stay at the firm Leonard Street and Deinard for twenty-six years. He would earn a small fortune and gain recognition as one of the Twin Cities' leading lawyers, along the way working to advance affordable housing with clients including for-profit and not-for-profit community developers.

Leonard Street was also one of the nation's most progressive law firms. McElhatton explained that after his first child was born, he held out for a legal position where he could work at 75 percent of a full-time schedule. In the ultracompetitive legal industry, this was, to put it mildly, a very unusual ask. In fact, McElhatton said, "I only interviewed if firms had part-time policies, and there were at least half a dozen interviews where I asked about part-time policies and you could tell that their demeanor completely changed. The interview was effectively over because I'd asked the question."

At Leonard Street, McElhatton finally found a professional home, a place accepting of what McElhatton calls this "kind of alternative lifestyle." This was a place, McElhatton explains, that hired the first female attorney in the area "probably two decades before any other firm hired any female attorney" and which was a refuge for Jewish lawyers who had been blacklisted from other firms. It was a place that at one time was the only law firm in the country with a pro bono legal aid clinic, operating directly in the poor urban neighborhood that it served. So it was also a place that allowed McElhatton to carve out a practice focused on the needs of the needy. Looking back, McElhatton says, "I feel tremendous satisfaction driving around the Twin Cities and seeing the projects that I worked on. I'm very proud of the work that I did as an attorney."

Climbing in the Mountains

Summarizing his career, McElhatton says, "If you're in a situation that's not working, get out." *Freakonomics* author and University of Chicago economist Stephen Levitt (2016) tested the wisdom of this proposition by recruiting participants who were unable to decide whether to quit their jobs. Levitt asked them to participate in a virtual coin flip, in which those landing on heads would quit their jobs, and those landing on tails would stay. Levitt then followed up with participants two months and six months later. Supporting McElhatton's theory, Levitt found those who had quit their jobs or otherwise made major life changes were substantially happier than those who stuck around.

By age fifty, McElhatton was back to his old tricks: he quit his job. Energized to find a new and challenging way to serve, he made a most unusual leap from law firm partner to Peace Corps volunteer. McElhatton explains that the "Peace Corps didn't have a big presence in my college, but I've met a lot of interesting people who'd been in Peace Corps. You know, it's my tribe. There's something about Peace Corps people. At the same time, I was a little bored at work, and looking for a different kind of challenge."

Reflecting an attitude of abundance over scarcity, McElhatton recalls asking himself, "Do you really need to be doing this for thirty, forty, fifty years, and there's other people that are dying to do the job? Having enough money to be comfortable, not to worry about it, is a big deal. But most of us in the United States get to a point where we're beyond that [worry]."

Once beyond the elemental fight for enough, McElhatton explains, intrinsic rather than extrinsic motivation ought to take precedence. "It's what kind of juice are you getting out of the work you're doing? Are you happy going to work? And people don't think about that. A lot of people think, 'I'll keep making more money. I'll get the new car and that's what it's all about.' But that's not what it's all about. There's a lot of unhappy lawyers. And a lot of unhappy rich people."

This is how McElhatton would find himself in a small, former Soviet nation. Socrates reputedly said, "I am not an Athenian or a Greek, but a citizen of the world" (Plutarch, 1874). McElhatton seems to share this perspective, despite his work in support of the Twin Cities. "Certainly there's a lot of Americans who are disadvantaged. But we consume so much of the world's resources, we have so many opportunities, and there are so many places in Kyrgyzstan where it's a lot tougher."

McElhatton's professional status meant he likely could have handpicked his Peace Corps posting. He could have asked for a cushy position in Bishkek, the tree-lined capital city, or an assignment to a prominent university. But

McElhatton didn't do that. Instead, he accepted a position in the mountains of Naryn City, population forty thousand, which even in the gritty world of Peace Corps–Kyrgyzstan is considered a hardship post. McElhatton explains it this way: "When I was in the Peace Corps, my goal was really to give back. I feel really lucky to have had the opportunities that I had in life. And I know there are a lot of people, especially outside the US, who don't have that. So my attitude was, 'I'll go anywhere and do anything.' I was hoping to make a difference and do the best I could. And," McElhatton said with a shrug, "it worked out great."

"One of the things that I try to do in my [legal] practice is be nice to everyone. And not just people who supervise me, but everybody," McElhatton emphasizes. He would take this mentality to his new home, whether while socializing with young Peace Corps volunteers or when interacting with Kyrgyz residents who saw McElhatton as someone rather alien. He walked the streets of his new town, a place where a Harvard lawyer was practically a myth. "You're sort of a freak . . . I'm a tall white guy, so even after two years of walking around—and I walked a lot—people will stare at you still. [But] I was really touched by how I was accepted by everyone. People, they were just nice."

Beyond the bouts of frostbite, loss of income, and separation from wife and family, what did McElhatton get out of all this? "It makes you feel good, you know? That's something that I knew before, but after being in the Peace Corps, helping other people makes me feel good."

He got all of this by relentlessly pursuing his vision of communal service even when the first few tries didn't work out. As University of Pennsylvania psychologist Angela Duckworth (2016) explains, "Dogged perseverance towards a top-level goal requires, paradoxically, some *flexibility* at lower levels in the goal hierarchy. It's as if the highest-level goal gets written in ink—and the lower-level goals get written in pencil, so you can revise them and sometimes erase them altogether, and then figure out new ones to take their place."

McElhatton is truly an ESI. In acting with enlightened self-interest, he subordinates material wealth without demeaning the value of money; he transcends ego, accepting relative anonymity in his new and remote home, in order to exercise noncompetitive and nonjudgmental mudita; and he uses his substantial intellect and experiences—sources of power—to enhance others' lives.

McElhatton confirms his ESI identity by denying that he's the hero of this story. "I thought about this a lot when I was in the Peace Corps. I had a rewarding career and a healthy family and plenty of money in the bank, so it was an easy choice for me to make." He evokes the horizontal, globally minded collectivist. A self-described "adventurer," he also evokes the horizontal individualist. When speaking to the personal pleasures of his twenty-seven-month adventure, for instance, he said, "I was in pretty good shape physically, so I was able to enjoy trekking in the mountains of Kyrgyzstan."

McElhatton is, like most everyone featured in this book, highly ambitious. In his early career he needed that ambition to keep going while burning through jobs. Importantly, however, when (if) he seeks money, power, and fame at all, he seeks it not only for himself—but also, and primarily, on behalf of others. In this way McElhatton is not just ambitious. He is *ethically ambitious.*

We have seen already that the vertically individualistic pursuit of money, power, and fame are all widely and predictably harmful and, at the same time, beneficial in the context of ESIs. The same is true of ambition. When matching a horizontal individualist with an other-oriented collectivist, many of ambition's negative outcomes are reversed.

Horizontal individualists, driven by passion and purpose, are, for instance, more likely to act on their ambitions, rather than passively daydream under the bedcovers. Like McElhatton, they are more resilient to setbacks than an extrinsic verticalist (Duckworth, 2016). Even if ambitions go unattained, they are more likely to express satisfaction with the journey (Van Hiel & Vansteenkiste, 2009). Moreover, they are more likely to possess optimal self-esteem, leaving them less reliant on outward achievements for inner worth.

As for the horizontal collectivist, McElhatton is but a continuation of a theme. Recall Reza Marvasti explaining, "I am so ambitious." For what? To build more playgrounds. Or Jerry White advocating a "shift from personal ambition for yourself and your tribe and your family, or money or bank account, to ambition for the *other.*" Recall Alice Mukashyaka saying "It's not that I want to become a billionaire, no. That's not my main drive." Instead, "Money can help you make more of an impact and reach more people."

Mike Brady, too, presents a case study for other-oriented ambition. Speaking about a certain malaise that characterized his early career—one spent on long airplane rides and working with people who were sometimes doing good, and some who "aren't that good"—he found his ambitions flagging (Brady, 2021). Brady needed purpose, and he found it when taking the helm at Greyston Foundation. There, he said, he again learned to find joy in simple hard work. He gained motivation to help the many people of New York who, like him, wanted to work hard but who weren't being given the chance. By extending Greyston's success, he knew that the foundation and its bakery-subsidiary would be able to take on more and more workers like Dion Drew.

As McElhatton claimed, service "makes me feel good"; Brady said of joining Greyston, "It was partly about this purpose-driven work and thinking that was important, but it was also because I wanted to be personally happy and satisfied in what I was doing every day." This is the essence of ambitions characterized by ESIs, and indeed of ESI writ large: it is selfless and, for that reason, perfectly selfish.

This consequently draws upon the enlightened self-interest of ubuntu, described by one scholar as "a gift of the African community to Western individualism for the sake of building a vision of global interdependence" (Battle, 2009). In considering ubuntu as a philosophy that holds space for the ambitious, achievement-oriented American, however, we must acknowledge that ubuntu remains more a philosophy of the few than a culture of the many.

Recall that it's most famous advocate, Bishop Desmond Tutu, fought against the tide in his own vertically individualistic and deeply unequal South Africa. If ubuntu is only partially accepted on its continent of birth, what hope does the vertically individualistic West have of embracing an ideology of enlightened self-interest?

15

Minting the Future

Jump-Starting Your Own Transition

Jerry White, the land mine eradication activist who accepted a Nobel Peace Prize on behalf of his social enterprise, argues that society is in a "collective neurosis." In this state, he explained in our interview, "most of us are walking around numb like zombies" (White, 2020). Unlike in the movies, however, these zombies are not eternally doomed. Like a bear waking from a long slumber, it's possible for the winter of despair to give way to a fruitful spring. "Getting as many zombies as we can to wake up to discover their inner capabilities—*which are powerful*—will reverberate out to the world," White says. Those who do awaken are "exhilarated about the prospects of really knowing themselves and then being in service."

White is describing the transition to enlightened self-interest. He believes this change is possible, and the research bears him out. Just as the coherence of the Nile region harmonized and solidified into Egyptian culture, the globalization of the twenty-first century can inevitably create supranational and even global norms. The resulting convergences are neither inherently good nor bad, though its consequences include some of both.

On the negative side of the ledger, there is a cultural convergence underway, which is disproportionately Western in style and appearance. One result is the inexorable rise of vertical individualism and the self-interested pursuit of money, power, and fame, all of which are on the rise everywhere from Latin America to Africa to East Asia (McCauley, 2013; Podoshen et al., 2011).

In addition to the inherent costs of vertical individualism, the rapid abandonment of ancient cultural practices also risks destabilizing societies. The tension is famously documented by Nigerian novelist Chinua Achebe, who in his 1953 short story *Dead Men's Path* writes of a "progressive"—read Westernized—headmaster. In the spirit of progress, this headmaster closes a path to a village shrine that meandered through school grounds. The later death of a young woman in labor is blamed on the headmaster's impetuous decision, and a local medicine man recommends "heavy sacrifices" to appease the offended spirits. In response, school grounds and a building are destroyed by irate locals. A school supervisor visiting the ruins writes of a "tribal-war situation developing... arising in part from the misguided zeal of the new headmaster" (Achebe, 2009).

Achebe's publication anticipates years of civil strife across Africa. He suggests through the headmaster's actions that well-intentioned though visions of "progress" may be, long-standing cultural practices serve as the glue holding societies together; though that glue may ultimately give way to new bonding agents, too rapid change risks collapsing the whole edifice.

Today's global convergence harkens to Achebe's warnings. While absorbing the toxicity of vertical individualism—of inequality, hypercompetition, materialism, and diminished psychological well-being—it also leaves in its wake the ruined or removed cultural practices of community and family that long held together sometimes fragile, impoverished societies.

And yet, another convergence appears underway. As vertical individualism radiates abroad from the United States, and as vertical individualism remains the dominant American ideology, some of its progenitors are busy building a global identity (Cleveland, Laroche, & Papadopoulos, 2009). Within the workplace, for instance, many reportedly hope to see more egalitarian and inclusive arrangements (House et al., 2004; Marks, 1997)—a finding that may signal frustration with the limited returns on a vertically individualistic and materialistic lifestyle. University of Michigan political scientist Ronald Inglehart goes so far as to argue that post-materialism is exploding across the globe (Inglehart & Abramson, 1999). Admittedly, scholars have for decades debated the true extent of post-materialism (Marks, 1997; Giacolone & Jurkiewicz, 2004), yet Inglehart's post-materialism represents a construct closely associated with enlightened self-interest, wherein the variables of horizontal individualism, such as self-expression and equity, are combined with horizontal collectivist variables such as belongingness, sense of community, and quality of life.

Whatever the current levels of horizontalism in the United States, there is a strong basis to support the hope that those acting out of an enlightened self-interest will increase as younger generations take center stage. Studies suggest heightened levels of horizontal individualism among American students compared to the overall population (Soh & Leong, 2002). Research from Meera Komarraju and Kevin Cokley (2008) goes further, showing a racially diverse segment of American college students already adhere to horizontally individualistic *and* collectivistic values. In their study, African American students had a mean score of 61.80 on horizontal individualism, on a scale ranging from 8–72. European American students scored only slightly lower, at 58. Even more surprising, both were reasonably high in horizontal collectivism as well: African Americans at 52.47 and European Americans at 55.04. These scores are substantially higher than the scores on vertical individualism and collectivism, which ranged for African American and European American students from 37 to 45 on the same 72-point scale.

Other research finds that young people are more likely to prioritize the purchase of experiences over things, in contrast to vertical individualists who use conspicuous consumption to signal achievement and professional victory. More promising still, 84 percent of young people believe "they are duty-bound to change the world" (Headlee, 2020: 70). They are in consequence choosing to balance compensation with the value of meaningful work (Headlee, 2020).

There are also the studies conducted for this book that introduced University of Florida students to the fictional characters Robin and Lauren. The foundational text read:

> Robin was born to a family of privilege. Growing up, Robin attended some of the best schools in the country. In high school, Robin received tutoring on the SAT test, as a result of which Robin's score improved significantly. In addition, Robin's family leveraged its academic connections to help Robin gain admission into a prestigious university. Upon graduation, Robin was quickly hired. Robin then received numerous promotions and gained recognition as one of the company's top performers.
>
> By contrast, Lauren was born to a family of limited financial means. Lauren attended schools growing up that were chronically underfunded. However, Lauren worked long hours in school, and studied long hours for the SAT, eventually gaining admission to a prestigious university. Upon graduation, Lauren was quickly hired. Like Robin, Lauren also received numerous promotions and gained recognition as one of the company's top performers.

We asked the undergraduates—students at a university of which around half of the students are raised by families in the top 20 percent of the economic ladder—whether Robin's advantages imposed any societal obligations. The vast majority believed that Robin had no responsibility to donate one penny extra to the society that had given her so much. Even fewer believed that Robin had an additional responsibility to accept a service-oriented job that would have allowed her to give substantially back to society, but at a salary well below her current level. A few participants felt Robin and Lauren ought both to give back; but most believed that any advantages Robin accrued during her upbringing were irrelevant to her societal obligations as an adult. After all, several students wrote in explanation, it's not Robin's "fault" that she had so many advantages.

Finally, the study revealed that students valued earning power and contributing to the public good in about equal measure, ranking both as somewhere between their third- and fourth-most-valued goal out of seven. These results suggest that while indeed many young people desire to contribute to the public good, doing so may conflict with self-interests.

The students valued job satisfaction, however, more than either wealth or societal contributions. This intrinsic motivation is consistent with high levels of horizontal individualism and is what one might expect from undergraduate youth—less desire to gain wealth or power over others, but also an occasionally aloof perspective toward others. Consistent with broader research, therefore, vertical individualism is low among these University of Florida students; horizontal individualism is meanwhile flourishing and horizontal collectivism is beheld with some ambivalence.

Anthropologist Clifford Geertz (2014) has written that human beings are "unfinished animals." National cultures, too, are living, breathing things subject to continual adaptation (Schwartz, 2015). Societies adopt cultural norms to serve needs, but they must discard norms that outlive their utility lest their cultures ossify or regress. In the United States, vertical individualism remains the norm. There is hope for change, however, not only from our youth, but from among the small yet growing number of horizontal ideologues pushing against the fossilization of contemporary culture.

COIN: The Historic Transition Toward Enlightened Self-Interest

ESIs may, in fact, represent a natural progression in American society, and possibly many others. This progression holds that at least dating back to the agricultural revolution, most human societies operated at a vertically collectivistic stage. Later in time, however, some societies moved toward vertical individualism, gaining some benefits of individualism but losing much value with the decline of collectivism. In the modern era fewer still progressed to the enlightened self-interest paradigm of horizontalism, in which noncompetitive individualism is paired with inclusive collectivism.

We term this the COIN (collectivist, individualistic) evolution, emphasizing the monetary relevance of the progression toward enlightened self-interest.

TABLE 15.1 The COIN Evolution

Ancient Era	Industrial Era	Modern Era
Predominantly vertically collectivistic societies fight for survival.	Newly wealthy societies rise in vertical individualism.	Long wealthy (and dissatisfied) societies trend toward horizontal individualism and horizontal collective (ESI).

Collectivism often arises in response to material scarcity (Biggs et al., 2019; Triandis, 1994). A surprising claim, perhaps, given the affluence of traditionally collectivist societies such as Hong Kong, Japan, and South Korea. Recall that rates of individualism in Hong Kong and Japan have increased rapidly along with rapid economic growth. Individualism likely will increase even more over time, with Japanese college students consistently rating *more* individualistic than their American peers (Yi, 2018).

Prosperous yet strongly collectivistic South Korean culture represents an exception, yet globally the robust, inverse correlation between collectivism and societal wealth is well documented (Hofstede, 1984; House et al., 2004). Nearly all the world's wealthy nations are high in individualism, moreover. And though there is inequality aplenty in vertically individualistic societies, one is hard-pressed to identify a single impoverished nation among the world's most individualistic.

Why does collectivism arise in materially scarce environments? If I cannot afford a nursing home in old age, as just one example, then I resort to my children as caretakers. In a society where few can afford nursing homes, children are inculcated with values relating to sacrificing and caring for elders. Similarly, these societies are often vertical and competitive (Triandis et al., 1990), because as in-group cooperation is key to survival, so too may limited resources lead to out-group competition. In these environments of scarcity, you're either with me or against me.

But as that society and its members grow wealthier, parents can afford to outsource their care while state revenues increase social safety nets and subsidize such support. Consequently, children are no longer discouraged from pursuing their own individualistic interests—taking jobs in faraway cities, working more hours, spending time with their immediate family or friends rather than caring for their elders. No longer is the close cooperation of an in-group required, and—as seen in Japan and Hong Kong and in earlier generations across the West—individualism takes hold (Triandis, 1994).

Nevertheless, the competitive, vertical instinct tends to initially remain intact. There is little longitudinal data tracking historical trends along the vertical and horizontal dimensions. However, no society appears to have transitioned from vertical collectivism directly to horizontal individualism (much less horizontal collectivism). Instead, vertical collectivism unfolds into vertical individualism in newly affluent nations, which in turns opens a portal to later reach the horizontal dimension.

The West's more horizontally individualistic nations have enjoyed generations of material abundance—and the perception that material goods are abundant rather than scarce appears crucial to the transition from a vertical to a horizontal mindset. By contrast, it may be that anxiety about falling back into poverty is higher among the newly affluent (Ahuvia & Wong, 2002). For instance, adults raised in resource-scarce environments are more likely to seek quick rewards (Griskevicius, Delton, Robertson, & Tybur, 2011; Griskevicius et al., 2013). These individuals continue to see the world as scarce even as their economic conditions improve (White, Li, Griskevicius, Neuberg, & Kenrick, 2013). The result is self-interested competition along the vertical dimension.

It is in this context that "robber barons" like the Rockefellers and Vanderbilts are most at home. This competition may even prove useful, initially, as a fear-driven work ethic creates a virtuous cycle of rising prosperity (Arrindell et al., 1997). As that prosperity increases yet further and society is eventually able to provide enough for all its members, however, that same competition can backfire (Arrindell et al., 1997). Instead, more useful is cooperation to manage the excess wealth and the damage aroused by all of that disregard for broader societal interests (such as climate change, refugee populations, and income inequality).

Eventually this incompatibility between a seemingly prosperous but simultaneously wounded society motivates change—though perhaps only after enduring much pain. The United States may be approaching this stage, as reflected in outrage against economic elites, in protests, and in documentaries, books, and the arts, which in various modalities all denounce the status quo. The disenfranchised may prevail, however, only when their opposition loses the will to fight. While earlier generations fought with daggers out to combat their fears of falling into poverty, subsequent generations feel more insulated from such dangers. The children of a society long rich grow secure— perhaps reasonably so—in their societal place. After all, their ancestors spent generations building a sturdy foundation. At the same time, they witness the dejection of ultramaterialists and come to reject a lifestyle that equates wealth with happiness. They begin exploring alternatives in parallel with the disenfranchised, and the wheels of cultural evolution accelerate.

This new set—educated, relatively prosperous—remain individualistic and self-interested, yet seek new outlets. Like the University of Florida student-participants and American college students more generally, they are more focused on self-development and their personal passions than on material accumulation. Viewing the world as abundant rather than scarce, they need not compete quite so hard to accumulate wealth, for they perceive there is plenty to go around. Thus the horizontal individualist is born, intrinsically rather than extrinsically motivated amid a world of plenty.

It is at this horizontal individualistic stage that musicians, artists, and writers enrich their societies—poorer societies can less ably accommodate such crafts, and those fearing a descent back into poverty spend their lives accumulating rather than living the romantic but materially risky life of an artist. This progression echoes Revolutionary War hero and second US president John Adams, who declared in a letter to his wife that he would study war so that his children could study math and philosophy, so that their children could study painting, poetry, and music (MHS, 2022).

This stage is also a time for entrepreneurs willing to gamble with success. Studies show that individuals who grow up in socioeconomically advanced households are more likely to take big, risky bets in the face of challenges. Children of poverty, by contrast, are more likely to hedge and diversify in the same environment (White et al., 2013). Similarly, this is a time for professionals who look to build rather than merely enrich. This viewpoint was echoed by the many University of Florida students who disagreed that business is a competition with others, and rather saw business as a tool for societal innovation and progress.

For all his flaws—and it seems there are many—Elon Musk may partially fall into this category. Far from choosing a safe professional path, Musk dropped out of a Stanford graduate program on his second day. Far from choosing safe investments, he opted for not one, but three, ultra-risky businesses—solar panels, electric cars, and space rockets. Tesla teetered on the verge of bankruptcy for years, with Musk spending nights sleeping on a cot at his Texas production facility in a desperate attempt to stay afloat (Ball, Kluger, & Garza, 2021).

Today, Musk is the world's richest person. Tesla is America's first new successful automotive company since Chrysler was started in 1925, which, *Time* magazine writes, makes Musk "arguably the biggest private contributor to the fight against climate change." At the same time, Musk's rockets are busy shooting into space on the force of a NASA contract. Yet Robert Zubrin, founder of the Mars Society and a partner with Musk in solar exploration, says Musk is driven by motives other than money. "He wants eternal glory for doing great deeds," Zubrin explains, "and he is an asset to the human race because he defines a great deed as something that is great for humanity. He is greedy for glory. Money to him is a means, not an end." This status-seeking behavior suggests a strong dose of vertical individualism runs through Musk's veins. This vies, however, with the profile of an aloof, free-thinking type, almost an artist's sensibilities, and in that we see the telltale signs of the horizontal individualist (Ball et al., 2021).

Nonetheless, something is missing for the horizontal individualist—and it is an absence that facilitates the final metamorphoses to the ideal of ESIs. This individualistic, go-it-alone mindset fosters a certain nihilism. Individualistic Westerners have disproportionately high rates of suicide (Harari, 2016), rising rates of perfectionism (Curran & Hill, 2019), depression (Manson, 2019), and weaker social ties than their more collectivistic counterparts (Triandis et al., 1988). Consider that the highly collectivistic Amish have suicide rates that are an incredible 70 percent lower than other Americans (McDougall, 2019).

Freed from the pains of cutthroat competition, however, a certain segment of horizontal individualists recognizes that something essential is lost during the transition from collectivism to individualism. They have their art, their business, their self-mastery, but they lack human connection. Returning to the sharply vertically collectivistic distinctions of old, of in-groups and out-groups, us versus them, is inconceivable. The horizontal individualist, remember, does not see others as better or worse, so verticalism of all sorts is a cognitive nonstarter.

The global identity of the horizontal collectivist is, however, within reach of the inclusive horizontal individualist. Already the horizontal individualist operates from a place of noncompetition; to spring from that place into active cooperation is not so great a leap. Already the horizontal individualist recognizes others as equals; to see others as possessing interlinked interests and rights requires but a modest change in vision.

Thus the trajectory from vertical collectivism, as early humans feasted around a campfire, to vertical individualism, as steam-billowing trains carried supplies for the rapidly rising cities of the West, to horizontal individualism, as the cosmopolitan children of the prosperous pursued lives of meaning and creativity, and finally to ESIs, as individualists who are at home everywhere but nowhere, only faintly recalls the camaraderie lost around the campfires of old.

The COIN evolution unfolded slowly, subtly, but now gains momentum, as those acting with enlightened self-interest take their prominent places. We've seen how the ideal of ESIs improves quality of life through the paradigm of money, power, and fame. We've also seen how optimal self-esteem and an interconnected identity can open the doors to enlightened self-interest. We now present a shock treatment of sorts to initiate change.

Forging the Future: Your A-Ha! Moment

Saint Francis of Assisi transforms from playboy to saint following a seemingly simple interaction with a beggar. Paul is blinded by light for three days, after which he sees again and becomes a devoted disciple of Jesus (Keltner & Haidt, 2003). Archimedes shouts "Eureka" as he discovers the principles of buoyancy, while legend has it that a falling apple leads Isaac Newton to a theory of gravitation.

"A-ha moments," sometimes referred to by social scientists as "peak experiences" or "insights," are flashes of great clarity often accompanied by a conversion to a new way of thinking. Those experiencing A-ha moments express feelings of greater authenticity and an elevation of the intrinsic over the extrinsic. A-ha moments regularly enhance feelings of connectedness with all others and bring about more communal and altruistic behaviors as well. These experiences are, consequently, perhaps the most direct route to the ideal of ESIs, whether for yourself or those around you.

So just how are A-ha moments initiated? Often, though thankfully not only, by moments of crisis. Jerry White's and Reza Marvasti's stories both began with near-death experiences, creating the launchpads for their rebirths as humanitarians on a grand scale. For Marvasti, his survival and the death of his close friend in a nearly identical accident just one week later left him deeply shaken. But the Reza Marvasti we know—the one building playgrounds in some of the world's most dangerous places—was not yet born. First the old Marvasti had to crumble.

A-ha moments arise when a previously held worldview falters. The result is cognitive dissonance or a mental disconnect. This is where Marvasti was situated following his accident—lost and trying to find his way. Psychologists Jonathan Haidt and Dacher Keltner (2003) explain that in response to a faltering understanding, the mind eventually resolves the conflict by, essentially, changing its mind—with old views replaced by new ones in a process known as accommodation.

Marvasti, again: "[Following the accident] I just knew I needed to hear my inner voice, my calling. I wanted to go somewhere deep in nature, away from all souls. I went to the Amazon in northern Peru and lived in the forest for two weeks alone." Recalling the noises emanating from an abundant and alien wildlife, he said, "Living in the forest by far was the scariest experience I have ever had." It was also the "most beautiful, and profound experience."

There, Marvasti confronted not just his recent pain and loss, but recalled a childhood marred by war. "In the solitude, I [reflected on] my childhood. I was born in Iran, and the first six years of my life was during the Iran and

Iraq War. I remembered how we used to get bombed, usually at night. When we heard the sirens, we ran to my aunt's home, which was on the lower floor, like a bunker. All the families would gather, turn the lights off, hide under the tables. There was this darkness, this fear in the air.

"Many of my friends are still carrying trauma and fear from those times," Marvasti continues. "As adults they are still scared of loud noises. [But] I remember anytime they turned the lights off, for me it was time to play hide-and-seek with my cousins. I had found the light in the darkness."

Giving light to darkness: in the forest Marvasti was beginning to hear again what he described as his "inner voice," his "calling." Just a couple of weeks later, while passing through La Paz, Bolivia, he observed homeless children as young as three or four. Every day for a week Marvasti visited these children—bringing them treats and small gifts. He recalls the heaviness of their lives, saying, "These children looked like adults in tiny sizes. Something was missing for them to be kids. [Then] it all clicked: for kids to be kids, they *need to play*."

That "click" was an A-ha moment, as the "accommodation" described by Keltner and Haidt took place. But the mind doesn't simply replace old views with new ones during this process of accommodation. Importantly, the new views are seen as genuine moments of epiphany or revelation (Topolinski & Reber, 2010). Research shows that this perception is largely correct; insights derived from A-ha moments are on average more accurate than insights drawn from more prosaic processes (Salvi, Bricolo, Kounios, Bowden, & Beeman, 2016). The more certain one is of an A-ha moment's value, furthermore, the more valuable it in fact is (Danek & Wiley, 2017).

James Hollis (1993), a scholar devoted to understanding the A-ha moments arising from so-called midlife crises, would not be surprised to learn that Marvasti's insight occurred while so far from home—as did Jerry White's. Hollis highlights the extrinsic orientation that leaves so many looking to others for guidance and a sense of self-worth. He then notes that A-ha moments often occur when the world is finally seen unfiltered by familiar societal standards and expectations—that is, through the intrinsic lens and from a position of authenticity.

Speaking specifically of vertically individualistic societies, Hollis suggests a "withdrawal of projections" (27) with respect to money and power, questioning instead one's higher life purpose. From this position of doubt, Hollis argues, the foundation is set to be "radically stunned into consciousness" (18). He writes, "Apart from shock, confusion, even panic, the fundamental result . . . is to be humbled" (41). Maslow (1959), the progenitor of the theoretically similar peak experiences concept, also emphasized the role of humility during peak experiences, writing of strong emotions including "reverence, humility, and surrender before the experience as before something great" (1999: 89).

White's A-ha moment, meanwhile, took over ten years to arrive. While traveling through Cambodia in 1996, White met a young girl with only one leg. While he had received a seventeen-thousand-dollar prosthetic leg following his accident in Israel, this child from one of the world's poorest and most traumatized nations leaned unsteadily on a homemade crutch. It was with a child's innocence that she did not comment on their differences, but instead their shared histories. She looked into White's eyes and said in local Khmer, "You are one of us" (2008: 2).

"I realized she was right," White writes in his book *I Will Not Be Broken*. "I asked myself what I could do to help support that little girl and the hundreds of thousands like her—people who, through no fault of their own, had slammed into some kind of horrible date with destiny" (2008: 2). He expanded on that in our interview: "After an A-ha moment, you can no longer think the same way. Once you have a conversion moment to the humility of our interdependence, the humility of our dignity and equality, and the humility of belonging to Mother Earth—yes, from that space, you can work miracles" (White, 2020). University of California–Irvine's Paul Piff similarly finds that moments of awe often reveal one's insignificance and thus interdependence, with the result that prosocial behaviors increase dramatically (Piff, Dietze, Feinberg, Stancato, & Keltner, 2015). Other researchers describe A-ha moments as energizing a "sense of oneness with the broader universe . . . self-realization, and impulses toward honesty and goodness" (Bethelmy & Corraliza, 2019: 2). Finally, participants in a separate study reported significantly higher levels of "communitarianism and empathy" following peak experiences, which, the authors write, "seem to be associated with holistic understandings of the self, one's role in an ordered universe, one's role in society" (Christopher, Manaster, Campbell, & Weinfeld, 2002).

As Marvasti created The Power of Play, meanwhile, White co-founded Survivor Corps. "Corralling the voices of mine victims around the world," White writes, "we set out to ban the use of land mines and help survivors get legs and find work" (White, 2008: 2). And corral he did, gaining the support of luminaries including Princess Diana, Senator John McCain, Jordan's King Hussein and Queen Noor, and our old favorite, the Dalai Lama. Together White and his team of royals helped secure the landmark 1997 Mine Ban Treaty—a treaty that now boasts 164 national signatories and led to the coalition's receipt of the Nobel Peace Prize.

Evidently A-ha moments that are the product of deep suffering may result in positive revelations (Topolinski & Reber, 2010). Thankfully, however, personal transformations do not have to only come from loss or tragedy. We may, for instance, seek A-ha moments by following that which is awesome, in the literal sense of the word. Scholars describe how moments of "awe," the sense of the vast, powerful, and mysterious, are awakened in what is an overwhelmingly positive experience (Bethelmy & Corraliza, 2019). Research similarly suggests that among the very best ways to provoke A-ha moments is through close connection to nature, such as being atop a mountain or while skiing down it, observing wild animals, or beholding a storm or the ocean's vastness (McDonald, Wearing, & Ponting, 2009). In May 1903, Theodore Roosevelt camped in the Sierra Nevada Mountains. He describes the experience in terms of the sacred, writing, "The first night we camped in a grove of giant sequoias. It was clear weather, and we lay in the open, the enormous cinnamon-colored trunks rising about us like the columns of a vaster and more beautiful cathedral than was ever conceived by any human architect" (1915). As author Annie Paul (2021) relates, Roosevelt, perhaps recalling his awe-inspiring experience, would go on to triple America's natural forests, double its national parks, and declare seventeen national monuments.

For those who prefer strong air-conditioning and few insects, exposure to sublime art and music may also evoke awe (Shiota, Keltner, & Mossman, 2007). The late Eugene d'Aquili and colleagues (1999), moreover, studied the neurobiology of religious revelation. They reported that religious revelations, like A-ha moments, are perceived as true and even "more real" than postrevelation reality. In response, religious revelations often "alter the way the experiencers live their lives," d'Aquili and the Andrew Newbergs write (192). The scholars suggest that new neural connections are made during these moments, which allows for the rapid formation of new beliefs.

Psychedelic experiences are, perhaps paradoxically, another pathway to A-ha moments (Majić, Schmidt, & Gallinat, 2015). Guided and intentional uses of psilocybin (the active ingredient in psychedelic mushrooms), ayahuasca, LSD, and even MDMA (from which ecstasy is derived) are all well-documented transformational agents. Along with increased prosocial motivation and global identification, users report increased empathy, mindfulness, creativity, and overall well-being, the trademarks of A-ha moments (Jungaberle et al., 2018).

Don't like nature, or the idea of a psychedelic trip? You're in luck. These lucid moments may occur during ordinary moments as well. Archimedes's eureka moment is said to have come during nothing more than bathtime. Research suggests, however, that the more thought is devoted to an idea initially, the more likely a spontaneous solution is to eventually arise (Gruber, 1981). Archimedes, for instance, is believed to have been deeply considering theories of water displacement long before he soaped up (Gruber, 1981). White, similarly, did not experience his A-ha moment until years after his injury, while Marvasti was months into a period of contemplation before his trip to South America unlocked life's mysteries. This is partly because the subconscious mind continues to work even while the conscious mind moves onto other ideas (Laukkonen, Schooler, & Tangen, 2018). When the subconscious mind identifies a solution—say, in a bathtub—it is experienced by the conscious mind as revelation. Thus scholars suggest that one of the best ways to initiate sudden, A-ha moments in ordinary life is, paradoxically, through slow, methodological consideration (Gruber, 1981).

Marvasti's and White's stories affirm the research: A-ha moments are powerful, transformative experiences that can stimulate the intrinsic, altruistic, and interdependent path of ESIs. To get there, we can seek awe in nature. We can deepen our religious commitment and perhaps initiate religious revelation. We can—under safe and guided conditions—use psychedelics. And we can grind away at problems, increasing the likelihood that one fine day, perhaps in a bathtub near you, a solution to your troubles will spontaneously rise with the bubbles.

Finally, there is another way to gain if not full A-ha moments, then at least greater clarity on your transition to enlightened self-interest. It is to surround yourself with role models like the ones featured throughout this book. Dacher Keltner and Jonathan Haidt (2003) note that bearing witness to remarkable displays of virtue or character may lead to a sense of elevation which, at the very least, hints at peak experiences, awe, and A-ha moments. This admiration, as is seen with healthy upward comparisons, can motivate the observer to live up to that model.

Wonder, then, at the sublimity of nature, of the arts, even of sports, but wonder, too, at the sublimity of others—those we know well and those observed from afar. Role models are unusual, it is true; but they are not rare. As mentioned at the beginning, I found my first and most lasting role model in coauthor Henry Biggs, an individual who prioritizes passion and purpose over dollars and cents. Without that formative influence in the uncertain days of my fledgling legal career, I can only wonder where I would be today.

You, too, can find role models who exemplify your most cherished ideals. As Jerry White told me, "There are many role models in every community with whom you can surround yourself." We need only look.

Conclusion

I awoke today to a message from a top student—we'll call her Meriam—from my time at the American University of Central Asia, in Bishkek, Kyrgyzstan. Meriam was applying to a digital education master's program at Stanford University and asked if I might review her statement of purpose. I, perhaps unusually among my profession, enjoy the opportunity to provide feedback on a student's application package, finding it—too rare in the life of a teacher—an opportunity to help a student see a direct and nearly immediate impact.

Her statement began with these words: "I am the child of a forced marriage, born in rural Kyrgyzstan, to a woman who did not choose her path in life." She went on to explain that as a child she expected to fall prey to this same merciless tradition in which Central Asian women are forced—often by kidnapping—to marry men they do not love and may not even know. Through pluck and luck, however, her mother saw to it that her daughter received an education in the capital city, which eventually brought her on scholarship to my English-speaking university. She later received a one-year scholarship to the United States, learned of the wider world, and saw her ambitions grow accordingly.

But Meriam saw her mother's suffering and her own fears as a preventable illness. She used the open doors the world had so narrowly provided to return home and educate other girls from her rural homeland. She climbed a ladder, first as leader of a US Peace Corps–sponsored summer camp for rural women and then to found a young women's leadership organization. She envisions much, much more in the years to come.

This week it was Meriam from Kyrgyzstan. Another it was Aloysius, a natural leader, rising writer, and social entrepreneur accomplishing amazing things through the Rotary Club, despite a humble upbringing in rural Uganda; then it was Esther, a Kenyan with an intellect that will shake the world in the years to come; by the rightfully self-assured student who hopes to lead her Liberian home country as president, as she did the university student body; or by another who hopes to gain wealth and connections in finance so that he may run a people's candidacy for governor of his Kenyan home province.

They may not all achieve all that they aspire toward. But, as the saying goes, aim for the stars and land on the moon. As for me, this is the fuel on which I run. As for you, perhaps these pages will have fueled you to turn, even if partially, toward the ideal of enlightened self-interest. Every available instrument has been deployed in this book, from dispassionate facts and emotional claims about the plight of the forgotten half of humanity, to highlighting your innate sense of altruism, to promoting your self-interests. We have together seen the costs to self of vertical individualism, and the sharp contrast this presents with enlightened self-interest. We have also seen the costs to others of vertical individualism and the debt we owe for our privileged positions in the world.

Whichever of these resonates in your life, you may agree that the time has come to initiate, or more likely accelerate, your change—not just believing in enlightened self-interest, but acting upon it. To break out of the bubble in which you may live now and confront the painful realities of the world around you, but also to open yourself to incredible beauty, love, compassion, and connection. To see the world as a surf competition on which the privileged few float above, and to share your life raft with those who most need to rise above the roiling waters.

You have received the knowledge and tools to, at the very least, initiate change. Recall that one of the very best ways we can use money is to give it away or spend it on deepening both new and long-established relationships. Recall that power is enhancing when seen as a responsibility to the benefit of others. Know that social comparisons grow healthier and more beneficial when, like the Dalai Lama, we no longer look down or up, but only across to our equals.

As the experience of lawyer-cum-Peace-Corps-volunteer Sean McElhatton shows, change may require resilience in seeking a job, a career, or a lifestyle in which your enlightened self-interest is able to shine. Do not be intimidated by the size of the endeavor. You need not relocate to Kyrgyzstan like McElhatton did, nor do you need to sell all your worldly goods like Marvasti did, nor donate everything you have (and then some) like Jim Doty. You simply need to start somewhere and recognize that incremental change multiplied by millions across the nation and globe is *radical evolution*. "There is," as educator Henry B. Eyring has written, "power in steadiness and repetition" (McKeown, 2020: 197).

Recall Greyston CEO Mike Brady, too, who graduated from Wharton and "did a lot of traditional things early on, without having a real mindset around what will make me happy. I was taking long business trips and spending hours on flights to meet with other businesspeople to discuss business issues I did not care about. I did not want to do that any longer and committed to finding work that aligned with my values. I was very fortunate to have an opportunity to take a pause and say, 'Hey, can I do something else?' And just began moving down that different branch" (Mann, 2022). At that point, Brady (2021) explains, the momentum began to carry itself. "That step in the one direction makes you want to walk more quickly to help people. You realize there's so many things that you can do and so many opportunities to make change. You begin to get really motivated. And I very much encourage people to take that first step in the thousand-mile journey that they want to get to."

It must be acknowledged that acting with enlightened self-interest represents a break, at times sharp, from the norms of American society. Thus, there must be first movers: those willing to buck the trends of society, risking the condemnation of others for violating sacrosanct though often-unquestioned norms.

Who is most likely to make this change? It is those who have experienced the clarity of A-ha moments, yes. But it also those, like Brady, Calderon, and McElhatton, who have, through long-standing resilience, sought lifestyles that are more compatible with their values than are America's dominant vertical practices. For these ESIs, conforming to social norms that were incongruent with their personal values was even more harmful than the price of nonconformity. These are first movers. These are our role models.

Ironically, to forgo the American expectation of self-interested individualism is in many ways an act of even greater individualism. She who lives her life seeking the esteem of her neighbors lives a life for others. She who lives her life according to her own deepest passions and values lives a life that might be, in the purest of senses, self-interested. And yet, the change will still be difficult, for it is easier to follow than to lead. Ayn Rand, despite her philosophical shortcomings, demonstrated the pull of conformity when her anti-hero Peter Keating asked: "Why do they always teach us that it's easy and evil to do what we want and that we need discipline to restrain ourselves? It's the hardest thing in the world—to do what we want. And it takes the greatest kind of courage. I mean, what we really want."

To all of you—to all of us: courage.

References

Abellard, Natasha. 2021. Parents are now paying more than half of their kids' college costs. *Bloomberg Wealth*. Accessed July 23. https://www.bloomberg.com/news/articles/2021 -07-23/university-tuition-per-year-parents-pay-higher-percentage-of-costs.

Abra, Jock C. 1993. Competition: Creativity's vilified motive. *Genetic Social and General Psychology Monographs* 119(3): 289–342. https://www.semanticscholar.org/paper /Competition%3A-creativity%27s-vilified-motive-Abra/3610d896c2fc48e4b28db2651 f9941a1e6d48d71.

Achebe, Chinua. 2009. *Dead men's path*. (4th ed.). Edited by R. S. Gwynn. New York: Penguin.

Acton, Lord. 1887. Letter to Bishop Creighton. Acton-Creighton Correspondence, available at Liberty Fund online, https://oll.libertyfund.org/quote/lord-acton-writes-to-bishop -creighton-that-the-same-moral-standards-should-be-applied-to-all-men-political-and -religious-leaders-included-especially-since-power-tends-to-corrupt-and-absolute-power -corrupts-absolutely-1887.

Ahuvia, Aaron C., & Wong, Nancy Y. 2002. Personality and values based materialism: Their relationship and origins. *Journal of Consumer Psychology* 12(4): 389–402.

Aknin, Lara B., Barrington-Leigh, Christopher P., Dunn, Elizabeth W., Helliwell, John F., Burns, Justine, Biswas-Diener, Robert, Kemeza, Imelda, Nyende, Paul, Ashton-James, Claire E., & Norton, Michael I. 2013. Prosocial spending and well-being: Cross-cultural evidence for a psychological universal. *Journal of Personality and Social Psychology* 104(4): 635.

Alexander, Ruth. 2012. Where are you on the global pay scale? *BBC News*, March 12. https:// www.bbc.com/news/magazine-17512040.

Ali, Muhammad. 2003. *The soul of a butterfly: Reflections on life's journey*. New York: Simon and Schuster.

Alighieri, Dante. 1996. *The divine comedy of Dante Alighieri, vol. 3, Paradiso*. New York: Oxford University Press.

Allport, Gordon Willard, Clark, Kenneth, & Pettigrew, Thomas. 1954. *The nature of prejudice*. Boston: Addison-Wesley.

Alvarado, Lorriz Anne. 2010. Dispelling the meritocracy myth: Lessons for higher education and student affairs educators. *Vermont Connection* 31(1): 2.

American Institute of Stress. 2019. 42 worrying workplace stress statistics. September 25. https://www.stress.org/42-worrying-workplace-stress-statistics.

Anderson, Cameron, & Kilduff, Gavin J. 2009. The pursuit of status in social groups. *Current Directions in Psychological Science* 18(5): 295–298.

Annenberg Space for Photography. 2017. Juliet Schor on keeping up with the Joneses vs. keeping up with the Kardashians. Accessed July 1, 2023. https://www.youtube.com /watch?v=m_NPXcbz1g8.

Anonymous interviews with author. 2018. Colombia.

Apicella, Coren L., Marlowe, Frank W., Fowler, James H., & Christakis, Nicholas A. 2012. Social networks and cooperation in hunter-gatherers. *Nature* 481(7382): 497–501.

APLU (Association of Public and Land-Grant Universities). 2022. How does a college degree improve graduates' employment and earnings potential? Last accessed January 18, 2022. https://www.aplu.org/our-work/4-policy-and-advocacy/publicuvalues /employment-earnings/.

Ariely, Dan. 2008. *Predictably irrational*. New York: Harper Perennial.

Ariely, Dan. 2011. *The upside of irrationality*. New York: Harper Perennial.

Ariely, Dan, & Levav, Jonathan. 2000. Sequential choice in group settings: Taking the road less traveled and less enjoyed. *Journal of Consumer Research* 27(3): 279–290.

Arrindell, Willem A., Hatzichristou, Chryse, Wensink, Jeroen, Rosenberg, Ellen, van Twillert, Björn, Stedema, Joke, & Meijer, Diane. 1997. Dimensions of national culture as predictors of cross-national differences in subjective well-being. *Personality and Individual Differences* 23(1): 37–53.

Asch, Solomon E. 1956. Studies of independence and conformity: I. A minority of one against a unanimous majority. *Psychological Monographs: General and Applied* 70(9): 1.

Aten, Jason. 2021. HBO MAX spent $70 million on Zach Snyder's remake of the $300 million "Justice League" flop: Why that's brilliant. *Inc.*, March 20. https://www.inc.com/jason -aten/hbo-max-spent-70-million-on-zach-snyders-remake-of-300-million-justice-league -flop-why-thats-brilliant.html.

Ball, Molly, Kluger, Jeffrey, & Garza, Alejandro de la. 2021. Person of the year: Elon Musk. *Time Magazine*, December 13. https://time.com/person-of-the-year-2021-elon-musk/.

Ball, Richard. 2001. Individualism, collectivism, and economic development. *Annals of the American Academy of Political and Social Science* 573(1): 57–84.

Bandura, Albert. 1988. Self-regulation of motivation and action through goal systems. In Hamilton, Vernon, Bower, Gordon, & Frijda, Nico (Eds.), *Cognitive perspectives on emotion and motivation*: 37–61. Dordrecht: Kluwer Academic.

Barrick, Murray R., & Mount, Michael K. 1991. The big five personality dimensions and job performance: A meta-analysis. *Personnel Psychology* 44(1): 1–26.

Barro, Robert J., & Lee, Jong Wha. 2013. A new data set of educational attainment in the world, 1950–2010. *Journal of development economics* (104): 184–198.

Barth, Brian. 2016. The secrets of chicken flocks' pecking order. *Modern Farmer*, March 16.

Bartolini, Stefano, & Sarracino, Francesco. 2017. Twenty-five years of materialism: Do the US and Europe diverge? *Social Indicators Research* 133(2): 787–817.

Bateson, Gregory. 1958. *Naven: A survey of the problems suggested by a composite picture of the culture of a New Guinea tribe drawn from three points of view.* Palo Alto, CA: Stanford University Press.

Battle, Michael. 2009. *Ubuntu: I in you and you in me.* New York: Church.

BBC News. 2005. Hairdressers "happiest at work." March 4. http://news.bbc.co.uk/2/hi /business/4296975.stm.

Beach, Steven R. H., & Tesser, Abraham. 2000. Self-evaluation maintenance and evolution. In Suls, Jerry, & Wheeler, Ladd (Eds.), *Handbook of social comparison*: 123–140. Boston: Springer.

Beauchamp, Tom L., Bowie, Norman E., & Arnold, Denis Gordon (Eds.). 2004. *Ethical theory and business*. London: Pearson Education.

Beckman, Steven R., Formby, John P., Smith, W. James, & Zheng, Buhong. 2002. Envy, malice and Pareto efficiency: An experimental examination. *Social Choice and Welfare* 19(2): 349–367.

Belk, Russell W. 1988. Possessions and the extended self. *Journal of Consumer Research* 15(2): 139–168.

Belk, Russell W. 2001. Materialism and you. *Journal of Research for Consumers* 1. http:// jrconsumers.com/academic_articles/issue_1/Belk_.pdf.

Belk, Russell W., & Pollay, Richard W. 1985. Images of ourselves: The good life in twentieth century advertising. *Journal of Consumer Research* 11(4): 88–297.

BER (Berkeley Economic Review). 2018. Beyond GDP: Economics and happiness. Accessed October 31. https://econreview.berkeley.edu/beyond-gdp-economics-and-happiness/.

Berdahl, Jennifer L., Cooper, Marianne, Glick, Peter, Livingston, Robert W., & Williams, Joan C. 2018. Work as a masculinity contest. *Journal of Social Issues* 74: 422.

Bethelmy, Lisbeth C., & Corraliza, José A. 2019. Transcendence and sublime experience in nature: Awe and inspiring energy. *Frontiers in Psychology* 10: 509.

Bickman, Leonard. 1971. The effect of social status on the honesty of others. *Journal of Social Psychology* 85(1): 8–22.

Biggs, Henry, Bussen, Thomas, & Ramsey, Lenny. 2019. *Shaping the global leader: Fundamentals in culture and behavior for optimal organizational performance*. Philadelphia: Routledge.

Blaker, Nancy M., Rompa, Irene, Dessing, Inge H., Vriend, Anne F., Herschberg, Channah, & Van Vugt, Mark. 2013. The height leadership advantage in men and women: Testing evolutionary psychology predictions about the perceptions of tall leaders. *Group Processes & Intergroup Relations* 16(1): 17–27.

Bonta, Bruce D. 1997. Cooperation and competition in peaceful societies. *Psychological Bulletin* 121(2): 299.

Brady, Mike. 2021. Author interview.

Brady, Mike, & Drew, Dion. 2022. Why we hire "unemployable" people. TED@Unilever. Last accessed January 19, 2022. https://www.ted.com/talks/mike_brady_and_dion_drew _why_we_hire_unemployable_people/up-next.

Braun, Ottmar L., & Wicklund, Robert A. 1989. Psychological antecedents of conspicuous consumption. *Journal of Economic Psychology* 10(2): 161–187.

Bregman, Rutger. 2020. *Humankind: A hopeful history*. London: Bloomsbury.

Breiter, Hans C., Aharon, Itzhak, Kahneman, Daniel, Dale, Anders, & Shizgal, Peter. 2001. Functional imaging of neural responses to expectancy and experience of monetary gains and losses. *Neuron* 30(2): 619–639.

Breznican, Anthony. 2021. "*Justice League*: The shocking, exhilarating, heartbreaking true story of #TheSnyderCut." *Vanity Fair*, February 22. https://www.vanityfair.com /hollywood/2021/02/the-true-story-of-justice-league-snyder-cut?utm_social-type =owned&utm_source=twitter&mbid=social_twitter&utm_medium=social&utm _brand=vf.

Brickman, P., D. Coates, & R. Janoff-Bulman. 1978. Lottery winners and accident victims: Is happiness relative? *Journal of Personality and Social Psychology* 36(8): 917.

Briggs, Jessica Sarah. 2015. If I am not for myself, who will be for me? Female autonomy, human rights-consciousness, and the right to exit from haredi communities in Israel. Unpublished doctoral dissertation, Columbia University, New York.

Brooks, David. 2015. *The road to character*. New York: Random House.

Brown, Kirk Warren, & Kasser, Tim. 2005. Are psychological and ecological well-being compatible? The role of values, mindfulness, and lifestyle. *Social Indicators Research* 74(2): 349–368.

Brown, Stuart L. 2009. *Play: How it shapes the brain, opens the imagination, and invigorates the soul*. London: Penguin.

Bruner, Jerome S., & Goodman, Cecile C. 1947. Value and need as organizing factors in perception. *Journal of Abnormal and Social Psychology* 42(1): 33.

Bryce, James. 2013 [1888]. *The American commonwealth, volume 2*. New York: Cosimo.

Buchan, Nancy R., Brewer, Marilynn B., Grimalda, Gianluca, Wilson, Rick K., Fatas, Enrique, & Foddy, Margaret. 2011. Global social identity and global cooperation. *Psychological Science* 22(6): 821–828.

Buffett, Howard G. 2013. *40 Chances: Finding hope in a hungry world*. New York: Simon and Schuster.

Buffett, Peter. 2011. *Life is what you make it*. New York: Crown.

Burger, Jerry M., Messian, Nicole, Patel, Shebani, Del Prado, Alicia, & Anderson, Carmen. 2004. What a coincidence! The effects of incidental similarity on compliance. *Personality and Social Psychology Bulletin* 30(1): 35–43.

Burgmer, Pascal, & Englich, Birte. 2013. Bullseye! How power improves motor performance. *Social Psychological and Personality Science* 4(2): 224–232.

Burroughs, James E., & Rindfleisch, Aric. 2002. Materialism and well-being: A conflicting values perspective. *Journal of Consumer Research* 29(3): 348–370.

Busbee, Jay. 2017. Chris Long will donate every game check for 2017 to charity. *Yahoo! Sports*, October 18. https://sports.yahoo.com/chris-long-will-donate-every-game-check -2017-charity-134552444.html.

Buss, David M. 1989. Sex differences in human mate preferences: Evolutionary hypotheses tested in 37 cultures. *Behavioral and Brain Sciences* 12(1): 1–14.

Cagnassola, Mary Ellen. 2021. Jobs requiring no work experience jumped 18 percent in early 2021. *Newsweek*, September 2. https://www.newsweek.com/jobs-requiring-no-work -experience-jumped-18-percent-early-2021-amid-labor-shortage-1625456.

Calderón, Jerónimo. May 2021. Author virtual interview.

Campbell, Charlie. 2021. In his speech to Congress, Joe Biden sets out a vision for "Competition, not conflict" with China. *Time Magazine*, April 29. https://time.com/5995109 /biden-congress-speech-china/.

Campbell, Colin. 1987. *The romantic ethic and the spirit of modern consumerism*. Oxford: Basil Blackwell.

Caprariello, Peter A., & Reis, Harry T. 2013. To do, to have, or to share? Valuing experiences over material possessions depends on the involvement of others. *Journal of Personality and Social Psychology* 104(2): 199.

Caro, Robert A. 2011. *The path to power: The years of Lyndon Johnson, volume 1*. New York: Vintage.

Carter, Nathan T., Guan, Li, Maples, Jessica L., Williamson, Rachel L., & Miller, Joshua D. 2016. The downsides of extreme conscientiousness for psychological well-being: The role of obsessive compulsive tendencies. *Journal of Personality* 84(4): 510–522.

Carter, Travis J., & Gilovich, Thomas. 2012. I am what I do, not what I have: The differential centrality of experiential and material purchases to the self. *Journal of Personality and Social Psychology* 102(6): 1304.

Cates, James A. 2014. *Serving the Amish: A cultural guide for professionals*. Baltimore: JHU.

Chambers, John R., Swan, Lawton K., & Heesacker, Martin. 2014. Better off than we know: Distorted perceptions of incomes and income inequality in America. *Psychological Science* 25(2): 613–618.

Chen, Chao C., Meindl, James R., & Hunt, Raymond G. 1997. Testing the effects of vertical and horizontal collectivism: A study of reward allocation preferences in China. *Journal of Cross-Cultural Psychology* 28(1): 44–70.

Chernow, Ron. 2010. *Washington: A life*. London: Penguin.

Cheung, Felix, & Lucas, Richard E. 2016. Income inequality is associated with stronger social comparison effects: The effect of relative income on life satisfaction. *Journal of Personality and Social Psychology* 110(2): 332.

Chiu, Chi-Yue, & Hong, Ying-Yi. 2013. *Social psychology of culture*. London: Psychology Press.

Chodron, Pema. 2022. Practicing non-judgment. *Yoba Lounge* (blog). Last accessed January 18, 2022. https://www.yobabalounge.com/blog/2017/1/25/non-judgment.

Choi, Yeon, & Mai-Dalton, Renate R. 1998. On the leadership function of self-sacrifice. *Leadership Quarterly* 9(4): 475–501.

Choi, Yeon, & Mai-Dalton, Renate R. 1999. The model of followers' responses to self-sacrificial leadership: An empirical test. *Leadership Quarterly* 10(3): 397–421.

Christopher, John Chambers, Manaster, Guy J., Campbell, Robert L., & Weinfeld, Michael B. 2002. Peak experiences, social interest, and moral reasoning: An exploratory study. *Journal of Individual Psychology* 58(1): 35–51.

Cialdini, Robert B., & Trost, Melanie R. 1998. Social influence: Social norms, conformity and compliance. In Gilbert, Daniel, Fiske, Susan, & Lindzey, Gardner (Eds.). *The handbook of social psychology*: 151–192. New York: McGraw-Hill.

Cialdini, Robert B., Vincent, Joyce E., Lewis, Stephen K., Catalan, Jose, Wheeler, Diane, & Darby, Betty Lee. 1975. Reciprocal concessions procedure for inducing compliance: The door-in-the-face technique. *Journal of Personality and Social Psychology* 31(2): 206.

CIA World Factbook. 2022. Gini index coefficient—Distribution of family income. Accessed January 18. https://www.cia.gov/the-world-factbook/field/gini-index-coefficient-distribution-of-family-income/country-comparison.

Clark, Andrew E. 1999. Are wages habit-forming? Evidence from micro data. *Journal of Economic Behavior & Organization* 39(2): 179–200.

Clark, Andrew E., & Oswald, Andrew J. 1994. Unhappiness and unemployment. *Economic Journal* 104(424): 648–659.

Cleveland, Mark, Laroche, Michel, & Papadopoulos, Nicolas. 2009. Cosmopolitanism, consumer ethnocentrism, and materialism: An eight-country study of antecedents and outcomes. *Journal of International Marketing* 17(1): 116–146.

Cohen, Patricia, & Cohen, Jacob. 2013. *Life values and adolescent mental health*. London: Psychology Press.

Collins, Rebecca L. 1996. For better or worse: The impact of upward social comparison on self-evaluations." *Psychological Bulletin* 119(1): 51.

Colquitt, Jason, Lepine, J. A., & Wesson, M. J. 2014. *Organizational behavior: Improving performance and commitment in the workplace (4e)*. New York: McGraw-Hill.

Coughenour, Courtney, Abelar, James, Pharr, Jennifer, Chien, Lung-Chang, & Singh, Ashok. 2020. Estimated car cost as a predictor of driver yielding behaviors for pedestrians. *Journal of Transport & Health* 16: 100831.

Coughlan, Sean. 2016. UN says 69 million teachers needed for global school pledge. *BBC News*, October 5. https://www.bbc.com/news/business-37544983.

Covey, Stephen R., & Collins, Jim (Foreword). 2013. *The 7 habits of highly effective people*. New York: Simon & Schuster.

Cragun, Ormonde Rhees, Olsen, Kari Joseph, & Wright, Patrick Michael. 2020. Making CEO narcissism research great: A review and meta-analysis of CEO narcissism. *Journal of Management* 46(6): 908–936.

Crisp, Roger, Ed. 2000. *Aristotle: Nicomachean ethics*. Cambridge: Cambridge University Press.

Csikszentmihalyi, Mihaly, & Rochberg-Halton, Eugene. 1981. *The meaning of things: Domestic symbols and the self*. Cambridge: Cambridge University Press.

Cuddy, Amy J. C., Fiske, Susan T., & Glick, Peter. 2007. The BIAS map: Behaviors from intergroup affect and stereotypes. *Journal of Personality and Social Psychology* 92(4): 631.

Curran, Thomas, & Hill, Andrew P. 2019. Perfectionism is increasing over time: A meta-analysis of birth cohort differences from 1989 to 2016. *Psychological Bulletin* 145(4): 410.

Curry, Richard O., & Valois, Karol E. 1991. The emergence of an individualistic ethos in American society. In Curry, Richard, & Goodheart, Lawrence (Eds.), *American chameleon: Individualism in trans-national context*. Kent: Kent State University Press.

Dahl, Melissa. 2015. Powerful people are messier eaters, maybe. *The Cut*, January 13. https://www.thecut.com/2015/01/powerful-people-are-messy-eaters-maybe.html.

Dalai Lama, & Cutler, Howard C. 2010. *The essence of happiness: A guidebook for living*. New York: Riverhead.

Dalai Lama, Tutu, Desmond, & Abrams, Douglas Carlton. 2016. *The book of joy: Lasting happiness in a changing world*. London: Penguin.

"Dalai Lama on Masterchef." 2012. Part 3. **YouTube**, August 28. https://www.youtube.com/watch?v=WuXlLk-PD3I.

Dalsky, David. 2010. Individuality in Japan and the United States: A cross-cultural priming experiment. *International Journal of Intercultural Relations* 34(5): 429–435.

Danek, Amory H., & Wiley, Jennifer. 2017. What about false insights? Deconstructing the Aha! experience along its multiple dimensions for correct and incorrect solutions separately. *Frontiers in Psychology* 7: 2077.

d'Aquili, Eugene G., Newberg, Andrew B., and Newberg, Andrew. 1999. *The mystical mind: Probing the biology of religious experience*. Philadelphia: Fortress.

Data Commons. 2021. United States of America. Accessed July 1, 2023. https://datacommons.org/place/country/USA?utm_medium=explore&mprop=income&popt=Person&cpv=age%2CYears15Onwards&hl=en.

Dawkins, Richard, & Davis, Nicola. 2017. *The selfish gene*. Oxfordshire: Macat Library.

Deaton, Angus. 2008. Income, health, and well-being around the world: Evidence from the Gallup World Poll. *Journal of Economic Perspectives* 22(2): 53–72.

DeCelles, Katherine A., DeRue, D. Scott, Margolis, Joshua D., & Ceranic, Tara L. 2012. Does power corrupt or enable? When and why power facilitates self-interested behavior. *Journal of Applied Psychology* 97(3): 681.

Deci, Edward L., & Ryan, Richard M. 1995. Human autonomy. In Kernis, Michael (Ed.), *Efficacy, agency, and self-esteem*: 31–49. Boston: Springer.

Deci, Edward L., & Ryan, Richard M. 2013. *Intrinsic motivation and self-determination in human behavior*. Berlin: Springer Science & Business Media.

De Cremer, David. 2002. Respect and cooperation in social dilemmas: The importance of feeling included. *Personality and Social Psychology Bulletin* 28(10): 1335–1341.

De Graaf, John, & Batker, David. 2011. Americans work too much for their own good. **Bloomberg**, November 3. https://www.bloomberg.com/opinion/articles/2011-11-03/americans-work-too-much-for-their-own-good-de-graaf-and-batker.

Della Cava, Marco, & Jones, Charisse. 2016. For older CEOs, issue is knowing when to bow out. *USA Today*, April 19. https://www.usatoday.com/story/money/business/2016/04/19/older-ceos-issue-knowing-when-bow-out/83114728/.

Deri, Sebastian, Davidai, Shai, & Gilovich, Thomas. 2017. Home alone: Why people believe others' social lives are richer than their own. *Journal of Personality and Social Psychology* 113(6): 858.

De Rivera, Joseph, & Carson, Harry A. 2015. Cultivating a global identity. *Journal of Social and Political Psychology* 3(2): 310–330.

Dessì, Ugo. 2017. Japanese Buddhism, relativization, and glocalization. *Religions* 8(1): 12.

de Waal, Frans B. M. 2008. Putting the altruism back into altruism: The evolution of empathy. *Annual Review of Psychology* 59: 279–300.

Dickens, Charles. 2004 [1850]. *David Copperfield*. London: Penguin.

Diener, Ed, & Biswas-Diener, Robert. 2002. Will money increase subjective well-being? *Social Indicators Research* 57(2): 119–169.

Diener, Ed, Lucas, Richard E., & Scollon, Christie Napa. 2009. Beyond the hedonic treadmill: Revising the adaptation theory of well-being. In Diener, Ed (Ed.), *The science of well-being*: 103–118. Dordrecht, the Netherlands: Springer.

Diener, Ed, & Seligman, Martin E. P. 2002. Very happy people. *Psychological Science* 13(1): 81–84.

Diener, Ed, Suh, Eunkook M., Smith, Heidi, & Shao, Liang. 1995. National differences in reported subjective well-being: Why do they occur? *Social Indicators Research* 34(1): 7–32.

Dittmar, Helga. 2005. Compulsive buying—A growing concern? An examination of gender, age, and endorsement of materialistic values as predictors. *British Journal of Psychology* 96(4): 467–491.

Dittmar, Helga, Bond, Rod, Hurst, Megan, & Kasser, Tim. 2014. The relationship between materialism and personal well-being: A meta-analysis. *Journal of Personality and Social Psychology* 107(5): 879.

Donaldson, Thomas. 1989. *The ethics of international business*. Oxford: Oxford University Press.

Doty, James R. 2017. *Into the magic shop: A neurosurgeon's quest to discover the mysteries of the brain and the secrets of the heart*. New York: Penguin.

Doty, James R. 2013. The science of compassion. **TedxUN Plaza**, October 2. https://www.youtube.com/watch?v=zJW5-0tjFDg.

Doty, James R. 2021. Author interview.

Drucker, Peter. 1981. Behind Japan's success. *Harvard Business Review*. https://hbr.org/1981/01/behind-japans-success.

Duckworth, Angela. 2016. *Grit: The power of passion and perseverance*. New York: Scribner.

Duffy, Michelle K., & Shaw, Jason D. 2002. The Salieri syndrome: Consequences of envy in groups. *Small Group Research* 31(1): 3–23.

Dunn, Elizabeth W., Aknin, Lara B., & Norton, Michael I. 2008. Spending money on others promotes happiness. *Science* 319(5870): 1687–1688.

Dunn, Elizabeth W., Biesanz, Jeremy C., Human, Lauren J., & Finn, Stephanie. 2007. Misunderstanding the affective consequences of everyday social interactions: The hidden benefits of putting one's best face forward. *Journal of Personality and Social Psychology* 92(6): 990.

Dunn, Elizabeth W., Gilbert, Daniel T., & Wilson, Timothy D. 2011. If money doesn't make you happy, then you probably aren't spending it right. *Journal of Consumer Psychology* 21(2): 115–125.

Duriez, Bart, Vansteenkiste, Maarten, Soenens, Bart, & De Witte, Hans. 2007. The social costs of extrinsic relative to intrinsic goal pursuits: Their relation with social dominance and racial and ethnic prejudice. *Journal of Personality* 75(4): 757–782.

DW (Deutshe Welle). 2017. UNESCO: 264 million children don't go to school. Last accessed January 18, 2022. https://www.dw.com/en/unesco-264-million-children-dont-go-to-school/a-41084932.

Eagly, Alice H., & Karau, Steven J. 2002. Role congruity theory of prejudice toward female leaders. *Psychological Review* 109(3): 573.

Earley, P. Christopher. 1989. Social loafing and collectivism: A comparison of the United States and the People's Republic of China. *Administrative Science Quarterly* 34(4): 565–581.

Earley, P. Christopher. 1993. East meets West meets Mideast: Further explorations of collectivistic and individualistic work groups. *Academy of Management Journal* 36(2): 319–348.

Easterlin, Richard A. 1973. Does money buy happiness? *The Public Interest* 30: 3.

Eastern Oregon University. 2020. The psychology behind competitiveness: Human beings are competitive, sometimes to a truly absurd degree. *ZME Science*, November 10. https://www.zmescience.com/science/the-psychology-behind-competitiveness/.

El Baroudi, Sabrine, Fleischer, Chen, Khapova, Svetlana N., Jansen, Paul, & Richardson, Julia. 2017. Ambition at work and career satisfaction: The mediating role of taking charge behavior and the moderating role of pay. *Career Development International* 22(1): 87–102.

Envy Canterbury (blog). 2016. Historical/modern examples of envy. Last accessed January 19, 2022. https://envycanterburyblog.wordpress.com/2016/10/18/blog-post-title/.

Epstein, Diana. 2011. Measuring inequity in school funding. *Center for American Progress*. Last accessed June 1, 2023. https://files.eric.ed.gov/fulltext/ED535988.pdf.

Eriksson, Kimmo, & Simpson, Brent. 2012. What do Americans know about inequality? It depends on how you ask them. *Judgment and Decision Making* 7(6): 741–745.

Euronews. 2013. Give up luxury cars, Archbishop Tutu tells South Africa government ministers. April 12. https://www.youtube.com/watch?v=xpN0CB18ZV4.

Falahati, Leila, & Paim, Laily H. J. 2011. A comparative study in money attitude among university students: A gendered view. *Journal of American Science* 7(6): 1144–1148.

FAO (Food and Agricultural Organization of the United Nations). 2022. FAO in Rwanda. http://www.fao.org/rwanda/our-office-in-rwanda/rwanda-at-a-glance/en/.

Fast, Nathanael J., Halevy, Nir, & Galinsky, Adam D. 2012. The destructive nature of power without status. *Journal of Experimental Social Psychology* 48(1): 391–394.

Fast Company. 2019. The world's most innovative companies. Accessed January 18, 2022. https://www.fastcompany.com/most-innovative-companies/2019/sectors/not-for-profit.

Fehr, Ernst, & Fischbacher, Urs. 2003. The nature of human altruism. *Nature* 425(6960): 785–791.

Fehr, Ernst, & Gächter, Simon. 2002. Altruistic punishment in humans. *Nature* 415(6868): 137–140.

Festinger, Leon. 1954. A theory of social comparison processes. *Human Relations* 7(2): 117–140.

Fiske, Susan T. 1993. Controlling other people: The impact of power on stereotyping. *American Psychologist* 48(6): 621.

Flora, Carlin. 2017. Moderation is the key to life. *Psychology Today*, July 4. https://www.psychologytoday.com/us/articles/201707/moderation-is-the-key-life.

Flynn, Francis J., Gruenfeld, Deborah, Molm, Linda D., & Polzer, Jeffrey T. 2011. Social psychological perspectives on power in organizations. *Administrative Science Quarterly* 56(4): 495–500.

Ford, James Ishmael. 2006. *Zen master who?: A guide to the people and stories of Zen*. New York: Simon and Schuster, 2006.

Foschi, Martha. 2000. Double standards for competence: Theory and research. *Annual Review of Sociology* 26(1): 21–42.

Foulk, Trevor, Chighizola, Nicolais, Gencay, Oguz, & Chen, Gilad. 2021. Giving power to the people: Empowering leadership's impact on leaders' prosocial use of power. In Taneja, Sonia, *Academy of management proceedings* 1: 10570. Briarcliff Manor, NY: Academy of Management.

Frank, Robert H. 1985. *Choosing the right pond: Human behavior and the quest for status*. Oxford: Oxford University Press.

Frankl, Viktor E. 1985. *Man's search for meaning*. New York: Simon and Schuster.

Frederick, Denver. 2019. Mike Brady, CEO of Greyston Bakery, joins Denver Frederick. *The Business of Giving*. Accessed January 28. https://www.denver-frederick.com/2019/01/28/mike-brady-ceo-of-greyston-bakery-joins-denver-frederick/.

Frey, Bruno S., & Stutzer, Alois. 2000. Happiness, economy and institutions. *Economic Journal* 110(466): 918–938.

Frey, Bruno S., & Stutzer, Alois. 2002. What can economists learn from happiness research? *Journal of Economic Literature* 40(2): 402–435.

Frimer, Jeremy A., Walker, Lawrence J., Dunlop, William L., Lee, Brenda H., & Riches, Amanda. 2011. The integration of agency and communion in moral personality: Evidence of enlightened self-interest. *Journal of Personality and Social Psychology* 101(1): 149.

Fryer, Bronwyn. 2005. Are you working too hard? *Harvard Business Review*, November. https://hbr.org/2005/11/are-you-working-too-hard.

Fujita, Frank. 2008. The frequency of social comparison and its relation to subjective well-being. In Eld, Michael, & Larsen, Randy (Eds.), *The science of subjective well-being*: 239–257. New York: Guildford.

Fujita, Frank, & Diener, Ed. 1997. Social comparisons and subjective well-being. In Buunk, Bram, & Gibbons, Frederick (Eds.), *Health, coping and well-being: Perspectives from social comparison theory*: 329–357. Hillsdale, MI: Lawrence Erlbaum.

Gable, Shelly L., Gonzaga, Gian C., & Strachman, Amy. 2006. Will you be there for me when things go right? Supportive responses to positive event disclosures. *Journal of Personality and Social Psychology* 91(5): 904.

Gaines, Judith. 1990. New Hampshire's new homeless belie the stereotypes. *Boston Globe*: 85–86.

Galinsky, Adam D., Gruenfeld, Deborah H., & Magee, Joe C. 2003. From power to action. *Journal of Personality and Social Psychology* 85(3): 453.

Galinsky, Adam D., Magee, Joe C., Inesi, M. Ena, & Gruenfeld, Deborah H. 2006. Power and perspectives not taken. *Psychological Science* 17(12): 1068–1074.

Galinsky, Adam D., & Moskowitz, Gordon B. 2000. Perspective-taking: decreasing stereotype expression, stereotype accessibility, and in-group favoritism. *Journal of Personality and Social Psychology* 78(4): 708.

Galinsky, Adam D., Rucker, Derek D., and Magee, Joe C. 2015. Power: Past findings, present considerations, and future directions. In Mikulincer, Mario, Shaver, Philip, Simpson, Jeffrey, & Dovidio, John (Eds.), *APA handbook of personality and social psychology, vol. 3: Interpersonal relations*: 421–460. Washington, DC: American Psychological Association.

Gallup. 2013. Gallup releases new findings on the state of the American workplace. June 11. https://news.gallup.com/opinion/gallup/170570/gallup-releases-new-findings-state -american-workplace.aspx.

Gandhi, Mohandas Karamchand. 1968. *The collected works of Mahatma Gandhi, vol. 81*. New Delhi: Ministry of Information and Broadcasting Government of India Publications Division.

Gardner, Wendi L., Gabriel, Shira, & Hochschild, Laura. 2002. When you and I are "we," you are not threatening: The role of self-expansion in social comparison. *Journal of Personality and Social Psychology* 82(2): 239.

Gates, Melinda. 2019. *The moment of lift: How empowering women changes the world*. New York: Flatiron.

GDA Speakers. 2022. Peter Buffett. Last accessed January 18, 2022. https://www.gdaspeakers .com/speaker/peter-buffett/.

Gee, Michael. 2018. Why aren't black employees getting more white-collar jobs? *Harvard Business Review*. Last accessed June 1, 2023. https://www.google.com/url?sa=t&rct =j&q=&esrc=s&source=web&cd=&cad=rja&uact=8&ved=2ahUKEwj819S5pKT _AhWxb2wGHSSDBPoQFnoECBkQAQ&url=https%3A%2F%2Fhbr.org%2F2018 %2F02%2Fwhy-arent-black-employees-getting-more-white-collar-jobs&usg=AOvVaw3 XcisMyI65UpgPSqtSC9Fj.

Geertz, Armin W. 2014. Whence religion? How the brain constructs the world and what this might tell us about the origins of religion, cognition and culture. In Geertz, A. (Ed.), *Origins of religion, cognition and culture*: 31–84. New York: Routledge.

Geertz, Clifford. *Ideology*. 2014. Philadelphia: Routledge.

Gelfand, Michele J., Erez, Miriam, & Aycan, Zeynep. 2007. Cross-cultural organizational behavior. *Annual Review of Psychology* 58: 479–514.

Georgesen, John C., and Harris, Monica J. 1998. Why's my boss always holding me down? A meta-analysis of power effects on performance evaluations. *Personality and Social Psychology Review* 2(3): 184–195.

Georgesen, John C., & Harris, Monica J. 2000. The balance of power: Interpersonal consequences of differential power and expectancies. *Personality and Social Psychology Bulletin* 26(10): 1239–1257.

Ger, Güliz, & Belk, Russell W. 1996. Cross-cultural differences in materialism. *Journal of Economic Psychology* 17(1): 55–77.

Ger, Güliz, & Belk, Russell W. 1999. Accounting for materialism in four cultures. *Journal of Material Culture* 4(2): 183–204.

Giacalone, Robert A., & Jurkiewicz, Carole L. 2004. The interaction of materialist and postmate-rialist values in predicting dimensions of personal and social identity. *Human Relations* 57(11): 1379–1405.

Giattino, Charlie, Ortiz-Ospina Esteban, & Roser, Max. 2020. Working Hours. *Our World in Data*, updated December. https://ourworldindata.org/working-hours.

Gibbons, Frederick X., and Buunk, Bram P. 1999. Individual differences in social compari-son: development of a scale of social comparison orientation. *Journal of Personality and Social Psychology* 76(1): 129.

Gilbert, Paul, Price, John, & Allan, Steven. 1995. Social comparison, social attractiveness and evolution: How might they be related? *New Ideas in Psychology* 13(2): 149–165.

Gimpelson, Vladimir, & Treisman, Daniel. 2018. Misperceiving inequality. *Economics & Poli-tics* 30(1): 27–54.

Giridharadas, Anand. 2019. *Winners take all: The elite charade of changing the world*. New York: Vintage.

Gladwell, Malcolm. 2018. Malcolm Gladwell teaches writing. *Master class*, February 12. https://www.masterclass.com/classes/malcolm-gladwell-teaches-writing.

Goedde, Loetz, Ooko-Ombaka, Amandla, & Pais, Gillian. 2019. *Winning in Africa's agricul-tural market*. McKinsey & Company. Accessed February 15. https://www.mckinsey.com/industries/agriculture/our-insights/winning-in-africas-agricultural-market#.

Goldstein, N. J., Cialdini, R. B., & Griskevicius, V. 2008. A room with a viewpoint: Using social norms to motivate environmental conservation in hotels. *Journal of Consumer Research* 35(3): 472–482.

Goodwin, Stephanie A., Gubin, Alexandra, Fiske, Susan T., & Yzerbyt, Vincent Y. 2000. Power can bias impression processes: Stereotyping subordinates by default and by design. *Group Processes & Intergroup Relations* 3(3): 227–256.

Górnik-Durose, Małgorzata, & Jach, Łukasz. 2020. Functionality of materialism—Cultural and evolutionary perspectives. *Materializm—Przyczyny i konsekwencje*: 207.

Grabb, Edward, Baer, Douglas, & Curtis, James. 1999. The origins of American individualism: Reconsidering the historical evidence. *Canadian Journal of Sociology/Cahiers cana-diens de sociologie* 24(4): 511–533.

Grant, Adam. 2013. *Give and take: A revolutionary approach to success*. New York: Penguin.

Grant, Adam. 2021. *Think again: The power of knowing what you don't know*. New York: Viking.

Gray, Peter. 2014. The decline of play. **TEDxNavesink**, June 13. https://www.youtube.com/watch?v=Bg-GEzM7iTk.

Grijalva, Emily, Newman, Daniel A., Tay, Louis, Donnellan, M. Brent, Harms, Peter D., Robins, Richard W., & Yan, Taiyi. 2015. Gender differences in narcissism: a meta-analytic review. *Psychological Bulletin* 141(2): 261.

Griskevicius, Vladas, Ackerman, Joshua M., Cantú, Stephanie M., Delton, Andrew W., Robertson, Theresa E., Simpson, Jeffry A., Thompson, Melissa Emery, & Tybur, Joshua M. 2013. When the economy falters, do people spend or save? Responses to resource scarcity depend on childhood environments. *Psychological Science* 24(2): 197–205.

Griskevicius, Vladas, Delton, Andrew W., Robertson, Theresa E., & Tybur, Joshua M. 2011. Environmental contingency in life history strategies: The influence of mortality and socio-economic status on reproductive timing. *Journal of Personality and Social Psychology* 100(2): 241.

Griskevicius, Vladas, & Kenrick, Douglas T. 2013. Fundamental motives: How evolutionary needs influence consumer behavior. *Journal of Consumer Psychology* 23(3): 372–386.

Gruber, Howard E. 1981. On the relation between 'AHA experiences' and the construction of ideas. *History of Science* 19(1): 41–59.

Gruenfeld, Deborah H., Keltner, Dacher J., & Anderson, Cameron. 2003. The effects of power on those who possess it: How social structure can affect social cognition. In Bodenhausen, Galen, & Lambert, Alan (Eds.), *Foundations of social cognition: A festschrift in honor of Robert S. Wyer, Jr.*: 237–261. Hillsdale, MI: Lawrence Erlbaum.

Guimond, Serge, Branscombe, Nyla R., Brunot, Sophie, Buunk, Abraham P., Chatard, Armand, Désert, Michel, Garcia, Donna M., Haque, Shamsul, Martinot, Delphine, & Yzerbyt, Vincent. 2007. Culture, gender, and the self: Variations and impact of social comparison processes. *Journal of Personality and Social Psychology* 92(6): 1118–1134.

Gutierrez-Zotes, Alfonso, Labad, Javier, Martorell, Lourdes, Gaviria Ana, Bayon, Carmen, Vilella, Elisabet, & Cloninger, C. Robert. 2015. The revised Temperament and Character Inventory: Normative data by sex and age from a Spanish normal randomized sample. *PeerJ* 3: e1481.

Gyekye, Kwame. 1996. African cultural values: An introduction. Accra: Sankofa.

Haddad, Mohammed. 2021. Mapping major protests around the world. *Al Jazeera*, March 30. https://www.aljazeera.com/news/2021/3/30/mapping-major-protests-around-the-world.

Hafner, Katie. 2006. In web world, rich now envy the superrich. *New York Times*, November 21. https://www.nytimes.com/2006/11/21/technology/21envy.html.

Haidt, Jonathan. 2012. *The righteous mind: Why good people are divided by politics and religion*. New York: Vintage.

Halevy, Nir, Bornstein, Gary, & Sagiv, Lilach. 2008. "In-group love" and "out-group hate" as motives for individual participation in intergroup conflict: A new game paradigm. *Psychological Science* 19(4): 405–411.

Halliwell, Emma, & Dittmar, Helga. 2006. Associations between appearance-related self-discrepancies and young women's and men's affect, body satisfaction, and emotional eating: A comparison of fixed-item and participant-generated self-discrepancies. *Personality and Social Psychology Bulletin* 32(4): 447–458.

Han, Carolyn. 2022. Author interview.

Han, Young Jee, Nunes, Joseph C., & Drèze, Xavier. 2010. Signaling status with luxury goods: The role of brand prominence. *Journal of marketing* 74(4): 15–30.

Harari, Yuval Noah. 2016. *Homo Deus: A brief history of tomorrow*. New York: Random House.

Harari, Yuval Noah. 2018. *21 Lessons for the 21st century*. New York: Random House.

Harbaugh, William T., Mayr, Ulrich, & Burghart, Daniel R. 2007. Neural responses to taxation and voluntary giving reveal motives for charitable donations. *Science* 316(5831): 1622–1625.

Hardy, Charlie L., & Van Vugt, Mark. 2006. Nice guys finish first: The competitive altruism hypothesis. *Personality and Social Psychology Bulletin* 32(10): 1402–1413.

Headlee, Celeste. 2020. *Do nothing: How to break away from overworking, overdoing, and underliving*. New York: Harmony.

Heilman, Madeline E., & Parks-Stamm, Elizabeth J. 2007. "Gender stereotypes in the workplace: Obstacles to women's career progress." In Correll, Shelley (Ed.), *Social psychology of gender, vol. 24*: 47–77. West Yorkshire: Emerald.

Hellman, Dan. 2011. The go-to lawyer for developers and investors. *Finance & Commerce*, April 27. https://finance-commerce.com/2011/04/the-go-to-lawyer-for-developers-and-investors/.

Helson, Ravenna, Mitchell, Valory, & Moane, Geraldine. 1984. Personality and patterns of adherence and nonadherence to the social clock. *Journal of Personality and Social Psychology* 46(5): 1079.

Helson, Ravenna, & Wink, Paul. 1992. Personality change in women from the early 40s to the early 50s. *Psychology and Aging* 7(1): 46.

Henniger, Nicole E., & Harris, Christine R. 2015. Envy across adulthood: The what and the who. *Basic and Applied Social Psychology* 37(6): 303–318.

Henrich, Joseph, & Gil-White, Francisco J. 2001. The evolution of prestige: Freely conferred deference as a mechanism for enhancing the benefits of cultural transmission. *Evolution and Human Behavior* 22(3): 165–196.

Heritage Foundation. 2021. Index of economic freedom: Country rankings. Accessed January 14, 2022. https://www.heritage.org/index/ranking.

Herron, Janna. 2019. How many Americans with $1 million feel wealthy? Fewer than you may think. *USA Today*, July 17. https://www.usatoday.com/story/money/2019/07/17/what-wealthy-its-not-necessarily-becoming-millionaire/1744408001/.

Hess Johnson, Abigail. 2018. Here's how many paid vacation days the typical American worker gets. *CNBC*, July 6. https://www.cnbc.com/2018/07/05/heres-how-many-paid-vacation-days-the-typical-american-worker-gets-.html.

Higgins, E. Tory. 1987. Self-discrepancy: A theory relating self and affect. *Psychological Review* 94(3): 319.

Hill, Kim, & Kaplan, Hillard. 1988. "Tradeoffs in male and female reproductive strategies among the Ache: Part 1." In Betzig, L., Borgerhoff Mulder, M., & Turke, P. (Eds.), *Human reproductive behaviour: A Darwinian perspective*: 277–289. Cambridge: Cambridge University Press.

Hofstede, Geert. 1984. *Culture's consequences: International differences in work-related values*. Newbury Park: Sage.

Hoelzl, Erik, & Loewenstein, George. 2005. Wearing out your shoes to prevent someone else from stepping into them: Anticipated regret and social takeover in sequential decisions. *Organizational Behavior and Human Decision Processes* 98: 15–27.

Hollis, James. 1993. *The middle passage: From misery to meaning in midlife*. Toronto: Inner City.

Holt, Douglas B. 1995. How consumers consume: A typology of consumption practices. *Journal of Consumer Research* 22(1): 1–16.

Hoover, Herbert. 2016 [1922]. *American Individualism*. With an introduction by George H. Nash. Stanford, CA: Hoover Institution Press.

House, Robert J., Hanges, Paul J., Javidan, Mansour, Dorfman, Peter W., & Gupta, Vipin. (Eds.). 2004. *Culture, leadership, and organizations: The GLOBE study of 62 societies*. Newbury Park: Sage.

House, Robert J., Hanges, Paul J., Ruiz-Quintanilla, S. Antonio, Dorfman, Peter W., Javidan, Mansour, Dickson, Marcus, & Gupta, Vipin. 1999. Cultural influences on leadership and organizations: Project GLOBE. In Gesner, M. J., & Arnold, V. (Eds.), *Advances in global leadership*: 175–233, West Yorkshire: JAI.

Houston, John M., Queen, Jennifer S., Cruz, Nathalia, Vlahov, Rachel, & Gosnell, Mercedes. 2015. Personality traits and winning: competitiveness, hypercompetitiveness, and Machiavellianism. *North American Journal of Psychology* 17(1): 105–112.

Howard, Ann, & Bray, Douglas W. 1988. *Managerial lives in transition: Advancing age and changing times*. New York: Guilford.

Howell, Ryan T., & Hill, Graham. 2009. The mediators of experiential purchases: Determining the impact of psychological needs satisfaction and social comparison. *Journal of Positive Psychology* 4(6): 511–522.

Hsee, Christopher K., Zhang, Jiao, Cai, Cindy F., & Zhang, Shirley. 2013. Overearning. *Psychological Science* 24(6): 852–859.

Hudders, Liselot, & Pandelaere, Mario. 2012. The silver lining of materialism: The impact of luxury consumption on subjective well-being. *Journal of Happiness Studies* 13(3): 411–437.

Hunnicutt, Benjamin. 2013. *Free time: The forgotten American dream*. Philadelphia: Temple University Press.

Imhoff, Roland, & Erb, Hans-Peter. 2009. What motivates nonconformity? Uniqueness seeking blocks majority influence. *Personality and Social Psychology Bulletin* 35(3): 309–320.

Inglehart, Ronald, & Abramson, Paul R. 1999. Measuring postmaterialism. *American Political Science Review* 93(3): 665–677.

Isaac, Mike. 2017. Insider Uber's aggressive, unrestrained workplace culture." *New York Times*, February 22. https://www.nytimes.com/2017/02/22/technology/uber-workplace-culture.html.

James, William. 1983 [1899]. *Talks to teachers on psychology; And to students on some of life's ideals*. Glasgow: Good Press, 2019.

Johnson, Dominic D. P. 2009. The error of God: Error management theory, religion, and the evolution of cooperation. In Levin, Simon (Ed.), *Games, groups, and the global good*: 169–180. Berlin: Springer.

Johnson, Dominic, & Bering, Jesse. 2006. Hand of God, mind of man: Punishment and cognition in the evolution of cooperation. *Evolutionary Psychology* 4(1). DOI: 147470490600400119.

Johnson, Dominic, & Krüger, Oliver. 2004. The good of wrath: Supernatural punishment and the evolution of cooperation. *Political Theology* 5(2): 159–176.

Jonason, Peter K., Li, Norman P., & Madson, Laura Madson. 2012. It is not all about the Benjamins: Understanding preferences for mates with resources. *Personality and Individual Differences* 52(3): 306–310.

Jones, Jeffrey. 2020. Donald Trump, Michelle Obama Most Admired in 2020. *Gallup*, December 29. https://news.gallup.com/poll/328193/donald-trump-michelle-obama-admired-2020.aspx.

Judge, Timothy A., Cable, Daniel, Boudreau, John, & Bretz Jr., Robert. 1995. An empirical investigation of the predictors of executive career success. *Personnel Psychology* 48(3): 485–519.

Judge, Timothy A., Heller, Daniel, & Mount, Michael K. 2002. Five-factor model of personality and job satisfaction: A meta-analysis. *Journal of Applied Psychology* 87(3): 530.

Judge, Timothy A., & Kammeyer-Mueller, John D. 2012. On the value of aiming high: The causes and consequences of ambition. *Journal of Applied Psychology* 97(4): 758–775.

Judge, Timothy A., & Locke, Edwin A. 1993. Effect of dysfunctional thought processes on subjective well-being and job satisfaction. *Journal of Applied Psychology* 78(3): 475.

Jungaberle, Henrik, Thal, Sascha, Zeuch, Andrea, Rougemont-Bücking, Ansgar, von Heyden, Maximilian, Aicher, Helena, & Scheidegger, Milan. 2018. Positive psychology in the investigation of psychedelics and entactogens: A critical review. *Neuropharmacology* 142: 179–199.

Kahneman, Daniel, & Deaton, Angus. 2010. High income improves evaluation of life but not emotional well-being. *Proceedings of the National Academy of Sciences* 107: 16489–16493.

Kaiser, David. 2018. A physicist's farewell to Stephen Hawking. *New Yorker*, March 15. https://www.newyorker.com/tech/annals-of-technology/a-physicists-farewell-to-stephen-hawking.

Kasser, Tim. 2002. *The high price of materialism.* Boston: MIT Press.

Kasser, Tim, & Ahuvia, Aaron. 2002. Materialistic values and well-being in business students. *European Journal of Social Psychology* 32(1): 137–146.

Kasser, Tim, & Ryan, Richard M. 1993. A dark side of the American dream: Correlates of financial success as a central life aspiration. *Journal of Personality and Social Psychology* 65(2): 410.

Kasser, Tim, & Ryan, Richard M. 1996. Further examining the American dream: Differential correlates of intrinsic and extrinsic goals. *Personality and Social Psychology Bulletin* 22(3): 280–287.

Kasser, Tim, & Ryan, Richard M. 2001. Be careful what you wish for: Optimal functioning and the relative attainment of intrinsic and extrinsic goals. In Schmuck, Peter, & Sheldon, Kennon (Eds.), *Life goals and well-being: Towards a positive psychology of human striving*: 116–131. Gottingen: Hogrefe & Huber.

Kasser, Tim, Ryan, Richard M., Couchman, Charles E., & Sheldon, Kennon M. 2004. Materialistic values: Their causes and consequences. In Kasser, Tim, & Kanner, Allen, (Eds.), *Psychology and consumer culture: The struggle for a good life in a materialistic world*: 11–28. New York: American Psychological Association.

Kasser, Tim, Ryan, Richard M., Zax, Melvin, & Sameroff, Arnold J. 1995. The relations of maternal and social environments to late adolescents' materialistic and prosocial values. *Developmental Psychology* 31(6): 907.

Kasser, Tim, Vansteenkiste, Maarten, & Deckop, John R. 2006. The ethical problems of a materialistic value orientation for businesses. *Human Resource Management Ethics*: 283–306.

Kaushal, Ashish. 2021. How the pandemic made the "last acceptable prejudice" worse. *Foreign Policy*, February 11. https://foreignpolicy.com/2021/02/11/how-the-pandemic-made-the-last-acceptable-prejudice-worse/.

Kazeem, Yomi. 2016. African countries are facing the world's worst teacher shortage. *Quartz Africa*, October 6. https://qz.com/africa/801571/world-teacher-day-unesco-estimates-show-africa-has-the-worlds-largest-teacher-shortage/.

Keeling, D. M. 2017. Feral rhetoric: Common sense animals and metaphorical beasts. *Rhetoric Society Quarterly* 47(3), 229–37.

Kellerman, Barbara. 2010. *Leadership: Essential Selections on Power, Authority and Influence*. New York: McGraw Hill Education.

Keltner, Dacher, Gruenfeld, Deborah H., & Anderson, Cameron. 2003. Power, approach, and inhibition. *Psychological Review* 110(2): 265.

Keltner, Dacher, & Haidt, Jonathan. 2003. Approaching awe, a moral, spiritual, and aesthetic emotion. *Cognition and Emotion* 17(2): 297–314.

Kemmelmeier, Markus, & Oyserman, Daphna. 2001. The ups and downs of thinking about a successful other: self-construals and the consequences of social comparisons. *European Journal of Social Psychology* 31(3): 311–320.

Kennedy, Jessica A., & Kray, Laura J. 2014. Who is willing to sacrifice ethical values for money and social status? Gender differences in reactions to ethical compromises. *Social Psychological and Personality Science* 5(1): 52–59.

Kernis, Michael H. 2003. Toward a conceptualization of optimal self-esteem. *Psychological Inquiry* 14(1): 1–26.

Khadjavi, Menusch, & Nicklisch, Andreas. 2018. Parents' ambitions and children's competitiveness. *Journal of Economic Psychology* 67: 87–102.

Kidder, Tracy. 2010. *Strength in what remains*. London: Random House.

Kierkegaard, Søren. 2008 [1849]. *The sickness unto death*. Radford, VA: Wilder.

Killingsworth, Matthew A. 2021. Experienced well-being rises with income, even above $75,000 per year. *Proceedings of the National Academy of Sciences* 118(4): 1–6.

Kim, Heejung, & Markus, Hazel Rose. 1999. Deviance or uniqueness, harmony or conformity? A cultural analysis. *Journal of Personality and Social Psychology* 77(4): 785.

Kim, Hee Young, and Pettit, Nathan C. 2015. Status is a four-letter word: Self versus other differences and concealment of status-striving. *Social Psychological and Personality Science* 6(3): 267–275.

Knight, John, & Gunatilaka, Ramani. 2011. Does economic growth raise happiness in China? *Oxford Development Studies* 39(1): 1–24.

Kohn, Alfie. 1992. *No contest: The case against competition*. Boston: Houghton Mifflin Harcourt.

Komarraju, Meera, & Cokley, Kevin O. 2008. Horizontal and vertical dimensions of individualism-collectivism: A comparison of African Americans and European Americans. *Cultural Diversity and Ethnic Minority Psychology* 14(4): 336.

Kotov, Roman, Gamez, Wakiza, Schmidt, Frank, & Watson, David. 2010. Linking "big" personality traits to anxiety, depressive, and substance use disorders: a meta-analysis. *Psychological Bulletin* 136(5): 768.

Krishnan, Venkat R. 2008. Impact of MBA education on students' values: Two longitudinal studies. *Journal of Business Ethics* 83(2): 233–246.

Kunkle, Fredrick. 2017. U.S. citizens among least likely to travel abroad, British firm says. *Washington Post*, September 29. https://www.washingtonpost.com/news/tripping/wp/2017/09/29/u-s-citizens-among-least-likely-to-travel-abroad-british-firm-says/.

Kuwabara, Ko, Yu, Siyu, Lee, Alice J., & Galinsky, Adam D. 2016. Status decreases dominance in the West but increases dominance in the East. *Psychological Science* 27(2): 127–137.

La Barbera, Priscilla A., & Gürhan, Zeynep. 1997. The role of materialism, religiosity, and demographics in subjective well-being. *Psychology & Marketing* 14(1): 71–97.

LaBonte, Rachel. 2021. Zack Snyder comments on "Justice League" Josh Whedon abuse allegations. *Screen Rant*, March 15. https://screenrant.com/justice-league-joss-whedon-abuse-zack-snyder-response/.

Lan, George, Gowing, Maureen, Rieger, Fritz, McMahon, Sharon, & King, Norman. Values, value types and moral reasoning of MBA students. *Business Ethics: A European Review* 19(2): 183–198.

Landor, William S., 2019 [1829]. *Imaginary conversations and poems: A selection*. Glasgow: Good Press.

Laukkonen, Ruben E., Schooler, Jonathan W., & Tangen, Jason M. 2018. *The Eureka Heuristic: Relying on insight to appraise the quality of ideas*. Last accessed June 1, 2023. https://

www.researchgate.net/publication/323376778_Eureka_Heuristics_How_feelings_of
_insight_signal_the_quality_of_a_new_idea.

Le, Thao N., & Levenson, Michael R. 2005. Wisdom as self-transcendence: What's love (& individualism) got to do with it? *Journal of Research in Personality* 39(4): 443–457.

Leary, Mark R. 2004. Digging deeper: The fundamental nature of "self-conscious" emotions. *Psychological Inquiry* 15(2): 129–131.

Lee, Jim. 2021. Author interview.

Lee, Richard B. 1969. *Eating Christmas in the Kalahari*. New York: American Museum of Natural History.

Lemann, Nicholas. 2017. Hating on Herbert Hoover. *New Yorker*, October 23. https://www
.newyorker.com/magazine/2017/10/23/hating-on-herbert-hoover.

Le Page, Michael. 2008. Evolution myths: "Survival of the fittest" justifies "everyone for themselves." *NewScientist*, April 16. https://www.newscientist.com/article/dn13671
-evolution-myths-survival-of-the-fittest-justifies-everyone-for-themselves/.

Levitt, Stephen D. 2016. Heads or tails: The impact of a coin toss on major life decisions and subsequent happiness. *National Bureau of Economic Research, Working Paper 2287*. August. https://www.nber.org/papers/w22487.

Lévy-Garboua, Louis, & Montmarquette, Claude. 2004. Reported job satisfaction: What does it mean? *Journal of Socio-Economics* 33(2): 135–151.

Lichtenberg, Judith. 1996. Consuming because others consume. *Social Theory and Practice* 22(3): 273–297.

Lucas, Richard E., Clark, Andrew E., Georgellis, Yannis, & Diener, Ed. 2004. Unemployment alters the set point for life satisfaction. *Psychological Science* 15(1): 8–13.

Luttmer, Erzo FP. 2005. Neighbors as negatives: Relative earnings and well-being. *Quarterly Journal of Economics* 120(3): 963–1002.

Lutz, David W. 2009. African Ubuntu philosophy and global management. *Journal of Business Ethics* 84(3): 313–328.

Maathai, Wangari. 2009. *The challenge for Africa: A new vision*. London: Random House.

Macmurray, John. 1977. *Conditions of freedom*. Atlantic Highlands: Humanities Press.

Magee, Joe C., & Galinsky, Adam D. 2008. 8 social hierarchy: The self-reinforcing nature of power and status. *Academy of Management Annals* 2(1): 351–398.

Mahan, Brian J. 2002. *Forgetting ourselves on purpose: Vocation and the ethics of ambition*. San Francisco: Jossey-Bass.

Majić, Tomislav, Schmidt, Timo T., & Gallinat, Jürgen. 2015. Peak experiences and the after-glow phenomenon: When and how do therapeutic effects of hallucinogens depend on psychedelic experiences? *Journal of Psychopharmacology* 29(3): 241–253.

Maner, Jon K., & Mead, Nicole L. 2010. The essential tension between leadership and power: when leaders sacrifice group goals for the sake of self-interest. *Journal of Personality and Social Psychology* 99(3): 482.

Mann, Alice. 2022. An interview with Mike Brady, CEO of Greyston Bakery. *Mann Weekly*. Last accessed January 19, 2022. https://mannadvisors.com/an-interview-with-mike
-brady-ceo-of-greyston-bakery/.

Manson, M. 2019. *Everything is f*cked*. New York: HarperCollins.

Marcos, Laura. 2019. Stephen Hawking's greatest achievements. *Mega Interesting*, December 11. https://www.megainteresting.com/pictures/gallery/stephen-hawkings-greatest
-achievements-491573551864.

Marin, Gerardo, & Triandis, Harry C. 1985. Allocentrism as an important characteristic of the behavior of Latin Americans and Hispanics. *Cross-Cultural and National Studies in Social Psychology* 69: 80.

Marks, Gary N. 1997. The formation of materialist and postmaterialist values. *Social Science Research* 26(1): 52–68.

Markus, Hazel R., & Kitayama, Shinobu. 1991. Culture and the self: Implications for cognition, emotion, and motivation. *Psychological Review* 98(2): 224.

Marsh, Abigail. 2021. Everyone thinks Americans are selfish. They're wrong. *New York Times*, May 26. https://www.nytimes.com/2021/05/26/opinion/individualism-united-states-altruism.html.

Martin, Emmie. 2019. Here's how much American men earn at every age. *CNBC*, July 26. https://www.cnbc.com/2019/07/26/how-much-american-men-earn-at-every-age.html.

Martins, Luis L., Eddleston, Kimberly A., & Veiga, John F. 2002. Moderators of the relationship between work-family conflict and career satisfaction. *Academy of Management Journal* 45(2): 399–409.

Marvasti, Reza. 2021. Author interview.

Maslow, Abraham H. 1959. Cognition of being in the peak experiences. *Journal of Genetic Psychology* 94(1): 43–66.

Maslow, Abraham H. 1999. Cognition of being in the peak experiences. In Maslow A. H. (Ed.), *Toward a Psychology of Being*. New York: Wiley, 81–111.

Masters, Kim. 2021. Ray Fisher opens up about "Justice League," Joss Whedon and Warners: "I don't believe some of these people are fit for leadership." *Hollywood Reporter*, April 6. https://www.hollywoodreporter.com/movies/movie-news/ray-fisher-opens-up-about-justice-league-joss-whedon-and-warners-i-dont-believe-some-of-these-people-are-fit-for-leadership-4161658/.

Matos, Kenneth, O'Neill, Olivia, & Lei, Xue. 2018. Toxic leadership and the masculinity contest culture: How "win or die" cultures breed abusive leadership. *Journal of Social Issues* 74(3): 500–528.

Mayew, William J., Parsons, Christopher A., & Venkatachalam, Mohan. 2013. Voice pitch and the labor market success of male chief executive officers. *Evolution and Human Behavior* 34(4): 243–248.

McCauley, John F. 2013. Africa's new big man rule? Pentecostalism and patronage in Ghana. *African Affairs* 112(446): 1–21.

McClelland, David C., & Kirshnit, Carol. 1988. The effect of motivational arousal through films on salivary immunoglobulin A. *Psychology and Health* 2(1): 31–52.

McDonald, Matthew G., Wearing, Stephen, & Ponting, Jess. 2009. The nature of peak experience in wilderness. *Humanistic Psychologist* 37(4): 370–385.

McDougall, Christopher. 2019. *Running with Sherman: The donkey with the heart of a hero*. London: Penguin Random House.

McElhatton, Sean. 2021. Author interview.

McFarland, Sam, Webb, Matthew, & Brown, Derek. 2012. All humanity is my ingroup: A measure and studies of identification with all humanity. *Journal of Personality and Social Psychology* 103(5): 830.

McKeown, Greg. 2020. *Essentialism: The disciplined pursuit of less*. Sydney: Currency.

Mead, Nicole L., Baumeister, Roy F., Stuppy, Anika, & Vohs, Kathleen D. 2018. Power increases the socially toxic component of narcissism among individuals with high baseline testosterone. *Journal of Experimental Psychology* 147(4): 591.

Meaney, Thomas. 2020. The myth of Henry Kissinger. *New Yorker*, May 18. https://www.newyorker.com/magazine/2020/05/18/the-myth-of-henry-kissinger.

Menon, Tanya, & Thompson, Leigh. 2010. Envy at work. *Harvard Busines Review*, April. https://hbr.org/2010/04/envy-at-work.

Menon, Tanya, Thompson, Leigh, & Choi, Hoon-Seok. 2006. Tainted knowledge vs. tempting knowledge: People avoid knowledge from internal rivals and seek knowledge from external rivals. *Management Science* 52(8): 1129–1144.

MHS (Massachusetts Historical Society). 2022. John Adams letter to Abigail Adams, May 12, 1780. Accessed September 19. https://www.masshist.org/digitaladams/archive/doc?id=L17800512jasecond.

Michaelson, Christopher, and Tosti-Kharas, Jennifer. 2020. A world changed: What post-9/11 stories tell us about the position of America, purpose of business, and meaning of work. *Academy of Management Review* 45(4): 877–895.

Milgram, Stanley. 1963. Behavioral study of obedience. *Journal of Abnormal and Social Psychology* 67(4): 371.

Montaigne, Michel de. 2004. *The complete essays*. London: Penguin UK.

Morishima, Yosuke, Schunk, Daniel, Bruhin, Adrian, Ruff, Christian C. Ruff, & Fehr, Ernst. 2012. Linking brain structure and activation in temporoparietal junction to explain the neurobiology of human altruism. *Neuron* 75(1): 73–79.

Moschetti, Valeri. 2019. Japan: Immigration, a remedy for the aging population? *Japan Spotlight*, July–August. https://www.jef.or.jp/journal/pdf/226th_Cover_Story_10.pdf.

Mowen, John C. 2004. Exploring the trait of competitiveness and its consumer behavior consequences. *Journal of Consumer Psychology* 14(1–2): 52–63.

Mukashyaka, Alice. 2021. Author interview.

Murray, Gregg R., & Schmitz, J. David. 2011. Caveman politics: Evolutionary leadership preferences and physical stature. *Social Science Quarterly* 92(5): 1215–1235.

Myers, David G. 1999. Close relationships and quality of life. In Kahneman, Daniel, Edward Diener, & Norbert Schwarz (Eds.), *Well-being: Foundations of hedonic psychology*. New York: Russell Sage.

Niederle, Muriel, & Vesterlund, Lise. 2011. Gender and competition. *Annual Review of Economics* 3(1): 601–630.

Norton, Michael I., & Ariely, Dan. 2011. Building a better America—One wealth quintile at a time. *Perspectives on Psychological Science* 6(1): 9–12.

NPS (National Park Service). 2022. Franklin Delano Roosevelt memorial. Last accessed January 18, 2022. https://www.nps.gov/frde/learn/photosmultimedia/quotations.htm.

Nuwer, Rachel. 2012. The world's happiest man is a Tibetan monk. *Smithsonian Magazine*, November 1. https://www.smithsonianmag.com/smart-news/the-worlds-happiest-man-is-a-tibetan-monk-105980614/.

O'Brien, Barbara. 2011. The Buddhist art of nonjudgmental judging is subtle. *The Guardian*, July 11. https://www.theguardian.com/commentisfree/belief/2011/jul/20/buddhist-dalai-lama-masterchef.

O'Connor, Marleen A. 2002. The Enron board: The perils of groupthink. *University of Cincinnati Law Review* 71: 1233.

OECD (Organisation for Economic Co-operation and Development). 2019. Trade in fake goods is now 3.3% of world trade and rising. Accessed March 18. https://www.oecd.org/newsroom/trade-in-fake-goods-is-now-33-of-world-trade-and-rising.htm.

Oettingen, Gabriele, Mayer, Doris, & Portnow, Sam. 2016. Pleasure now, pain later: Positive fantasies about the future predict symptoms of depression. *Psychological Science* 27(3): 345–353.

Oishi, Shigehiro, Diener, Ed, Suh, Eunkook, & Lucas, Richard E. 1999. Value as a moderator in subjective well-being. *Journal of Personality* 67(1): 157–184.

Oliver, J. Eric, & Rahn, Wendy M. 2016. Rise of the Trumpenvolk: Populism in the 2016 election. *ANNALS of the American Academy of Political and Social Science* 667(1): 189–206.

O'Neill, J. 2006. Citizenship, well-being and sustainability: Epicurus or Aristotle? *Analyse & Kritik* 28(2), 158–72.

O'Rourke, Meghan. 2020. The shift Americans must make to fight the coronavirus. *The Atlantic*, March 12. https://www.theatlantic.com/ideas/archive/2020/03/we-need-isolate -ourselves-during-coronavirus-outbreak/607840/.

Otto, K., Roe, R., Sobiraj, S., Baluku, M. M., & Vásquez, M. E. G. 2017. The impact of career ambition on psychologists' extrinsic and intrinsic career success: The less they want, the more they get. *Career Development International* 22(1): 23–36.

Ouchi, William G. 1981. Organizational paradigms: A commentary on Japanese management and Theory Z organizations. *Organizational Dynamics* 9(4): 36–43.

Overbeck, Jennifer R., & Park, Bernadette. 2006. Powerful perceivers, powerless objects: Flexibility of powerholders' social attention. *Organizational Behavior and Human Decision Processes* 99(2): 227–243.

Oyserman, Daphna, Coon, Heather M., & Kemmelmeier, Markus. 2002. Rethinking individualism and collectivism: Evaluation of theoretical assumptions and meta-analyses. *Psychological Bulletin* 128(1): 3.

Parks, Craig D., Rumble, Ann C., & Posey, Donelle C. 2002. The effects of envy on reciprocation in a social dilemma. *Personality and Social Psychology Bulletin* 28(4): 509–520.

Patock-Peckham, Julie A., Ebbert, Ashley M., Woo, Jessica, Finch, Hannah, Broussard, Matthew L., Ulloa, Emilio, & Moses, Jennifer Filson. 2020. Winning at all costs: The etiology of hypercompetitiveness through the indirect influences of parental bonds on anger and verbal/physical aggression. *Personality and Individual Differences* 154: 109711.

Paul, Annie Murphy. 2021. *The extended mind: The power of thinking outside the brain.* New York: Eamon Dolan.

Phelan, Jo, Link, Bruce G., Moore, Robert E., and Stueve, Ann. 1997. The stigma of homelessness: The impact of the label "homeless" on attitudes toward poor persons. *Social Psychology Quarterly* 60(4): 323–337.

Pettersson, Henrik, Manley, Byron, & Hernandez, Sergio. 2002. Tracking covid-19's global spread. *CNN Health*. Accessed January 18. https://edition.cnn.com/interactive/2020 /health/coronavirus-maps-and-cases/.

Pettigrove, Glen. 2007. Ambitions. *Ethical Theory and Moral Practice* 10(1): 53–68.

Piff, Paul K., Dietze, Pia, Feinberg, Matthew, Stancato, Daniel M., & Keltner, Dacher. 2015. Awe, the small self, and prosocial behavior. *Journal of Personality and Social Psychology* 108(6): 883.

Piketty, Thomas. 2018. *Capital in the twenty-first century.* Boston: Harvard University Press.

Pink, Daniel H. 2011. *Drive: The surprising truth about what motivates us.* New York: Penguin.

Pinker, Steven. 2018. *Enlightenment now: The case for reason, science, humanism, and progress.* London: Penguin UK.

Pittinsky, Todd L., & Montoya, R. Matthew. 2016. Empathic joy in positive intergroup relations. *Journal of Social Issues* 72(3): 511–523.

Platek, Steven M., Mohamed, Feroze B., & Gallup Jr., Gordon G. 2005. Contagious yawning and the brain. *Cognitive Brain Research* 23(2–3): 448–452.

Plutarch. 75 AD. *Pyrrhus.* John Dryden (Trans.). Accessed June 1, 2023. http://classics.mit .edu/Plutarch/pyrrhus.html.

Plutarch. 1874. *Plutarch's morals.* Translated from the Greek by several hands. Corrected and revised by William W. Goodwin, PhD. Boston: Little, Brown; and Cambridge: John Wilson and Son. http://www.perseus.tufts.edu/hopper/text?doc=Perseus%3Atext%3A 2008.01.0308%3Asection%3D5.

Podoshen, Jeffrey S., Li, Lu, & Zhang, Junfeng. 2011. Materialism and conspicuous consumption in China: A cross-cultural examination. *International Journal of Consumer Studies* 35(1): 17–25.

Raheja, Ganesh. 2021. Zack Snyder on Joss Whedon's version of "Justice League": Destroyed 3 yrs of My Work. *Republic World,* May 28. https://www.republicworld.com /entertainment-news/hollywood-news/zack-snyder-on-joss-whedons-version-of-justice -league-destroyed-3-yrs-of-my-work.html.

Ramachandran, Vilayanur S., & Jalal, Baland. 2017. The evolutionary psychology of envy and jealousy. *Frontiers in Psychology* 8: 1619.

Rand, Ayn. 2014. *The fountainhead.* Toronto: Penguin Canada.

Reardon, Sean F., Matthews, Stephen A., O'Sullivan, David, Lee, Barrett A., Firebaugh, Glenn, Farrell, Chad R., & Bischoff, Kendra. 2008. The geographic scale of metropolitan racial segregation. *Demography* 45(3): 489–514.

Reynolds, Jeremy, & Xian, He. 2014. Perceptions of meritocracy in the land of opportunity. *Research in Social Stratification and Mobility* 36: 121–137.

Reysen, Stephen, & Katzarska-Miller, Iva. 2013. A model of global citizenship: Antecedents and outcomes. *International Journal of Psychology* 48(5): 858–870.

Richins, Marsha L. 1994. Special possessions and the expression of material values. *Journal of Consumer Research* 21(3): 522–533.

Richins, Marsha L., & Dawson, Scott. 1992. A consumer values orientation for materialism and its measurement: Scale development and validation. *Journal of Consumer Research* 19(3): 303–316.

Richter, Ruthann. 2007a. Former faculty entrepreneur digs deep into his own pockets to honor his commitment to Stanford. *Stanford News Release,* September 18. https:// web.archive.org/web/20080630014345/http:/med.stanford.edu/news_releases/2007 /september/doty.html.

Richter, Ruthann. 2007b. Former faculty entrepreneur sticks to his promise. *Stanford Report,* September 26. https://news.stanford.edu/news/2007/september26/med-doty-092607 .html.

Ringelmann, Max. 1913. Recherches sur les moteurs animés: Travail de l'homme. *Annales de l'Insitut National Agronomique* 12: 1–40.

Roberts, Brent W., & Helson, Ravenna. 1997. Changes in culture, changes in personality: The influence of individualism in a longitudinal study of women. *Journal of Personality and Social Psychology* 72(3): 641.

Roccas, Sonia. 2003. Identification and status revisited: The moderating role of self-enhancement and self-transcendence values. *Personality and Social Psychology Bulletin* 29(6): 726–736.

Roosevelt, Theodore. 1915. John Muir: An Appreciation. *Outlook* 109: 27–28.

Rosenberg, Tina. 2019. No background check, drug test or credit check: You're hired! *New York Times*, May 29. https://www.nytimes.com/2019/05/29/opinion/greyston-bakery -open-hiring.html.

Roser, Max, & Ortiz-Ospina, Esteban. 2013. Tertiary Education. **Our World in Data.** https:// ourworldindata.org/tertiary-education#citation.

Rousseau, Jean-Jacques. 2018. *Rousseau: The social contract and other later political writings*. Cambridge: Cambridge University Press.

Rubin, Gretchen. 2009. *The happiness project*. New York: HarperCollins.

Ryan, Lisa, & Dziurawiec, Suzanne. 2001. Materialism and its relationship to life satisfaction. *Social Indicators Research* 55(2): 185–197.

Ryan, Richard M., Chirkov, Valery I., Little, Todd D., Sheldon, Kennon M., Timoshina, Elena, & Deci, Edward L. 1999. The American dream in Russia: Extrinsic aspirations and well-being in two cultures. *Personality and Social Psychology Bulletin* 25(12): 1509–1524.

Ryckman, Richard M., Libby, Cary R., van den Borne, Bart, Gold, Joel A., & Lindner, Marc A. 1997. Values of hypercompetitive and personal development competitive individuals. *Journal of Personality Assessment* 69(2): 271–283.

Sagmeister, Stefan. 2014. The power of time off. **TED Talk.** March 4, 2014. https://www.ted .com/talks/stefan_sagmeister_happiness_by_design?language=en.

Salvi, Carola, Bricolo, Emanuela, Kounios, John, Bowden, Edward, & Beeman, Mark. 2016. Insight solutions are correct more often than analytic solutions. *Thinking & Reasoning* 22(4): 443–460.

Schindler, Ines, Paech, Juliane, & Löwenbrück, Fabian. 2015. Linking admiration and adoration to self-expansion: Different ways to enhance one's potential. *Cognition and Emotion* 29(2): 292–310.

Schindler, Ines, Zink, Veronika, Windrich, Johannes, & Menninghaus, Winfried. 2013. Admiration and adoration: Their different ways of showing and shaping who we are. *Cognition & Emotion* 27(1): 85–118.

Schlösser, Oliver, Frese, Michael, Heintze, Anna-Maria, Al-Najjar, Musaed, Arciszewski, Thomas, Besevegis, Elias, & Bishop, George D., et al. 2013. Humane orientation as a new cultural dimension of the GLOBE project: A validation study of the GLOBE scale and out-group humane orientation in 25 countries. *Journal of Cross-Cultural Psychology* 44(4): 535–551.

Schmuck, Peter, Kasser, Tim, & Ryan, Richard M. 2000. Intrinsic and extrinsic goals: Their structure and relationship to well-being in German and US college students. *Social Indicators Research* 50(2): 225–241.

Schwartz, Barry. 2015. *Why we work*. New York: Simon and Schuster.

Schwartz, Shalom H. 2012. An overview of the Schwartz theory of basic values. *Online Readings in Psychology and Culture* 2(1): 11–20.

Schwartz, Shalom H., & Bardi, Anat. 2001. Value hierarchies across cultures: Taking a similarities perspective. *Journal of Cross-Cultural Psychology* 32(3): 268–290.

Scott, Greg, Ciarrochi, Joseph, & Deane, Frank P. 2004. Disadvantages of being an individualist in an individualistic culture: Idiocentrism, emotional competence, stress, and mental health. *Australian Psychologist* 39(2): 143–154.

Scott, Kristin. 2009. *Terminal materialism vs. instrumental materialism: Can materialism be beneficial?* Unpublished doctoral dissertation, Oklahoma State University, Stillwater.

Seeyle, Katherine. 2018. Bernard Glassman, zen master and social activist, dies at 79. *New York Times*, November 23. https://www.nytimes.com/2018/11/23/obituaries/bernard -glassman-dead.html.

Seligman, Martin E. P., and Csikszentmihalyi, Mihaly. 2014. Positive psychology: An introduction. In Cooper, Harris (Ed.), *Flow and the foundations of positive psychology*: 279–298. Dordrecht, the Netherlands: Springer.

Shavitt, Sharon, Torelli, Carlos J., & Riemer, Hila. 2011. Horizontal and vertical individualism and collectivism: Implications for understanding psychological processes. In Gelfand, Michelle, Chiu, Chi-yue, & Hong, Ying Yi (Eds.), *Advances in culture and psychology*: 309–350. Oxford: Oxford University Press.

Shiota, Michelle N., Keltner, Dacher, & Mossman, Amanda. 2007. The nature of awe: Elicitors, appraisals, and effects on self-concept. *Cognition and Emotion* 21(5): 944–963.

Shutte, Augustine. 2009. Ubuntu as the African ethical vision. In Murove, Munyardzi (Ed.), *African ethics: An anthology of comparative and applied ethics*. Scottsville, South Africa: University of KwaZulu Natal Press.

Sinclair, Upton. 1994. *I, candidate for governor: And how I got licked*. Berkeley: University of California Press.

Singelis, Theodore M., Triandis, Harry C., Bhawuk, Dharm P. S., & Gelfand, Michele J. 1995. Horizontal and vertical dimensions of individualism and collectivism: A theoretical and measurement refinement. *Cross-Cultural Research* 29(3): 240–275.

Smith, Adam. 2010 [1822]. *The theory of moral sentiments*. New York: Penguin.

Smith, Deborah L., & Smith, Brian J. 2006. Perceptions of violence: The views of teachers who left urban schools. *High School Journal* 89(3): 34–42.

Smith, Richard H., Parrott, W. Gerrod, Ozer, Daniel, & Moniz, Andrew. 1994. Subjective injustice and inferiority as predictors of hostile and depressive feelings in envy. *Personality and Social Psychology Bulletin* 20(6): 705–711.

Smith, Richard H., Powell, Caitlin A. J., Combs, David J. Y., & Schurtz, David Ryan. 2009. Exploring the when and why of schadenfreude. *Social and Personality Psychology Compass* 3(4: 530–546.

Smith, Richard H., Turner, Terence J., Garonzik, Ron, Leach, Colin W., Urch-Druskat, Vanessa, & Weston, Christine M. 1996. Envy and schadenfreude. *Personality and Social Psychology Bulletin* 22(2): 158–168.

Soh, Star, & Leong, Frederick T. L. 2002. Validity of vertical and horizontal individualism and collectivism in Singapore: Relationships with values and interests. *Journal of Cross-Cultural Psychology* 33(1): 3–15.

Solnick, Sara J., & Hemenway, David. 1998. Is more always better? A survey on positional concerns. *Journal of Economic Behavior & Organization* 37(3): 373–383.

Sosis, Richard, & Bressler, Eric R. 2003. Cooperation and commune longevity: A test of the costly signaling theory of religion. *Cross-Cultural Research* 37: 211–239.

Stahl, Leslie. 2012. Born good? Babies help unlock the origins of morality." *CBS News*, November 18. https://www.youtube.com/watch?v=FRvVFW85IcU.

Statista. 2021. Median household income in the United States 2020, by race or ethnic group. **Statista Research Department**. Accessed October 28. https://www.statista.com/statistics /233324/median-household-income-in-the-united-states-by-race-or-ethnic-group/.

Stellar, Jennifer E., Manzo, Vida M., Kraus, Michael W., & Keltner, Dacher. 2012. Class and compassion: Socioeconomic factors predict responses to suffering. *Emotion* 12(3): 449.

Strom, Stephanie. 2015. Melvin J. Gordon, who ran Tootsie Roll Industries, dies at 95. *New York Times*, January 22. https://www.nytimes.com/2015/01/22/business/melvin-j-gordon-who-ran-tootsie-roll-industries-dies-at-95.html.

Suls, Jerry, Martin, Rene, & Wheeler, Ladd. 2002. Social comparison: Why, with whom, and with what effect? *Current Directions in Psychological Science* 11(5): 159–163.

Szegedy-Maszak, Marianne. 2005. Competition Freaks. *Los Angeles Times*, November 28. https://www.latimes.com/archives/la-xpm-2005-nov-28-he-competition28-story.html.

Tait, Marianne, Padgett, Margaret Y., & Baldwin, Timothy T. 1989. Job and life satisfaction: A reevaluation of the strength of the relationship and gender effects as a function of the date of the study. *Journal of Applied Psychology* 74(3): 502.

Tajfel, Henri, Billig, Michael G., Bundy, Robert P., & Flament, Claude. 1971. Social categorization and intergroup behaviour. *European Journal of Social Psychology* 1(2): 149–178.

Takahashi, Hidehiko, Kato, Motoichiro, Matsuura, Masato, Mobbs, Dean, Suhara, Tetsuya, & Okubo, Yoshiro. 2009. When your gain is my pain and your pain is my gain: Neural correlates of envy and schadenfreude. *Science* 323(5916): 937–939.

Tang, Thomas Li-Ping, & Chiu, Randy K. 2003. Income, money ethic, pay satisfaction, commitment, and unethical behavior: Is the love of money the root of evil for Hong Kong employees? *Journal of Business Ethics* 46(1): 13–30.

Tassi, Paul. 2021. An interview that will put you in Zack Snyder's corner for his "Justice League" cut. *Forbes*, February 23. https://www.forbes.com/sites/paultassi/2021/02/23/an-interview-that-will-put-you-in-zack-snyders-corner-for-his-justice-league-cut/?sh=3bdcab9c392c.

Tauer, John M., & Harackiewicz, Judith M. 1999. Winning isn't everything: Competition, achievement orientation, and intrinsic motivation. *Journal of Experimental Social Psychology* 35(3): 209–238.

Taylor, Merika. 2018. I was a student of Stephen Hawking's—Here's what he taught me. *The Conversation*, March 16. https://theconversation.com/i-was-a-student-of-stephen-hawkings-heres-what-he-taught-me-93508.

Tesser, Abraham, & Campbell, Jennifer. 1982. Self-evaluation maintenance and the perception of friends and strangers. *Journal of Personality* 50(3): 261–279.

Tesser, Abraham, Pilkington, Constance J., & McIntosh, William D. 1989. Self-evaluation maintenance and the mediational role of emotion: The perception of friends and strangers. *Journal of Personality and Social Psychology* 57(3): 442.

Thomas, Ashley J., Thomsen, Lotte, Lukowski, Angela F., Abramyan, Meline, & Sarnecka, Barbara W. 2018. Toddlers prefer those who win but not when they win by force. *Nature Human Behavior* 2(9): 662–669.

Thornton, Bill, Ryckman, Richard M., & Gold, Joel A. 2011. Hypercompetitiveness and relationships: Further implications for romantic, family, and peer relationships. *Psychology* 2(4): 269.

Thye, Shane R. 2000. A status value theory of power in exchange relations. *American Sociological Review* 65(3): 407–432.

Tocqueville, Alexis de. 2004. *Democracy in America*. Goldhammer, Arthur (Trans.). New York: The Library of America.

Tolle, Eckhart. 2006. *A new Earth: Awakening to your life's purpose*. London: Penguin Life.

Topolinski, Sascha, & Reber, Rolf. 2010. Immediate truth: Temporal contiguity between a cognitive problem and its solution determines experienced veracity of the solution. *Cognition* 114(1): 117–122.

Torelli, Carlos J., Leslie, Lisa M., Stoner, Jennifer L., & Puente, Raquel. 2014. Cultural determinants of status: Implications for workplace evaluations and behaviors. *Organizational Behavior and Human Decision Processes* 123(1): 34–48.

Tost, Leigh Plunkett. 2015. When, why, and how do powerholders "feel the power"? Examining the links between structural and psychological power and reviving the connection between power and responsibility. *Research in Organizational Behavior* 35: 29–56.

Triandis, Harry. 1994. Major cultural syndromes and emotion. In Kitayama, Shinobu, & Markus, Hazel Rose (Eds.), *Emotion and culture: Empirical studies of mutual influence*: 285–308. Washington, DC: American Psychological Association.

Triandis, Harry C. 1996. The psychological measurement of cultural syndromes. *American Psychologist* 51(4): 407.

Triandis, Harry C., Bontempo, Robert, Villareal, Marcelo J., Asai, Masaaki, & Lucca, Nydia. 1988. Individualism and collectivism: Cross-cultural perspectives on self-ingroup relationships. *Journal of Personality and Social Psychology* 54(2): 323.

Triandis, Harry C., Carnevale, Peter, Gelfand, Michele, Robert, Christopher, Wasti, S. Arzu, Probst, Tahira, & Kashima, Emiko S., et al. 2001. Culture and deception in business negotiations: A multilevel analysis. *International Journal of Cross Cultural Management* 1(1): 73–90.

Triandis, Harry C., Chen, Xiao Ping, & Chen, Darius K-S. 1998. Scenarios for the measurement of collectivism and individualism. *Journal of Cross-Cultural Psychology* 29(2): 275–289.

Triandis, Harry C., & Gelfand, Michele J. 1998. Converging measurement of horizontal and vertical individualism and collectivism. *Journal of Personality and Social Psychology* 74(1): 118.

Triandis, Harry C., McCusker, Christopher, & Hui, C. Harry. 1990. Multimethod probes of individualism and collectivism. *Journal of Personality and Social Psychology* 59(5): 1006.

Tupy, Marian. 2019. The great miracle of industrialization. **Human Progress**, May 6. https://www.humanprogress.org/the-miracle-of-industrialization/.

Turner, John C., & Reynolds, Katherine J. 2011. Self-categorization theory. *Handbook of Theories in Social Psychology* 2(1): 399–417.

Tutu, Desmond. 2009. *No future without forgiveness*. New York: Doubleday.

Tutu, Desmond. 2011. *God is not a Christian: Speaking truth in times of crisis*. New York: Random House.

Twain, Mark. 2014. *Mark Twain on common sense: Timeless advice and words of wisdom from America's most-revered humorist*. Brennan, Stephen (Ed.). New York: Simon and Schuster.

Twenge, Jean M. 2010. A review of the empirical evidence on generational differences in work attitudes. *Journal of Business and Psychology* 25(2): 201–210.

UN (United Nations). 2021. Vaccine hoarding will prolong COVID warns WHO, as agency mulls early Omicron data. *United Nations News*, December 9. https://news.un.org/en/story/2021/12/1107542.

UNICEF (United Nations Children's Fund). 2021. Data: Secondary education. https://data.unicef.org/topic/education/secondary-education/.

US Travel Association. 2022. Time off and vacation usage. Accessed January 18. https://www.ustravel.org/toolkit/time-and-vacation-usage.

Van Boven, Leaf. 2005. Experientialism, materialism, and the pursuit of happiness. *Review of General Psychology* 9(2): 132–142.

Van Boven, Leaf, & Gilovich, Thomas. 2003. To do or to have? That is the question. *Journal of Personality and Social Psychology* 85(6): 1193.

van der Linden, Sander. 2015. The psychology of competition. *Psychology Today*, June 24. https://www.psychologytoday.com/us/blog/socially-relevant/201506/the-psychology -competition.

Van de Ven, Niels. 2017. Envy and admiration: Emotion and motivation following upward social comparison. *Cognition and Emotion* 31(1): 193–200.

Van de Ven, Niels, Zeelenberg, Marcel, & Pieters, Rik. 2009. Leveling up and down: The experiences of benign and malicious envy. *Emotion* 9(3): 419.

Van de Ven, Niels, Zeelenberg, Marcel, & Pieters, Rik. 2011. Why envy outperforms admiration. *Personality and Social Psychology Bulletin* 37(6): 784–795.

Van Hiel, Alain, & Vansteenkiste, Maarten. 2009. Ambitions fulfilled? The effects of intrinsic and extrinsic goal attainment on older adults' ego-integrity and death attitudes. *International Journal of Aging and Human Development* 68(1): 27–51.

Van Kleef, Gerben A., Homan, Astrid C., Finkenauer, Catrin, Gündemir, Seval, & Stamkou, Eftychia. 2011. Breaking the rules to rise to power: How norm violators gain power in the eyes of others. *Social Psychological and Personality Science* 2(5): 500–507.

Van Kleef, Gerben A., Oveis, Christopher, Van Der Löwe, Ilmo, LuoKogan, Aleksandr, Goetz, Jennifer, & Keltner, Dacher. 2008. Power, distress, and compassion: Turning a blind eye to the suffering of others. *Psychological Science* 19(12): 1315–1322.

Van Knippenberg, Barbara, & Van Knippenberg, Daan. 2005. Leader self-sacrifice and leadership effectiveness: the moderating role of leader prototypicality. *Journal of Applied Psychology* 90(1): 25.

Van Reybrouck, David. 2014. *Congo: The epic history of a people*. Sam Garrett (Trans.). New York: Ecco.

Van Vugt, Mark, De Cremer, David, & Janssen, Dirk P. 2007. Gender differences in cooperation and competition: The male-warrior hypothesis. *Psychological Science* 18(1): 19–23.

Van Vugt, Mark J., & Tybur, J. M. 2015. The evolutionary foundations of status hierarchy. *Handbook of Evolutionary Psychology* 2: 788–809.

Vargas, Jose H., & Kemmelmeier, Markus. 2013. Ethnicity and contemporary American culture: A meta-analytic investigation of horizontal–vertical individualism–collectivism. *Journal of Cross-Cultural Psychology* 44(2): 195–222.

Vauchez, André. 2012. *Francis of Assisi*. New Haven, CT: Yale University Press.

Vedantam, Shankar. 2018. Romeo & Juliet in Kigali: How a Soap Opera Sought to Change Behavior in Rwanda. *NPR: Hidden Brain*, April 16. https://www.npr.org/transcripts /602872309.

Verkuyten, Maykel, & Lay, Clarry. 1998. Ethnic minority identity and psychological well-being: The mediating role of collective self-esteem. *Journal of Applied Social Psychology* 28(21): 1969–1986.

Walsh, Nick Paton. 2020. There is no getting "back to normal," experts say: The sooner we accept that, the better. *CNN Health*, updated September 30. https://edition.cnn.com /2020/09/30/health/back-to-normal-bias-wellness/index.html.

Warneken, Felix, & Tomasello, Michael. 2009. Varieties of altruism in children and chimpanzees. *Trends in Cognitive Sciences* 13(9): 397–402.

Watson, Paul J., Morris, Ronald J., & Miller, Liv. 1998. Narcissism and the self as continuum: Correlations with assertiveness and hypercompetitiveness. *Imagination, Cognition and Personality* 17(3): 249–259.

Wattles, Jackie, Wagner, Meg, Macaya, Melissa, Hayes, Mike, Mahtani, Melissa, & Rocha, Veronica. 2021. William Shatner goes to space on Blue Origin mission. *CNN Business*, October 13. https://edition.cnn.com/business/live-news/william-shatner-blue-origin-space-flight/index.html.

Wei, Jessica. 2021. Money is a great servant but a bad master—Francis Bacon. *Due* (blog). Accessed February 22. https://due.com/blog/money-is-a-great-servant-but-a-bad-master-francis-bacon/.

Wheeler, Ladd, & Miyake, Kunitate. 1992. Social comparison in everyday life. *Journal of Personality and Social Psychology* 62(5): 760.

White, Andrew Edward, Li, Yexin Jessica, Griskevicius, Vladas, Neuberg, Steven L., & Kenrick, Douglas T. 2013. Putting all your eggs in one basket: Life-history strategies, bet hedging, and diversification. *Psychological Science* 24(5): 715–722.

White, Jerry. 2008. *I will not be broken: Five steps to overcoming a life crisis*. New York: St. Martin's.

White, Jerry. 2020. Author interview.

White, Katherine, & Lehman, Darrin R. 2005. Culture and social comparison seeking: The role of self-motives. *Personality and Social Psychology Bulletin* 31(2): 232–242.

WHO (World Health Organization). 2021. Children: Improving survival and well-being. September 8. https://www.who.int/news-room/fact-sheets/detail/children-reducing-mortality.

Whyte, Kenneth. 2017. *Hoover: An extraordinary life in extraordinary times*. New York: Vintage.

Wiktionary. 2022. Ambition. Last edited January 4. https://en.wiktionary.org/wiki/ambition.

Widerquist, Karl. 2006. Rereading Keynes: Economic possibilities of our grandparents. *Dissent* 53(1): 85–87.

Wilkerson, Isabel. 2020. *Caste (Oprah's book club): The origins of our discontents*. New York: Random House, 2020.

Willer, Robb. 2009. Groups reward individual sacrifice: The status solution to the collective action problem. *American Sociological Review* 74(1): 23–43.

Williams, Geoffrey C., Hedberg, Viking A., Cox, Elizabeth M., & Deci, Edward L. 2000. Extrinsic life goals and health-risk behaviors in adolescents. *Journal of Applied Social Psychology* 30(8): 1756–1771.

Wills, Thomas A. 1981. Downward comparison principles in social psychology. *Psychological Bulletin* 90(2): 245.

Wisse, Barbara, & Rus, Diana. 2012. Leader self-concept and self-interested behavior. *Journal of Personnel Psychology* 11(1): 40–48.

Wong, Nancy Y., & Ahuvia, Aaron C. 1998. Personal taste and family face: Luxury consumption in Confucian and Western societies. *Psychology & Marketing* 15(5): 423–441.

Wood, Joanne V. 1996. What is social comparison and how should we study it? *Personality and Social Psychology Bulletin* 22(5): 520–537.

Woodson, Carter Godwin. 2012. *African myths and folk tales*. Mineola: Dover.

World Bank. 2020a. GDP per capita (current US$)—Costa Rica. Accessed January 18, 2022. https://data.worldbank.org/indicator/NY.GDP.PCAP.CD?locations=CR.

World Bank. 2020b. Poverty and equity brief: South Africa. April. https://databank.worldbank.org/data/download/poverty/33EF03BB-9722-4AE2-ABC7-AA2972D68AFE/Global_POVEQ_ZAF.pdf.

World Economic Forum. 2017. Travel and tourism competitiveness report. Accessed January 14, 2022. https://reports.weforum.org/travel-and-tourism-competitiveness-report-2017/sub-saharan-africa-results/.

Wuthnow, Robert. 1994. *God and Mammon in America*. New York: Simon & Schuster.

Yaden, David B., Iwry, Jonathan, Slack, Kelley J., Eichstaedt, Johannes C., Zhao, Yukun, Vaillant, George E., & Newberg, Andrew B. 2016. The overview effect: Awe and self-transcendent experience in space flight. *Psychology of Consciousness: Theory, Research, and Practice* 3(1): 1.

Yaffe, Nechumi Malovicki, McDonald, Melissa, Halperin, Eran, & Saguy, Tamar. 2018. God, sex, and money among the ultra-Orthodox in Israel: An integrated sociocultural and evolutionary perspective. *Evolution and Human Behavior* 39(6): 622–631.

Yi, J. 2018. Revisiting individualism-collectivism. *Journal of Intercultural Communication* 47(1). https://immi.se/oldwebsite/nr47/jung.html.

Yukl, Gary, & Chavez, Carolyn. 2002. Influence tactics and leader effectiveness. *Leadership* 1(1): 139–165.

Zakaria, Fareed. 2020. *Ten lessons for a post-pandemic world*. London: Penguin UK.

Zhong, Chen-Bo, Magee, Joe C., Maddux, William W., & Galinsky, Adam D. 2006. Power, culture, and action: Considerations in the expression and enactment of power in East Asian and Western societies. In Chen, Y. R. (Ed.), *National culture and groups 9 (Research on managing groups and teams)*. Bingley: Emerald.

Index

Note: Information in tables is indicated by *t*.

About the Authors

THOMAS J. BUSSEN is a former lawyer turned Peace Corps volunteer, now assistant teaching professor of management strategy at Miami University in Oxford, Ohio. Prior to his current role he was a faculty member at the Rwandan campus of African Leadership University. Based in Kigali, Rwanda, Bussen taught international subjects to students of diverse nationalities, while inside and outside the classroom striving to reject deeply ingrained competitively individualistic impulses in lieu of the enlightened self-interest ideal. He is an established author on cross-cultural research. His books include *Shaping the Global Leader: Fundamentals in Culture and Behavior for Optimal Organizational Performance* (Routledge, 2019), coauthored with Lenny Ramsey; and *Compliance Management: A How-to Guide for Executives, Lawyers, and Other Compliance Professionals* (Praeger, 2015), coauthored with Nitish J. Singh. Bussen holds a DBA from the University of Florida and a joint JD-MBA from Saint Louis University School of Law.

HENRY BIGGS is founder and CEO of the higher education software company Eusabian Technologies. Since 2013 he has taught courses in international intellectual property law at Washington University in St. Louis. He holds a PhD in romance linguistics from the University of California, Los Angeles, an MBA from the Olin Business School at Washington University, and a JD in international law from Saint Louis University School of Law.

TIMOTHY BONO is associate dean of student affairs and a lecturer in psychological and brain sciences at Washington University in St. Louis, where thousands of students have taken his courses on the psychology of young adulthood and the science of happiness. An award-winning teacher and researcher, Bono is the author of *Happiness 101: Simple Secrets to Smart Living and Well-Being* (Grand Central, 2020). He is an expert consultant on psychological health and happiness for a number of national media outlets (including CNN, *Fast Company*, the Associated Press, and several public radio stations). He holds a PhD from Washington University in St. Louis.